Surviving Post-communism

STUDIES OF COMMUNISM IN TRANSITION

General Editor: Ronald J. Hill

*Professor of Comparative Government
and Fellow of Trinity College
Dublin, Ireland*

Studies of Communism in Transition is an important series which applies academic analysis and clarity of thought to the recent traumatic events in Eastern and Central Europe. As many of the preconceptions of the past half century are cast aside, newly independent and autonomous sovereign states are being forced to address long-term, organic problems which had been suppressed by, or appeased within, the Communist system of rule.

The series is edited under the sponsorship of Lorton House, an independent charitable association which exists to promote the academic study of communism and related concepts.

Surviving Post-communism
Young People in the Former Soviet Union

K. Roberts
Professor of Sociology, University of Liverpool, UK

with

S.C. Clark
Department of Sociology, Social Policy and Social Work Studies, University of Liverpool, UK

C. Fagan
Department of Sociology, University of Manchester, UK

J. Tholen
Head, Department of Knowledge Transfer, University of Bremen, Germany

assisted by
A. Adibekian, G. Nemiria and L. Tarkhnishvili

STUDIES OF COMMUNISM IN TRANSITION

Edward Elgar
Cheltenham, UK • Northampton, MA, USA

Published by
Edward Elgar Publishing Limited
Glensanda House
Montpellier Parade
Cheltenham
Glos GL50 1UA
UK

Edward Elgar Publishing, Inc.
136 West Street
Suite 202
Northampton
Massachusetts 01060
USA

A catalogue record for this book
is available from the British Library

Library of Congress Cataloguing in Publication Data

Surviving post-communism: young people in the former Soviet Union / K. Roberts, with S.C. Clark, C. Fagan, J. Tholen; assisted by A. Adibekian, G. Nemiria, L. Tarknishvili.
     (Studies of communism in transition)
   Includes bibliographical references and index.
   1. Youth—Former Soviet republics—Economic conditions. 2. Youth— Former Soviet republics—special conditions. I. Roberts, Kenneth, 1940– II. Clark, S.C. III. Adibekian, A. IV. Series.

HQ799.F59 S87 2000
305.235'0947—dc21

                                                                99–053194

ISBN 1 84064 103 7

Electronic typesetting by Lorton Hall
Printed and bound in Great Britain by MPG Books Ltd, Bodmin, Cornwall

Contents

Figures and Tables

FIGURES

TABLES

Preface

The research on which most of this book is based was funded by INTAS (award 93-2693). INTAS stands for International Association for the Promotion of Co-operation with Scientists from the New Independent States of the former Soviet Union. The INTAS members are the European Union countries plus Iceland, Israel, Norway and Switzerland. Our research among young people in the former Soviet Union began as one of the first-wave INTAS projects. Funding was secured in 1993 then extended, and the actual research was undertaken between 1995 and 1999. We should like to express our appreciation to INTAS for enabling us to collaborate.

Like all INTAS projects, our research was a partnership between scientists from former Soviet and Western countries. The data collection was basically by the Armenian, Georgian and Ukrainian partners, but all other aspects of the research – the design of the enquiries and the interpretation of the findings – were thoroughly collaborative.

There have been several streams of output. The researchers from the New Independent States have produced reports in the national languages, mostly with strong policy orientations. This book is written by the Western partners to explain post-communism to a primarily Western audience, but we know that some readers will be from the New East and we hope that they will recognize the portrait that we offer. We are fairly confident here because all our interpretations and conclusions have been agreed with our partners in Georgia, Armenia and Ukraine.

There are dozens of individuals whom we need to thank for their work on the projects, mostly postgraduates in Yerevan, Tbilisi, Donetsk and Lviv who were the data gatherers. We describe our working methods in some detail in Appendix I to this book. We are also grateful to Clare Minghella and Hilary McDonagh who word processed successive drafts of our manuscript.

Needless to say, the authors alone are responsible for any errors and omissions.

K. ROBERTS
S.C. CLARK
C. FAGAN
J. THOLEN

1. After Communism

TRANSITIONS TO WHAT?

At the start of this new millennium most people in most former communist countries are still net losers. It is true that they have gained new religious and political freedoms but in terms of living standards post-communism is still delivering less than communism.

The countries are usually described as in transition. This is the preferred view of their situations in the West and inside the countries themselves where neither the authorities nor the people wish to believe that they have already reached their ultimate destinations. The countries are supposed to be becoming Western-type democracies with buoyant market economies. At any rate, no one has publicized an alternative goal. The following chapters show that the prospect of Westernization is attractive to most of their people, certainly the young people. Most still believe that the goal is realizable but this optimism is unlikely to last indefinitely. Whether it is well founded will become known only later in the twenty-first century. If international capital were confident about the countries' futures then, presumably, it would already be gushing in.

In fact, all the countries are heading into uncharted territory. There have been no previous transitions from communism. At present all forecasts are guestimates. There are no experts. Post-communism is a wholly new subject. Russia and the Baltic states apart, none of the ex-Soviet countries has a modern history of independence. Their viability is unproven.

All the countries have been deluged with Western advice, all less authoritative than the bearers like to pretend. A blunt fact of the situation is that no one has any soundly based knowledge on how to manage a transition from communism. This has not inhibited outside advisers from applying measurements of the countries' progress: monetary stabilization, the proportions of the economies transferred to the private sectors, and so on. There is a similar set of indicators of democratization. Among other uses, the indices have been used to place countries in a queue for European Union (EU) membership. Yet inside their own countries the Western advisers would not remain in post, or governments that continued to listen could not expect to remain in office, on the basis of their track records in the East. The Eastern countries that have fared best have owed this not to the quality of the Western advice that they have received, or to their having acted upon it, but to their geographical proximity to the EU. However, Western advice and influence have achieved what was probably the primary goal all along: dismantling the old systems so rapidly and thoroughly, whatever the immediate damage to people's day-to-day quality of life and living standards, as to make the resurrection of communism highly improbable. The main threat to the West from 1945 until the 1980s has vanished. What the East has gained is far less certain.

This book offers a glimpse into the everyday realities of post-communism. It goes beneath the economic indicators and studies of political elites and structures to examine the everyday lives of ordinary young people. They are always an interesting age group since their lives are touched by all the major social institutions: the family, education, employment and politics. And since young people's own lives are in transition they are usually exceptionally sensitive to changes in the surrounding social, economic, political and cultural orders. They are usually the most receptive age group to new fashions in dress, upturns and downturns in labour demand, and new political causes. Moreover, the first post-communist generations may offer some useful indications of the kinds of adult populations that the former communist countries are most likely to produce and reproduce.

Our book is deliberately restrained in offering advice and predictions. It is essentially an account of what post-communism actually is. Most of the evidence is from three former Soviet countries – Armenia, Georgia and Ukraine – but comparisons are drawn throughout with the situations in other ex-communist countries, including those in Central Europe, and with studies of young people in the West. This makes it possible to distinguish what is common among young people in all modern societies, East and West, features that distinguish the entire post-communist bloc, and variations among the former communist countries.

EX-COMMUNIST AND EX-SOVIET

A recurrent contrast in the following chapters is that between former Soviet and Central European countries. There were always solid reasons for believing that these two groups of countries would experience different post-communist trajectories.

History

In the early 1990s most former Soviet republics became new independent states, members of the Commonwealth of Independent States (CIS). At that time most of these countries, including the three on which this book focuses, had no prior modern histories of independence. Ukraine had never been independent except for a brief period (1918–21) following the Bolshevik revolution. Armenia and Georgia had substantial histories of independence but these ended in the fourteenth century. This is just one respect in which the former Soviet republics differ from Central European countries such as Poland and Hungary.

Another contrast is that the ex-Soviet countries had no pre-communist histories as modern industrial societies. Central Europe is different. In the longer term, in these countries communism may appear to have been but a brief interlude in their modern histories whereas republics such as Armenia, Georgia and Ukraine were modernized by communism. Previously most of their people were peasants, living in villages with no modern services or amenities. These countries have no pre-communist modern histories to resume.

How communism ended

There have been further differences: in the length of time the countries were communist, and in exactly how communism collapsed. Protest movements in Central Europe – Solidarity in Poland and Civic Forum in Czechoslovakia (as it then was) – played a crucial role in undermining communism. The reforms in Central Europe, particularly the lifting of Soviet domination, were a response to pressure from below. Once conceded, these reforms fuelled a mounting crisis within Soviet communism. It was at this time, between 1988 and 1991, that political

4 *Surviving Post-communism*

reform movements and religious revivals mushroomed in many of the Soviet republics. Young people, especially students, were heavily involved in these movements. By 1991 there was widespread support for reform and rather less uniform and more equivocal support for independence. However, these were delivered to countries such as Armenia, Georgia and Ukraine not through the force of internal pressure but because Yeltsin took Russia out of the Soviet Union. Suddenly the reform movements in the other Soviet republics had everything that they had asked for. Indeed, reform became a necessity rather than a choice.

Although the changes have subsequently been referred to as revolutions there were not necessarily sweeping changes in political personnel. In many of the new independent states there were no major changes in the structures of government. In some countries the old communists remained in office, having been reborn as nationalists and democrats. This usually occurred without any shakeouts in the state apparatuses. The old bureaucracies and officials remained in place and continued to operate in most of their customary ways. It was different in Poland and Czechoslovakia, for example, where, for a few years at any rate, not only the Communist Parties but also the old communist politicians were swept out of office. In most of the former Soviet Union it was less a case that communism was toppled by reform movements than that it was transformed from above or within.

Economic decline and recovery

Another difference between Central Europe and the former Soviet Union is that in the latter countries the reforms have led to deeper and longer-lasting economic crises. Everywhere, most of Central Europe included (the Czech Republic being the exception), the end of central economic planning led to steep drops in economic output of 30 per cent, 50 per cent and more. An inevitable result was a plunge in living standards of a type akin to the impact of a major war. One cause of the decline was market reforms, the so-called shock therapy of withdrawing subsidies from state enterprises thereby obliging them to slim, to cut unit costs or to do whatever was necessary to trade their output at market prices or shut down. However, the principal reason for the economic collapse was the breakdown in the Soviet bloc's trading relationships in which the administratively set prices often bore little resemblance to world market prices (see Gros, 1997). Inevitably the countries that were the most integrated into this Soviet-led system – namely, the countries of the former Soviet Union – were the most severely affected by its demise. When the planning system was dismantled many of the trading relationships simply collapsed. Plants lost various combinations of their supplies, sales and incomes, and these were domino-type repercussions. This was at the time when the new independent states were introducing their own currencies. These, and the Russian rouble, lost value rapidly, eliminating people's savings unless these had already been banked in the West or otherwise converted into hard currency. Rapidly depreciating currencies were hardly a good basis on which to revive trade and industry. The experience of citizens in many parts of the former Soviet Union was that industry simply stopped.

The steepest declines in output occurred between 1989 and 1992. Thereafter recovery commenced in the Central European countries where the declines had been painful but relatively shallow. In most of the old Soviet Union, in contrast, the economies either continued to contract, albeit more slowly, or merely stabilized. In 1999 recovery was still a forecast rather than an event in most of these countries. Recovery in Central Europe was stimulated by an influx of Western money: for exports, as investment, and through tourism. In 1997 foreign investors injected $5000 million into Poland but just $623 million into Ukraine, an adjacent, larger country in both territory and population. Except in honeypots such as Moscow and St Petersburg, the former Soviet Union has enjoyed no comparable stimulus. Up to 1997 no Western airlines had scheduled flights into Georgia or Armenia. Communism had developed the countries' economies and at the dawn of the twenty-first century it remains unclear whether post-communism can offer a more attractive status than underdevelopment.

MARKET REFORMS: CHOICE OR NECESSITY?

Before we all succumb to amnesia we should remind ourselves that the reform movements that gained popular support at the end of the 1980s were not demanding market reforms. The common denominator was a demand for self-determination: by the country or republic, or some-times by the oblast (regional authority). Sometimes, but not always, the movements sought to replace existing elites. Everyone was in favour of democracy, a word with elastic definitions, but always meaning that governments become representative and responsive to the people's will. A common demand was for more effective government, to arrest the economic decline which had been occurring virtually everywhere since the 1970s. Environmental issues were sometimes high on the (post-Chernobyl) agendas.

There were no popular demonstrations in favour of selling state enterprises to politicians or plant directors or to foreigners. The demon-strators were not seeking reforms that would shut down workplaces or decimate the workforces, or cut back state spending on pensions and child care, or raise the prices of transport, telephones and electricity to market levels. In so far as there was widespread support for private enterprise, the kinds of enterprise that people were most likely to have in mind were those that they had experienced: growing produce for sale, repairing neighbours' cars, and importing and selling Western goods, for example. People wanted all this to become legal and open but did not usually envisage any enterprise of their own becoming subject to new commercial laws and taxation.

In Poland, Solidarity was basically a trade union at the start. Its original demands were for better socialism: for enterprises and the country to become responsive to and to be run in workers' interests. The leaders of the Eastern reform movements and their active supporters were most likely to be reform communists, though rarely Gorbachev supporters: he was generally (outside the West) regarded as ineffective. Reformers who wanted to tear down the iron curtain envisaged their countries becoming part of or equal partners with, not subordinate to, the West.

Market reforms were not so much a choice, a response to people's pleas, but a necessity when the state economies folded. This dis-empowered the governments. None was able to prevent the run down. They differed only in the extent to which they attempted to retain formal control. In practice the politicians and central planners could do no better than to allow plant managements to do their best. This was the context of the 'honest robbery' privatizations. No one but the existing managers would have been willing to take over, let alone to purchase and try to run, the establishments profitably.

Assistance and at least the prospect of inward investment were available from the West, and a condition was always market reforms. These measures were sometimes embraced by the original reform movements. Hence the paradox (from a Western perspective) of trade unions (in parts of Poland for example) demanding faster privatization and speedier market reforms and the replacement of too hesitant ex-communist bureaucrats, managers and politicians.

It has been easiest to make market reforms popular where there are obvious benefits; this means, in the main, in the countries where Western capital has flowed in. In the old Soviet Union people certainly like the larger number of shops and the wider choice of goods. Yes, the people would like the 'Western way of life'. But few approve of the privatizations which have transformed old communists into the new bourgeoisie, or their countries' transformation from being among the world's most equal societies to being among its most unequal.

By the mid-1990s the Central European countries were being manifestly Westernized. Further east, the old systems had been dismantled to various extents, living standards had plunged, insecurity had spread, and what would follow was still unclear (see Wallace and Haerpfer, 1998). The former Soviet Union has endured plenty of shock, but in most places the therapy is still invisible (see Gerber and Hout, 1998).

In Central Europe the pace of change has been remarkable. Up to 1992, visiting Poland from the West was an adventure. It was necessary to obtain a visa. Warsaw airport had Soviet-style customs checks for inward and outward travellers. Hotels had higher prices for foreigners and wanted to hold on to passports until guests departed. The most vivid evidence of the new market economy was the spontaneous bazaars in Warsaw's central square and at the football stadium. It used to be difficult to find picture postcards to buy or all the other standard tourist items. By 1995 Warsaw had a new airport terminal, visa requirements had been lifted (for EU citizens), customs had been Westernized, hotels charged uniform prices and wanted only a record of passport numbers, there was an up-market shopping district in Warsaw, tourist goods were on sale everywhere, virtually all the stores had been Westernized, and the city was jammed with private motor traffic.

Further east the changes had been equally remarkable and shocking. By the mid-1990s Kiev, Tbilisi and Yerevan (the capitals of Ukraine, Georgia and Armenia) all had modern airports, but otherwise their procedures remained Soviet. The conditions in Yerevan's modern airport were really dreadful. There were no refreshments or heating, even in the depth of winter. The toilets became primitive, especially when passengers had to wait all day and night for delayed Aeroflot flights. At that time the Armenian national airline could offer no reliable flights due to a shortage of aviation fuel. Any aircraft wishing to depart from Yerevan needed to land with full fuel tanks. Visiting Armenia was still an adventure: it was impossible to know in advance exactly how and when one would leave the country.

THE SECOND ECONOMIES

It is necessary to qualify this grim picture by acknowledging that all the ex-communist countries have second, grey or unofficial economies of unknown size but estimated as ranging from 30 per cent to over 50 per cent of all gainful economic activity. Much private sector economic activity has remained 'in the shade', where it was under communism. There have been substantial gaps everywhere between official statistics on incomes and what people are recorded as spending and are seen to be spending on cars and in restaurants. In Central Europe, after a brief period of wild and free capitalism, the new market economies slowly became subject to the rule of law. Further east the second economies have remained as huge as ever.

Knowledge of this can encourage a blasé attitude towards the countries' predicaments: nudges and winks convey the impression that most people are managing well and that in reality many are benefiting from the reforms. Be that as it may, a plain fact of the situation has been that for most people the second economies have done no more than ease the pain. The age-old, apparently universal law, 'Whosoever hath, to him shall be given', operates ruthlessly 'in the shade'. In many places the reforms have led to acute shortages and breakdowns in basic services: water supplies function for only a few hours per day and there are frequent interruptions to electricity supplies, for example. In many cities of the former Soviet Union families have spent years living in dark and cold conditions, repairing rather than replacing clothing. Rates of mortality have risen. It has been common everywhere to see people trying to raise money through the street sale of garden produce and personal or household possessions. Young adults have seen their parents impoverished, their savings eliminated and the value of their pensions decimated. They have seen public buildings, roads, schools and hospitals become physically dilapidated. When they have remained optimistic this has usually been in spite of rather than on the basis of their own experiences of post-communism.

Needless to say, the story of post-communism has not been one of unalleviated suffering. There have been new religious and political freedoms. Everywhere there are more varied shops and television programmes. 'Everything is born in pain', said one of the young Ukrainians we interviewed. Many appear to have subscribed to an Eastern version of the maxim that 'If it's hurting it might be working'. It has only subsequently become fully apparent how deeply communism was detested. Most young people have been willing to trade the old guarantees for the mere chance that the Western way of life might spread to their countries.

COUNTRY SPECIFICITIES

When the reforms commenced, all the ex-communist countries started the new era from similar positions. They had all spent decades with basically the same systems of political authority and economic planning. Communism built similar blocks of flats and offices everywhere. There was a common, though not completely uniform, way of life. Even the elites enjoyed only modest advantages compared with their equivalents in the West.

While conducting research in the New East we have held research meetings in some of the old elite haunts: the Holiday Home of the Council of Ministers in Bulgaria and Smolenice Castle in Slovakia, for instance. The local participants were surprised to find that the Bulgarian facility was definitely below four-star standard. Smolenice's presidential suite is huge, but it is neither as well-equipped nor as comfortable as the equivalent in Bratislava's new Forum Hotel. The 1998 market rate in both of the ex-elite facilites was $30 a night (compared with $150 for a standard room in the Bratislava Forum). It is true that the East's old elites had privileged access to scarce Western goods, city centre flats, official cars and dachas, but it would have been hard to find even junior executives in the West who would have traded their own salaries and perks for Eastern privileges. By all international standards, the communist elites lived modestly.

As soon as communism collapsed, inter-national and intra-country differences, some of these being blatant inequalities, began to widen rapidly. Widening inter-country differences were due partly to the different paces at which the market economies developed and the extent to which the state sectors contracted. In other instances, however, the widening contrasts between countries have been due to a resuscitation of national characteristics. In much of the former communist world an older 'nationalities question' has been reopened (see Mestrovic, 1994).

All countries have unique histories, cultures, geographical and other circumstances. Even if these do not explain, they usually help to shape or at least form the context for events and how these are experienced by those concerned. Throughout the following chapters there are constant references to how the reforms took somewhat different courses, or at any rate had varying consequences in the 1990s in Georgia, Armenia and Ukraine, albeit within a shared post-Soviet context; hence the need to preface everything with an introduction to these countries.

Georgia and Armenia are both small states today (and always have been), with populations of over five million and over three million respectively. Up to 1998 there had been no post-Soviet censuses, so all up-to-date population figures are estimates. Both countries are on the southern fringe of the CIS, situated between the Black Sea and the Caspian Sea (see Figure 1.1). They share a common border: Armenia is to Georgia's south; Russia is on the other side of Georgia's northern and western borders. Both countries have Turkey as a common southern neighbour and Azerbaijan as a common neighbour in the east. In the south Armenia is also bordered by Iran. The Georgians and Armenians are both Middle Eastern peoples, except that both became Christian in the fourth century AD and, as a result, have subsequently had an occidental orientation. They would like to be regarded (by the EU especially) as present-day Europe's Far East.

Ukraine is more European in its history and location. It is a large country, equivalent in area to Britain and France combined, situated on and extending westward from the northern perimeter of the Black Sea. Its current population is over 50 million. Ukraine is surrounded by Russia to its east and north; then, moving from the north-west

Figure 1.1 Map of Central and Eastern Europe

southwards, its neighbours are Belarus, Poland, Slovakia, Hungary, Romania and Moldova.

Like most other European peoples, the Ukrainians have existed for less than a thousand years. The Armenians and Georgians differ from them in this respect: they have much longer histories, as do many Eastern peoples. Armenia and Georgia are both Caucasian nations. There are similarities with the Balkans: Caucasia is another region where Christianity met, and still meets, Islam; it is also mountainous. The peoples of this region have lived close together, or so it appears on the map, but they are separated by mountains across which there has been little regular communication. So although Georgia and Armenia are both small countries with a common border, their peoples have rarely visited each other. This was true before and during communism, when Armenians and Georgians were most likely to meet in Moscow. There has been little inter-marriage. When our research project meetings were held in Tbilisi and Yerevan, most of the Georgian and Armenian participants were making their first visits to each other's countries. The peoples of the Caucasus have lived there for millennia without merging into a single Caucasian nation.

Armenia

Armenians, like many Eastern peoples, can trace their history to beyond 2000 BC. Some regard Tigranes II as their greatest king. He reigned from 95 to 55 BC. Armenia has been a great power in the Middle East but this was very long ago. It can claim to have become the first Christian country, having officially adopted the religion in 314 AD since when the Armenians have maintained their own Christian church, neither Orthodox nor Catholic. The Armenian language (in written form) dates from 404 AD. Their own language, church and culture have been crucial in maintaining the Armenians' identity. Throughout their history they have usually been living in, fighting against or ruled by some other state. The country has rarely enjoyed long periods of peace. Indeed, its history has been described as 'perpetual warfare' (Walker, 1991). In Soviet times Armenia produced far more Soviet army generals than might have been expected from a republic of its size.

Armenia was an independent state, a great power in its region, from 885 AD until 1375 AD. It then fell under Ottoman, followed by Russian

and Soviet rule until 1991, except for a brief period between 1918 and
1921 following the collapse of the Tsarist regime but before the Soviet
Union incorporated the territory. Until the late 1980s a *pax Sovietica*
operated. Indeed, Armenia flourished under communism. In 1920,
outside Yerevan, the capital, most of the people lived in typical Middle
Eastern villages without any modern amenities. By the 1980s, 80 per
cent of the population lived in urban areas and Armenia had become
one of the three best-educated republics in the Soviet Union and was
top in terms of Candidates of Science (the equivalent of PhDs) per
capita. Soviet communism modernized Armenia, and most Armenians
were grateful for this. They were proud to be Armenians and, simultaneously, citizens of the Soviet Union. Unlike the Georgians (see
below), the Armenians feel close to Russia. Before and during
communism Russia protected Armenia from its enemies to the south.
And the Soviet Union did more than this: it placed Armenia where its
people felt they belonged – within the modern occidental world.

When the Soviet Union ended, the *pax Sovietica* evaporated and
Armenia resumed its normal history (of warfare). Armenia and Azerbaijan were already locked in a dispute over the status of Nagorny
Karabakh, a mountainous part of Azerbaijan with a mainly Armenian
population. When the Soviet referee and controller of the armed forces
in the area withdrew, the dispute between Armenia and Azerbaijan
intensified and armed conflict erupted. Since 1994 there has been an
official ceasefire but no settlement. Since independence Armenia has
felt it necessary to maintain a substantial army. The military (and the
police) have high profiles throughout Armenia. They have drained the
state's already depleted resources. And in the early 1990s the economic
crisis in Armenia was intensified by a blockade imposed by all the
country's Muslim neighbours (Iran and Turkey as well as Azerbaijan).
Armenia is landlocked. It has some mineral ores but all the country's
main industries which developed in Soviet times depended on imported
energy and raw materials. Its main communications (in Soviet times)
were through Azerbaijan. Subsequently Armenia's only reasonably
reliable land routes to the outside world have been through Georgia
with whom relationships have never been better than just acceptable.
The rail link remained closed up to 1997 and even the main road was in
poor condition. Since independence, as in earlier centuries, Russia has
in fact been Armenia's main ally – its main source of diplomatic
support and essential supplies, including military hardware.

There are only just over three million people in present-day Armenia, but roughly the same number of Armenians live outside the country: there is a substantial diaspora. Those abroad have been an important source of aid in the 1990s, typically sending cash gifts to their families and supporting non-governmental organizations (NGOs) with projects in Armenia. The diaspora has been responsible for funding the Armenian American University, the best-resourced higher education institute in Yerevan in the 1990s. Under communism the diaspora resulted in Armenians having more links with and greater awareness of the outside (Western) world than did the populations in most other Soviet republics.

By 1997 Armenia's relationship with Iran had improved, but not with Azerbaijan or Turkey. Present-day Armenia is not located on the territory of historical Armenia: this (which includes Mount Ararat) is in Turkey. There was a substantial Armenian population in north-east Turkey until 'the massacre' in 1915 (which the Armenians regard as an attempted genocide), when the Armenians from the area who survived did so by fleeing eastward, into present-day Armenia. Exactly what happened in 1915 is still fiercely disputed, both in the people's memories and at government level, between Armenia and Turkey.

Since independence Armenia's population has been depleted by emigration. Up to 1995 the country lost roughly three-quarters of a million people, mainly young people who were seeking to escape from the dire economic conditions and military service. In the first half of the 1990s there was widespread pessimism about Armenia's future. Surveys suggested that more than 80 per cent of the population were potential emigrants (see Adibekian, 1991, 1992, 1995). Inside the country conditions were described as not just 'grim' but 'heavy'. By the mid-1990s Armenia's cities, towns and villages contained scores of young war veterans suffering various combinations of physical and psychological injuries. There were also roughly 400,000 war refugees (mainly from Azerbaijan), plus young war widows.

Political conditions within Armenia were contributing to the 'heavy' atmosphere. Upon independence the old political elite was swept aside. The old rulers were replaced by a new group with popular support, the Karabakh Committee, most of whose members had been in the Communist Party though not in elite positions (see Fischer and Grigorian, 1993). The Karabakh Committee achieved power on a platform of settling (winning) the dispute with Azerbaijan. The ruling personnel changed but the old political structures remained intact and effective one-party rule was maintained. Opposition to the government was treated as almost treachery.

However, the economic situation quickly became the most depressing feature of Armenia's post-communist condition. By 1991, 85 per cent of the country's industry had stopped. Armenia's industries had depended heavily on imported raw materials and energy, so when the supply lines closed so did the Armenian economy. Until 1996 there were daily interruptions in electricity and water supplies. Then in 1996 the nuclear power station at Medzamor, which had been closed following the Chernobyl disaster, was reopened and conditions eased. In fact, in 1994 Armenia became the first CIS country to begin to recover economically, but this recovery was from a very low base. Armenia has no natural resources which could be its economic salvation as an independent state. In practice, throughout the 1990s Armenia remained heavily dependent on Russia from whom many Armenians never wanted to be separated.

Although Armenian was the republic's official language in Soviet times, Russian language schools were popular. In Yerevan in the 1980s, 45 per cent of pupils attended schools in which Russian was the language of instruction. These schools tended to be the best resourced (they were used by elite groups) and, equally relevant, there were larger literatures in Russian than in Armenian in most subjects, especially the sciences, and Russian was the main language of education in the USSR. It was the language of Moscow, the main centre of official intellectual life and where academically ambitious young Armenians aspired to study.

Education and the arts have always been highly esteemed in Armenia. In the 1990s some of Yerevan's youth theatres were among the few facilities that remained reasonably resourced. State buildings became dilapidated and the roads became potholed while some theatres continued to renew their lighting and sound equipment, despite being unable to pay the performers and with the public ceasing to be able to afford admission charges. The funds for the theatres, as for much else, were from abroad. Their use says much about the values of the providers and the recipients.

Although they number only about three million, the Armenians are splintered into several groups. There are in fact two Armenian languages – Eastern and Western. Only the Eastern language is now spoken inside Armenia (though in over two dozen dialects). The use of Western Armenian became rare (except among the diaspora) when the Western lands were lost to Turkey and most of the language's speakers were massacred.

Armenians refer to their clan-like individualism; there are several major 'clans'. In Yerevan there is the established urban population, recent settlers from rural areas, and sections of the diaspora who have returned to Armenia from different places and at different times. One wave of in-migration occurred after the creation of the Soviet Union. However strange this might sound today, in the 1920s there was a great deal of enthusiasm about the socialism that was being constructed. One recently formed 'clan' within Armenia is composed of refugees from Azerbaijan. There are no formal organizations, and individuals' main loyalties are to their own families, but members of the 'clans' recognize their commonality and, for example, will often prefer to employ and do business with one another. Additional 'clans' have formed around particular kinds of careers; in the Communist Party under communism and in government and political office subsequently, for instance.

These forms of social organization helped the Armenian people to survive in earlier centuries, and they have been called on again in the 1990s. The scale of emigration since independence may suggest that many Armenians have concluded that they will be able to lead and protect their preferred ways of life only outside their own country. However, the decision to join the diaspora has a long history among the Armenian people. The need to flee in the 1990s was not a historical novelty. Armenians are accustomed to surviving adversity.

Georgia

In some ways Georgia is another Armenia, only slightly larger with a population of over five million and a Black Sea border. The countries' histories have many parallels. As with Armenia, there have been states on the territory of present-day Georgia to which the modern population traces its ancestry since before 1000 BC. The peoples of Georgia became Christian in the fourth century AD, at roughly the same time as Armenia, and have remained Christian but as part of the Orthodox confession. And it was not until the end of the first millennium that a unified Georgian state was first created. Independent Georgia then survived until the fourteenth century. As with Armenia, the preceding centuries were the nation's golden age, its classical period. Georgia, like Armenia, then fell into the hands of Muslim invaders from the south. Georgia came under Russian protection in 1783 but, unlike Armenia, always tended to experience this relationship as one of subjugation. Up to the nineteenth century parts of Georgia survived as small independent kingdoms. There were more or less continuous nationalist independence movements up to the 1980s. However, until 1991 Georgia's only post-fourteenth century period of independence as an entire country was between 1918 and 1921, during the interval between the collapse of the Tsarist regime and the spread of Soviet power.

Georgia produced Stalin but was never an acquiescent Soviet republic. Even so, like Armenia, it was modernized by communism; also like Armenia, it was among the Soviet Union's best-educated republics. And Georgia had additional advantages: its temperate climate permits diverse types of agriculture and the Black Sea coastal resorts were the base for a thriving tourist industry. All this was in addition to the modern industries that communism developed.

During the 1990s Georgia's experience of independence was similar to Armenia's in some ways, specifically in that the two countries' transitions were complicated by military conflicts. Georgia's communist rulers were replaced in elections in 1990 by dissident nationalists (albeit mostly former Communist Party members) led by Zviad Gamsakhurdia. As in Armenia, the new elite did not change Georgia's political structures and proceeded to establish its own authoritarian rule. Here the Georgian regime was less successful than Armenia's new rulers. Gamsakhurdia was ousted in a military coup in 1992, whereupon Georgia's politicians splintered into numerous factions. Eduard Shevardnadze, the former Soviet foreign minister, was initially installed as president by the military and subsequently confirmed by election. In the midst of these events the 'Tbilisi War' erupted, a shooting match between rival groups of Georgian politicians and their supporters. By then Georgia's territorial integrity was under threat. Three regions, South Ossetia (in the north of Georgia), Abkhazia (in the west) and Adjaria (in the south), were anxious to retain the autonomy that had been granted to them when Georgia was part of the Soviet Union. Between 1991 and 1994 there was a series of armed clashes in South Ossetia and Abkhazia in which 20,000 people died, mainly young soldiers. Since 1994 there have been ceasefires but no settlements: the

Georgian government has been unable to establish control in either
Abkhazia or South Ossetia. Nor has the government been fully secure
even in Tbilisi. By 1998 President Shevardnadze had survived two
assassination attempts, believed to be by dissident Georgian political
factions. During its civil wars Georgia acquired around 500,000 war
refugees, mainly Georgians from the unsettled regions. In 1998 some
were still squatting in what had once been Tbilisi's main hotel. By 1995
an estimated 800,000 people had left the country for much the same
reasons as in Armenia. Georgia has not been in official dispute with any
other state, though most Georgians have suspected, with or without
proper justification, that their historical subjugator, Russia, has been
influential in provoking trouble in the country's north and west where
the non-Georgian populations have always felt closer to Russia (in the
case of the Abkhazians) or to a national minority within the Russian
Federation (in the case of the South Ossetians) than to the Georgian
majority in the republic.

The types of warfare in which Armenia and Georgia became
involved in the early 1990s did not unify either country. These were
'dirty' rather than 'clean' wars. There were clashes between opposing
armies but much of the military action was against civilians. There was
looting, hostage taking and hostage selling. Neither the Armenian nor
the Georgian army won. Those who fought did not return home as
victorious heroes; many returned with serious physical and psychological damage. And the countries found themselves with thousands of
displaced persons who had lost all their possessions, their homes and
homelands, and their own people were unable or unwilling to right
these wrongs.

Georgia and Armenia in the 1990s became examples of how war can
damage economic life. The military turbulence in Georgia, as in
Armenia, exacerbated the disruption of trading relationships and
industry. Tourism simply ceased in the Black Sea regions within
or close to Abkhazia. Georgia shared many of Armenia's post-
independence problems but, whereas in Armenia these were managed
by a strong state, in Georgia economic and social life quickly became
chaotic, at least on the surface. Tbilisi's new airport was designed for
Soviet-style customs checks, but on most occasions inward and
outward passengers have simply walked through. Up to 1995 Western
visitors did not need visas in order to enter Georgia: the (weak)
government was unable to operate the necessary procedures. Road

traffic in Tbilisi appears to avoid even more collisions only by observing informal rules that visitors are unable to decipher.

Even in the 1980s much of the Georgian economy was being run not by the political elite or state planners but by unofficial 'partnerships' between plant directors, individual bureaucrats and businessmen. Subsequently these groups often became the 'legitimate' owners (see Gachechiladze, 1995). Underneath the surface in Georgia, as in Armenia, many traditional social practices and bonds acquired renewed importance in the 1990s. Like Armenians, Georgians are splintered into clan-like groups. In Georgia most of these groups have origins in particular regions (where surnames have a common ending – -vili or -adze, for example). These affinities and traditional extended family relationships survived communism in Georgia and became more important than previously in its aftermath. They helped people to survive the post-communist 1990s. Wellisz (1996) argues that these bonds have in fact saved many Georgians from starvation, but warns that the same loyalties could prevent Georgia developing into a 'normal' modern state and a Western-type market economy.

In the 1990s Georgia was advantaged, *vis-à-vis* Armenia, in not being blockaded. By 1996 Georgia was building a pipeline to carry Azerbaijan's oil to the Black Sea. This was to be the country's economic salvation, regenerating the economy and making Georgia as important to the West as Kuwait. However, other countries have been building pipelines to transport Azerbaijan's oil to world markets. Russia has been the traditional route (via Chechnia), and Turkey has high hopes of obtaining Western investment to fund a deal with its Muslim neighbour, Azerbaijan.

Ukraine

The latest birth of independent Ukraine has been less bloody though in some respects it inherited the most threatening example of the 'nationalities question'. Georgians (around 70 per cent) and Armenians (over 90 per cent) are by far the largest national groups in their respective countries. Ukraine is different. It has Russian (by language and origin) majorities in the east (in its most heavily industrialized regions surrounding the cities of Donetsk and Kharkiv) and in Crimea. Following the break-up of the Soviet Union, Russia claimed the greater part of the Black Sea fleet and control over its main bases, which are in

Crimea. Simultaneously, the Tartars who had been expelled from Crimea during Soviet times made claims upon 'their' homeland and property. Fortunately, all the parties in Ukraine, and in Moscow, have recognized a common interest in resolving these matters peacefully. And within Ukraine the main national groups have agreed on the need to maintain Ukraine's independence and integrity. None wants to divide the country.

Ukraine, unlike Georgia and Armenia, is a huge country, one of the largest in Europe. The people have existed for almost a thousand years but, until 1991, without a country of their own except between 1918 and 1921. From the Middle Ages onwards the territory was ruled (in whole or part) by Mongols, Lithuania, the Habsburgs, Poland and Russia. There were periodic invasions from the south, by Turks, in response to which the Cossacks were formed. Ukraine may have had no prior experience of independence but it was among the least acquiescent Soviet republics. Partisans (nationalists), based in the west of Ukraine, fought Soviet troops in the 1920s, during the Second World War and until the early 1950s.

The east of Ukraine was thoroughly industrialized during the Soviet period, beginning before the Second World War when the newly opened or expanded mines and factories were staffed largely by Russian migrants. Part of the west was integrated into Ukraine only after the Second World War. Previously a part of this region had been within Poland, and before that within the Habsburg Empire, so this particular part of Ukraine has a Western history. The main religion in the west is Uniate or Greek Catholic: the worship is Orthodox but the church recognizes the supremacy of Rome. The east of Ukraine is overwhelmingly Orthodox (or atheist) and the central regions are religiously mixed. Of the countries featured in this book it is Ukraine which contains the sharpest internal, regional contrasts, which is why our fieldwork in Ukraine was split between two centres, Lviv in the west and Donetsk in the east.

Following independence most of Ukraine's communist politicians stayed in power but were divided into new parties, though the Communist Party remained a force. Immediately a left–right split among the old and new parties became apparent but alongside another, equally clear division. With the exception of the Communist and Socialist Parties there have been entirely different parties organizing in and representing the populations of east and west Ukraine. In west Ukraine nationalist parties are not merely influential: nationalism has been the dominant, over-arching political position.

Nevertheless, Ukraine's main problems since independence have been economic rather than political. The centrally planned economy seized up when the Soviet Union ended, though not to the same extent as in Georgia and Armenia. Ukrainians had always regarded their land as blessed with natural resources. It used to be described as 'the bread basket of Russia'. In the east it has coal and other mineral resources. However, after the break-up of the Soviet Union Ukraine discovered that it was unable to market either food or coal at world prices; and in the mid-1990s repairing and containing the damage from the 1986 Chernobyl disaster was still consuming 10 per cent of Ukraine's GNP. This burden was equal to the costs of the country's armed forces.

CHOICE OF COUNTRIES

In practice there was no choice. The research partners would not have been equally qualified to tackle other countries; but Armenia, Georgia and Ukraine are probably as illustrative as any other three countries of post-communist situations. Our countries do not include Moscow, which is representative of nowhere but itself. Our countries are not Central Europe. The West tends to hear most about these adjacent countries. The transition experiences of Poland, Hungary and the Czech Republic are in fact highly untypical. The following chapters make comparisons with Central Europe but from a more typical, CIS-centred position.

A balanced selection?

Our focal countries are certainly not a representative sample. Could any selection be representative? Our claim is rather that the countries offer a spread of quite typical post-Soviet scenarios. Warfare has been common. The West knows about Jugoslavia (as was) and Chechnia, but perhaps less about the restive Georgian regions, Nagorny Karabakh and the numerous other conflagrations in the former Soviet Union. Economic decline has occurred in most places. The state sectors have been run down everywhere, though in some places the old order has proved perhaps surprisingly resilient. In some parts of Russia the state-owned factories were able to replace central planning with mutually agreed deals and sometimes with barter arrangements, thereby (wholly or partly) maintaining supplies, production and sales (see Clarke, 1995). The east of Ukraine, the Donbass (Donetsk coal basin) region, has been an example, albeit a weak one, of this. Whether in the longer term the resilience of its older structures in the 1990s will prove a help or hindrance to Ukraine's development remains uncertain. New market sector economies have developed everywhere, more rapidly in some ex-communist countries, especially in Central Europe, than in others, but in all the countries there are particular places, mostly (outside Central Europe) capital cities, where numerous Western firms and projects have established bases. Ukraine, Georgia and Armenia contain examples of all these developments.

All the countries of the former Soviet Union have additional features in common. Some have already been mentioned but deserve repetition. The countries modernized and became industrialized under Soviet communism. At the time the populations did not welcome all aspects of their modernization. The collectivization of agriculture in the 1930s was a bloody process and, in retrospect, probably one of communism's gravest mistakes. Nevertheless, it was communism that gave the countries their factories, mass education, health services and housing with modern amenities. None had a modern pre-communist history which it was able to resume in the 1990s. Moreover, none of the countries which are centre-stage in this book had a pre-communist modern history of independence. In the 1990s the countries' leaders, elected politicians and officials had to learn the arts of governing independent countries and handling international relationships. In many ways the challenges have been analogous to those that would confront Greater Birmingham or Greater Manchester if the cities' politicians and council officers had to transform themselves overnight into national governments. These conurbations' populations are of a similar size to those of Georgia and Armenia. Ukraine's problems have been larger and in some ways much more complicated on account of the country's regional divisions. An independent Scotland would be of comparable size to Georgia and Armenia, but the political transition would be different, probably smoother, because it has so many politicians with experience of national (and international) politics.

In the 1990s all the new independent states of the former Soviet

Union were obliged to step into the unknown. It has been up to them to test out and discover the senses in which such countries can be truly independent, sovereign, in control of their own affairs, in present-day global conditions. Some of the countries discovered very quickly that their real rulers appeared to be the World Bank, the International Monetary Fund, the EU and NATO. The adjacent countries of Eastern and Central Europe have been able to commence becoming integrated into the West. Meanwhile former Soviet countries have often found the West apparently indifferent to their plights. The closest neighbours of Ukraine, Georgia and Armenia are Middle Eastern states, plus Russia: their most powerful neighbour for centuries, gravely weakened in the 1990s but still a powerful influence.

Can we generalize?

Area specialists will insist that Armenia, Georgia and Ukraine are very different countries. We would expect specialists to dispute the wisdom of trying to generalize about them all, but area specialists have vested interests in highlighting particularities. Our own disciplinary backgrounds encourage different inclinations. Sociologists habitually generalize about the UK (sometimes describing it all as Britain); we generalize about Western countries and even about all modern societies.

We recognize, of course, that Armenia and Georgia, on the one hand, and Ukraine, on the other, have entirely different pre-modern histories. We are also aware, and indeed have drawn attention to the fact, that each of these countries has its own language(s), national identity(ies) and culture(s). That said, a crucial fact is that all ex-Soviet countries have massive similarities. Countries do not experience 70 years of Soviet communism without this leaving an impression. Communism modernized them all under basically the same system of political representation and authority and the same system of central economic planning. The types of housing that were built from the 1920s onwards, together with the education, health and social security systems, were all Soviet. Another legacy is that all the people are able to speak, read and write Russian. By the end of communism all this had applied for several generations. On top of this, the countries have shared typical post-Soviet transition experiences: reform movements at the end of the 1980s and in the early 1990s which mobilized popular support for change and independence; enthusiasm and celebration when these were delivered; then steep and deep economic decline accompanied by a dramatic widening of internal inequalities.

The rest of this book will demonstrate that it is possible to make generalizations about how young people have been affected by these events and their range of responses. We can add that it has been no more difficult to gain agreement among researchers from our different countries on matters such as sample selection and questionnaire design than would probably have been evident among collaborators from any one of the countries from which the authors of this book are drawn.

Appendix I gives a full account of the original research on which this book is based. Our original evidence is in fact from several research projects, conducted in different combinations of countries at various times during the 1990s. First, there were surveys of 900 young people, 300 from each from Ukraine, Georgia and Armenia, that were conducted in 1997. The Ukraine sample was split equally between Lviv and Donetsk. In Georgia all the respondents were from Tbilisi. In Armenia the sample was from districts and schools which were chosen so that the respondents would be representative of their age group across the entire country. Everywhere the sampling ensured that males and females, from all the main kinds of family and educational backgrounds, were adequately represented. All the young people were in their twenties, typically 24–25, at the time of the investigations. We describe this research as our 'main surveys' because these are in fact our main source of new evidence. The interview schedule that was used in these surveys is in Appendix II.

Our second source of new evidence is qualitative, loosely structured, opened-ended interviews that were conducted with selected groups of young people in Lviv, Donetsk, Tbilisi and Yerevan. The third source is interviews with 50 self-employed young people in each of the three CIS countries in 1996. The fourth source is interview surveys among samples of 800 unemployed young people, and 400 self-employed young people in four Eastern and Central European countries (Bulgaria, Hungary, Poland and Slovakia), that were conducted in 1997. Our fifth source is a survey of a total of 1800 young people in three regions of Poland – Gdańsk, Katowice and Suwałki – in 1993. Sixth, our analysis uses some comparable evidence that was gathered in the Economic and Social Research Council (ESRC) 16–19 Initiative, a longitudinal study of representative samples of young people in four parts of Britain, conducted between 1987 and 1989. All this evidence from enquiries in which authors of this book were directly involved is set in the context of findings from other studies, conducted throughout the 1990s, among young people in various countries of Eastern and Central Europe and the former Soviet Union.

All the chapters in this book identify country, and sometimes regional, specificities, but the emphasis is on generalities – not just in the trends that have affected young people in post-communist Armenia, Georgia and Ukraine, and in other former communist countries as well, but also in the divisions among the young people. Some of these divisions are traditional, meaning here that they were present during, and sometimes preceded, communism. Other divisions are new and are being created by the changes in labour, consumer and housing markets that began in the 1990s.

Chapter 2 deals with the economic restructuring that accompanied the all-round decline and persistent crisis conditions in the 1990s. It explains how new career groups have been created, the most visible being the self-employed and the chronically unemployed. But there are also new divisions among employees: according to whether their jobs are in the public or the private sector, and whether the jobs are 'regular', meaning full-time and properly paid, as opposed to 'bitty' or marginal. This chapter also explains how the new labour market processes tend to hold young people within one or another of the new career groups.

Chapter 3 deals with education and how the systems have been modified and swollen by rising stay-on rates rather than being radically restructured. In many respects it has been business as usual. Children from old elite families are continuing to succeed in academic education. Children from working-class homes are following other educational routes. As under communism, these educational backgrounds govern whether young people enter professional, management, other white-collar or manual jobs. However, the old determinants of life chances prove far less effective in predicting who will become self-employed, who will obtain a regular job, and who will be confined to marginal employment or unemployed. This is the context in which many young people (and adults) have become uncertain as to which types of home backgrounds, education and occupations are advantageous. A feeling has spread that, in the new conditions far more than in the past, more depends on the individual. Needless to say, this feeling is common in the West where, as in the new East, as our evidence demonstrates, the feeling reflects that the forces that now hold individuals into their respective positions have become opaque rather than non-existent.

Chapter 4 describes how the labour market problems that the majority of the young people have been experiencing have complicated their housing and family transitions. The systems of house ownership and allocation themselves have been changing everywhere: towards private ownership, with dwellings becoming marketable assets. These changes are advantaging some and disadvantaging other young people. In either event, family relationships are being subject to new tensions. Like much else, the detailed implications are rather different for young women and for young men.

Chapter 5 deals with young people's day-to-day ways of spending time and money. It demonstrates that their leisure has proved perhaps surprisingly resilient, given the grim economic conditions. It shows that new hierarchies are being created depending on how much money young people can afford to spend on themselves, but also how some older lifestyle divisions are surviving (so far): between males and females, and between young people from elites and those from other home and educational backgrounds.

Most of the young people whom we studied had strong feelings about their countries' condition. It would have been amazing had they been indifferent. Yet, as we explain in Chapter 6, most were wholly disengaged from formal politics. Attitudes towards politicians ranged from indifference through cynicism to outright hostility. Western-type party politics were, at best, embryonic. Attitudes towards the reforms were mixed. The same individuals could be in some senses in favour and in other ways critical of how their countries had changed. Public opinion, among young people at any rate, was fluid, finely poised, capable of swinging either way. Meanwhile, a tiny minority of young people have been building careers in politics. Such careers have sometimes progressed rapidly, though not reliably, just like careers in business, given that most of the political parties, like the market economies, are new.

The best way of summarizing what has happened so far to post-Soviet young people is this book's title. They have been surviving: neither defeated nor deflated nor obviously benefiting in any way yet, in most cases, from post-communism.

For most, the by far preferred eventual outcome of the transition will be the 'Western way of life'. It is still a possibility, though by no means a certainty or even the countries' most probable destination. For it to remain a genuine possibility the people of the new East, especially the young people, need to continue to believe. This is a 'bottom line'. It could easily fail, with worldwide implications. So our final chapter suggests some low-cost, short-term, eminently practical measures that will realize no one's wildest dreams, yet could still be decisive in keeping young people's hopes alive in this new millennium.

2. Jobs and Career Routes

THE CREATION OF LABOUR MARKETS

The most exposed age group

Employment is the best topic with which to commence an account of how young people in Armenia, Georgia and Ukraine survived post-communism in the 1990s. The countries' economies were the sites of the changes that affected young people most widely, directly, forcefully and sometimes with devastating effects. The ability to worship openly without fear of the consequences and to vote for one's choice of party and candidate in elections were significant developments. But these did not have as many consequences for everyday life as developments on the jobs front. Some sections of the populations were most affected by changes (reductions) in welfare rights in respect of pensions, child care and the rest. Young people were more affected by the disappearance or degradation of many of the careers which, under communism, they would have entered, and for which, in most cases, their education had prepared them.

Employment under central planning

Under communism there were no real labour markets. Employment was planned. The size of workforces in government departments, state factories and mines and so on, together with terms and conditions of employment, were determined in the planning apparatuses. Individual workers were not planned into jobs irrespective of their own inclinations, except that, with variations according to time and place, in the initial stages of their careers, higher education and some secondary school graduates could be required to work in the occupations for which they had been prepared and in regions to which they would not otherwise have gone. There were legal restrictions on the movement of labour between and within republics in the Soviet Union, but within their home areas most young people and older workers were legally free to choose and to change their employers. This was not always a purely nominal freedom. State departments and plants usually had vacancies at all levels. The centrally planned economies systematically generated shortages of all supplies, whether television sets or labour. So it was possible for dissatisfied workers to seek alternative jobs. It was plant managers who almost always and everywhere faced the seemingly intractable problem of labour shortages. Labour shortages were endemic because plant managers had vested interests in requesting more and more staff (along with the budgets to pay them) from the central planners. There were no penalties for carrying excess labour, and it was in every plant's interest to ensure that it had enough of all supplies for targets to be met; hence the paradox of underemployed workforces coexisting with official labour shortages.

There was supposed to be no unemployment. Rather, people had a legal obligation to work to support themselves. The planners sometimes made mistakes which created local labour surpluses but before long these were invariably absorbed into local factories or government departments. Many towns were dominated by single large plants, so there was sometimes precious little scope for individuals to switch employers. School and college students were not always able to enter courses leading to their preferred careers or to obtain their first-choice jobs subsequently. All this, needless to say, applies equally in market economies. Communism was different in that, once established in their careers and having gained some seniority, there was very rarely any need and usually little or no financial incentive for members of the workforce to seek a career change. In the latter decades of communism some market mechanisms were introduced (pay variations in response to local labour supply and demand imbalances, for example) but this was to assist in achieving planned outcomes rather to replace central planning.

The advent of markets

In the mid-1990s the old economic systems were still operating, albeit to different extents in different countries. The collapse of the state sectors when communism ended was uneven. In all regions some plants fared better than others (see Michailova and Mills, 1998). Sometimes this was because the plant managers were able to fix deals with local suppliers and customers. Managers had vested interests in keeping their sites in business, thereby preserving their own careers. There was also the potential reward of a profitable privatization. Inevitably, some managers proved more energetic and capable than others, but in some cases the difficulties were simply overwhelming. Munitions factories lost their sole customer, the Soviet army. In the 1990s marketing became an essential management skill: under communism it had been unnecessary, so marketing expertise was in short supply everywhere in the 1990s.

There were also inter-country variations in how state enterprises fared which depended, in part, on the governments' ability and willingness to manage the transition. Among the three countries in this study, the Ukraine government had retained the greatest control over economic life, thereby preserving, or at least slowing down, the disappearance of the old system. There were numerous indications of this which will appear throughout the following chapters. One was the level of trade union membership among the Ukraine samples in our main survey: 57 per cent of all respondents in Donetsk and 48 per cent in Lviv compared with just 4 per cent in both Tbilisi and Armenia. Under communism employees had obtained many of their welfare rights via the trade unions. In Ukraine most of these old structures were still in place but they had often become derelict, de-energized by breakdowns in supplies, orders and chronic shortages of cash.

In Lviv we interviewed the local branch secretary of the machine builders' union, Ludmila, who was aged 48. Ludmila's description of her job made it clear that in Ukraine the trade unions were still top-down organizations. In practice there was basically just one trade union with divisions in all regions and branches in different industries. Ludmila was a university graduate who had become employed in a factory: 'But I was socially active. I was elected to the trade union branch committee, and later on I was offered a job in the union.' The job of the union used to be to reach agreements with employers on the implementation of policies agreed at higher levels on recruitment, salaries and other benefits, and the union was involved in the administration of some of the benefits – sick pay, health care and holidays, for example:

The job has now become much more difficult. Employers see no need for

trade unions any longer. We have lost members due to the run downs and
closures at state plants. Also, people have just left: they have lost trust in the
unions. We have some members in private firms, but not many. An
advantage is that if you are a trade union member you cannot be dismissed
without the union's permission. This is still the law. But we have less funds
and it has become more difficult to help members with health care, holidays
and suchlike.

In practice the job security that went with union membership was
proving hollow. It was meaningless when sites closed. Otherwise firms
could simply lay off staff or fail to pay salaries. Ludmila believed that
the change to a market economy was basically a good idea.

But too many mistakes have been made by former communists who have
no relevant experience. The privatization has been too rapid. However, the
basic problem is that we lost our markets with the end of the Soviet Union.
I do not expect the situation to improve. Our industries are unable to
compete. Our technology is old. We need huge investment. At present we
are unable to use our own resources.

Private businesses were able to operate openly and legally; in all the
countries in this study the private sector labour markets were examples
of extreme deregulation. Whatever the letter of the law, employees had
little protection, given that so much private enterprise remained in the
second economies. In practice private sector employers could hire and
fire according to their own requirements and discretion. Hours of work
and rates of pay were fixed by each employer, subject only to market
forces.

Public sector employment was also being subjected to new market
disciplines. Even if basic terms and conditions, and the size of payrolls,
were still centrally planned, some establishments were able to pay
above the stipulated levels. In some cases the additional rewards would
be in cash and in other cases in goods, sometimes 'on' and sometimes
'off the record'. In some state enterprises it was possible (in practice,
though not in law) for managers and workers to use company
machines, materials and time for their own private enterprises. This
could be an important element in an overall compensation package, and
helps to make sense of the behaviour of workers who clung on,
apparently irrationally, to very low-paid public sector jobs. Many
public sector officials regularly charged members of the public (asked
for or demanded bribes) in exchange for their services. All this had

happened under communism but in the 1990s it escalated. This was another important element in the reward structure in some public service occupations. By the mid-1990s it had become expected and largely accepted. A 1997 survey of 17–30-year-olds in Russia found that over a half could see nothing wrong in looking for jobs where they stood a chance of being bribed (Meek, 1998). Western governments tax the workforces and use part of the proceeds to pay public officials' salaries. In CIS countries, until now, tax collection has been ineffective; so there has been insufficient cash to pay decent salaries; so members of the public have often acknowledged that public officials need to be paid directly. This has applied virtually everywhere when people have sought medical attention at state hospitals and clinics.

Another change in the 1990s was that some state departments and plants had too little work to keep their staffs occupied and insufficient cash to pay the stipulated wages and salaries. This meant that many people were nominally employed but laid off in practice, and salaries sometimes fell months into arrears. An end result was much greater variety than formerly in public sector terms and conditions of employment.

All the above could be viewed, and in fact were generally viewed within the countries, as abnormalities created by the exceptional crisis conditions of the 1990s. Alternatively, and probably more realistically, the trends could be viewed as evidence of market forces becoming sovereign and creating new normalities.

Open and hidden unemployment

An immediate consequence of the development of labour markets while the centrally planned economic sectors were in rapid decline was the spread of unemployment. This happened in all the former communist countries, but in many of them, including most from the old Soviet Union, officially registered unemployment remained low, often extremely low. In this sense most unemployment was hidden though its existence was not a secret.

Among young people the jobs deficit was concealed partly by their remaining longer in education; they completed secondary school then enrolled in higher education or other post-secondary courses. This was a way of sheltering from the labour market. Many young people hoped to shelter until the crisis passed. In Georgia and Ukraine an additional benefit for males was that they could thereby postpone, and perhaps escape altogether, military service. In Armenia this escape route was closed in 1993 when all 18-year-old males became eligible for conscription.

Another way in which levels of unemployment were concealed in all age groups, but especially among young people, was that most unemployed people failed to register at the Labour Offices. In our interviews all the respondents who had ever been unemployed for a month or longer were asked whether they had registered on the last occasion. Overall just 17 per cent had registered. Their reasons for not registering were usually that they would not have been eligible for benefit and that they did not believe that the Labour Offices would be able to offer suitable jobs. Benefit eligibility rules had been tightened everywhere, usually in ways that excluded most new school and college graduates altogether, or strict limits were set on the periods for which they could claim benefit. A related reason for not trying to claim was that any benefits received would be extremely low, nearly always less than $10 a month and sometimes as low as $2 unless the claimants had dependants. In Donetsk a danger in registering and claiming benefit was that a person was likely to be directed to a vacancy, probably in a state enterprise where the conditions of work, the level of pay and the irregularity of payments made the job unattractive even to the unemployed.

A further reason for not registering was that some of the unemployed were actually working, usually spasmodically, in their regions' 'grey' economies. Just over a quarter (28 per cent) of respondents who had ever been, or who were currently unemployed, reported that they had in fact earned money during their most recent spells of unemployment. Individuals with unofficial incomes had good reason to avoid the Labour Offices and the enquiries that might have resulted into their means and availability for work. A paradox of post-communism was the coexistence of substantial numbers of people in jobs who had neither work to do nor wages alongside pools of formally (though not usually registered) unemployed individuals, many of whom were actually earning. We shall see in Chapter 5 that the young unemployed in this study were not a particularly impoverished group: they were not being excluded from their age group's normal leisure activities.

Oleg was aged 23 and had been unemployed for two years. On

leaving secondary school he had been employed as a metal worker at a state plant which had subsequently trimmed its workforce from 5000 to 100:

> I went to the Labour Office but they have no jobs. All our industries have closed. They told me that I could not claim benefit. On your own you simply cannot get a job. I have to hope that relatives or acquaintances will help. All jobs go to relatives. If you don't have contacts it's impossible to get a job. The only exceptions are people who are very well qualified and who also have experience. Even university graduates have great difficulty. You find them doing the same odd jobs as me.

Oleg was earning occasional money in a warehouse.

The young people interviewed who held private sector jobs confirmed the importance of contacts. Vadim said initially that he had obtained his job by replying to a newspaper advert, but later on he explained that he had an acquaintance in the firm: 'You can't get a job that easily. Private firms work in a secretive way.' Ivanna's relatives had helped her to obtain her job in a small private business that installed aquariums in hotels, offices and private residences.

A final way in which unemployment could be concealed has already been described: by plants retaining and even recruiting new employees into public sector posts when there was neither sufficient work to keep them fully occupied nor cash to pay their salaries. The underemployment that had been widespread under communism became chronic in the early stages of the reforms. Young people who were clinging to such jobs, and depending on them for their livelihoods, were in fact among the most impoverished members of their age group.

Tania, aged 30, had such a job. After secondary school she had trained in librarianship and had then been employed at a state bookstore where she had worked ever since:

> It's so-so. You are able to take time off if you want. The salary is $25 a month. It's the same as in 1991 but you cannot buy as much with the money today.

Was Tania looking for another job?

> There's no choice. With my speciality there's nowhere else to work in this town. There are no private bookshops here.

This was untrue: there were several such bookshops in the town centre. What Tania meant was that in these jobs she would not be able to use her skills in librarianship and, in any case, she seemed to prefer the calmer regime in the state sector.

Myklos had spent seven years training to become a doctor:

> It's always been a prestigious occupation and it always will be. People need medicine. I had to work for two years as a hospital orderly before I could be admitted to medical school.

Since completing his training Myklos had been employed at a state clinic along with 20 other doctors. He was paid between $40 and $50 a month:

> It's not very good. You can't earn enough to live. But we are also paid by the patients. The medical facilities are poor. We rely on experience, not equipment.

Myklos advised that should we need medical attention while in the country we should find a state doctor and pay him privately, cash in hand, rather than try to use insurance policies.

THE REFORM OF EMPLOYMENT

In the 1990s school and college leavers in all former communist countries were offered a much wider variety of jobs than had formerly existed. There was much more variety (and inequality) in the hours worked, rates of pay, work intensity, career prospects and security.

Reformed employment in the public sector

Everywhere the public sector remained a major if not the dominant source of regular employment. Public sector employment was reduced but not decimated by the 'shock', and was rarely rapidly transformed in response to the 'therapy' of market forces. Some plants closed. There was an even sharper downturn in public sector output, which meant more underemployment (always a problem under communism) and reduced real earnings (Bouin, 1996; International Labour Office, 1995;

Jackson, 1996). However, as indicated previously, workflows and pay levels held up better in some places than in others. Among the areas in this study, public sector work was better paid and the work was more regular in Donetsk than anywhere else. Within Ukraine it was regarded as a political imperative that the Donbass mines had to be kept going, the miners in employment and paid regularly. In fact, the politics of Ukraine meant that no region with significant political representation could be stripped of its public sector jobs. So Lviv had large bus and television manufacturing plants which had employed 10,000 and 5000 repectively prior to the reforms, and which remained open, nominally in operation, with reduced but still substantial workforces, despite orders and supplies dwindling to a trickle.

Public sector employment changed everywhere, even in Donetsk, in so far as it lost its former almost absolute security. Workers who remained in the public sector knew that their jobs were no longer guaranteed for life. There was also a general degradation of public sector pay levels. Fringe benefits – entitlements to health, recreation, housing and other social services which had often been part of the job package, often delivered through the trade unions – were removed or reduced in scale. Under communism some large enterprises had been mini-societies: they had provided virtually everything that their workers needed, during their entire lives. In the 1990s this changed rapidly: enterprises dispensed with non-essential functions; some also off-loaded non-essential labour. However, there was general agreement among the young people in this study that the public sector remained the source of the most secure jobs, where rates of pay were guaranteed even if they were pathetically low and the payments often came months in arrears. Many young people were still taking such jobs. These gave them reasonably secure official positions in a context where a prevalent view was that before long, whether through the refreshment supplied by market forces or the empowerment of the new national govern-ments, levels of trade, production and pay would return to their normal levels. Public sector employees were more likely than any other groups of workers in this study to be earning less than $30 a month at the time of our main survey in 1997, but, unlike other 'bitty jobs' (see below), in the public sector this was regarded as a temporary aberration. A benefit of the relaxed public sector work regimes was that employees were often able to take second jobs and to take time off from their main jobs when their other activities required this.

The public sectors across all three countries were responsible for 51 per cent of the samples' current or most recent jobs. Everywhere they remained the base for substantial segments of the workforces. This was one of the two segments (employment in large private companies was the other) in which young people were most likely to obtain work that corresponded with their education. And those who entered public sector jobs on completing their full-time education were tending to remain: those employed in the public sector in 1997 were more likely than any other group of employees to have held just one job; they were the least likely to have quit jobs of their own accord, and also the least likely to have experienced unemployment.

Quality jobs in the private sector

Meanwhile, everywhere the private sectors were creating more jobs. A few (very few in fact) were quality jobs in firms with Western bases or joint ventures. Western firms that established sites in Eastern Europe and the former Soviet Union in the early 1990s were usually attracted by the well-educated, skilled workforces that were available, the low labour costs and the advantages of being first movers into potentially huge markets. Inward investors rarely mounted wholesale takeovers. They were able to cherry-pick parts of companies and carefully select the staff to be retained (see Pye, 1998). The introduction of Western pay systems soon overcame any reluctance to work hard and long hours or staff found that they were no longer required. Semenova's (1998) interviews with young Russians found that some who had moved from public into private sector employment likened the switch to migrating to a different country. In our study the young people who had taken jobs with Western-based or -linked organizations were experiencing Western work regimes: demands on employees were considerably heavier than in the public sector, but the rewards were correspondingly higher. Pay levels were not equal to those in Germany and other Western countries but they were well above the Eastern norms. These were among the best jobs that young people could aspire to but they were extremely scarce in all the areas in this study.

Olga, aged 24, had such a job with a London-based English language school. She had studied languages at university and while a student had worked as an interpreter for Western institutes of management and banking. She also had a brief period as a tourist guide. Olga's language skills were up to this because she had spent six months at a US high school during a family visit. On graduating she had obtained her present job as an office manager. Olga was one of the more prosperous young people whom we interviewed. She and her husband were renting their own flat.

Jobs in Western-based organizations had not always turned out so well. At the end of his college education Andrij had been directed to a job at a Kiev brewery: 'I had to go otherwise I would not have received the diploma. They provided hostel accommodation which was quite good.' Andrij had stayed in Kiev for just six months. He could have stayed indefinitely but preferred to return home, where his old college found him his next job, at a state tobacco factory. In 1994 this plant had been acquired by a Western multi-national:

> When they bought the factory working conditions worsened. They stopped helping with holidays and medical services. There was no increase in salaries. We were paid $70 and the Americans got $7000. But we were happy with what we got. The work regime became tougher. If we had orders we had to work day and night. After that we might stop working for a week. When it was a state factory we worked regularly all the time.

Its new owners had closed the factory in 1998: 'They were happy with the work but not with the taxes.' The overseas owners were probably tempted into the region by the rather attractive national tax regime but may not have understood about all the official and unofficial demands that they would face from regional and local officials. Andrij's wife had also worked at the tobacco factory. Since it closed they had both been unemployed.

Jobs in locally owned medium-sized and large private companies had become another distinctive labour market segment by 1997. Some of these businesses were privatized former state enterprises; others had grown from scratch. As in the state sector, employment in these businesses was likely to be in occupations corresponding to the employees' education. In this segment of the labour market and in Western-based or linked organizations, young people stood their best chances of earning in excess of $100 a month and were less likely than in any other segment to earn less than $30. But high levels of employment commitment were expected, as in Western-based organizations – long hours of work and no second jobs. This kind of private sector employment was expanding in the 1990s. In 1997 most of the young people who held these 'quality jobs' had begun their working lives somewhere else. They were unlikely to have held only the one job since completing their education. They were the career group (see below) who were most likely to have left previous jobs of their own accord, but having secured their (relatively) good jobs they were tending to stick. They were less likely to have applied for other jobs during the previous 12 months than any other groups of young workers.

Yury's move into the private sector had worked out rather well:

> When I left secondary school I tried to enter a physical education institute but I failed the entrance examination so I ended up at a clothing school. After that I did army service. It was quite interesting radio work.

On leaving the army Yury was offered a job at a state factory which manufactured military uniforms: 'It was a very low salary.' So Yury had resumed his studies on a specialized course in clothing design:

> In 1993 I entered a competition for fashion designers in the west of Ukraine and I won second prize. I was then offered my present job. The firm has around 500 employees now. It is owned by a husband and wife. Neither had any background in clothing but he does the commercial side and she does the clothes. They started with just a handful of orders. I do a bit of everything but my main jobs are buying materials and designing the clothes. Basically it is 10.00–19.00 but in practice it's often 8.00–23.00. The salary depends on the amount of business that we do.

Yury had no plans to leave but in the longer term he intended to develop a business of his own.

However, medium-sized and large private businesses were not a homogeneous employment sector. As explained above, some of the businesses were Western-based or -linked. These were the blue-chip employers – very few and far between in our research areas. Other businesses had grown from nowhere under local management and ownership during the 1990s. Others were privatized companies, which themselves were a varied group in terms of the actual patterns of ownership and control. Privatization had sometimes passed the business into the hands of one person or a group of individuals. In other cases privatization had been into the ownership of managers or of managers and workers. Sometimes a public authority was the new 'private'

owner. In the latter cases the businesses were most likely to be func-
tioning as if they were still state enterprises. However, the Western-
based or -linked businesses were the new role models in this sector in
terms of management practices and employment regimes.

Marginal firms, marginal jobs

Most new private sector employment was in fact being created by
small, locally owned and managed enterprises which had been created
de novo in the 1990s or had emerged surreptitiously from the second
economies (see Bilsen and Konings, 1996). Such businesses were for
the most part run by self-employed people and their families and
were most likely to be in trade or consumer services. The new private
sector economies had been quicker at opening shops, bars and
restaurants than factories. Most of these businesses were themselves
marginal in all senses of this word. Much of the employment that they
generated was temporary and part-time, as is the case in Western
countries. In the former Soviet countries the businesses usually
operated at least partly in the 'grey' economies. Workers were usually
hired without written contracts. Employees often had no fixed hours of
work or guaranteed monthly pay: they were engaged if and when the
need arose. Many private sector jobs created in the 1990s were
distinctly 'bitty'.

Many young people in this study had held such marginal jobs (self-
employed, in family businesses or with another employer) while
completing their secondary and higher education courses. Some had
taken employment in the private sector alongside main public sector
jobs. Public sector work regimes had always been indulgent and
became even more so in the 1990s. As explained earlier, when factories
could not provide regular work they had no reason to try to enforce
regular attendance. Individuals were able to take time off: weeks or
months if they wanted to do so, when their other jobs required this.
When public sector pay lagged months in arrears or when it had sunk
to 'nominal' levels, beneath $25 a month in many cases, and some-
times to less than $10 a month in Georgia and Armenia, the financial
penalty for taking leave was slight. Needless to say, it was one thing
to have a 'bitty job' in a shop or a bar or driving a taxi as a
secondary activity, and quite another to have such a job as one's main
occupation.

Igor had formerly been employed at a state plant which manufactured carved wood products: 'When I left I was really redundant. There was no job. I was really unemployed but I did not receive benefit because they said that I had left voluntarily.' During his last two years at the state plant Igor had also worked unofficially as a cashier in a shop. This job had become official and Igor's main job when the alternative was unemployment: 'At first it was difficult to adjust but now I'm used to it. I'm now paid regularly, usually $50 a month.'

Boris was at university studying banking and finance, but he was also employed in the office of a small private company for between 10 and 20 hours each week. He expected to continue in this job if he failed to find anything better on graduating.

Vera had given up her job as a tax inspector to work as a sales assistant in a small food store: 'The tax job was difficult and the salary was low. My present job is more satisfying. I'm valued by other people. The pay depends on how much business we do.' Vera was working seven 12-hour shifts during alternate weeks. She had opted for this arrangement (in effect job-sharing with another employee) because it enabled her to spend every other week looking after her young son.

Eva had once worked in a state factory that manufactured space equipment: 'It was a good job in an important factory. We were visited by Soviet cosmonauts. The factory once employed 5000 but the workforce has shrunk to 700.' When Eva left, 'Technically it was of my own accord but in practice I was redundant.' She had obtained her current job, in a small firm with just nine employees which installed aquariums, through a relative (see above):

> My previous [state] job was stable, calm. There was a fixed salary and opportunities for professional development. My present job is not so stable. Sometimes I get nervous. The pay depends on how the firm is doing. You have to be prepared to do everything here. I do not feel any better off. We could afford holidays in the past but we can't afford them now. The situation in Ukraine is getting worse. This is due to the state's wrong economic policies. If they change these policies, then things might get better.

Self-employment

If young people did not want or were unable to obtain jobs with public or private sector employers, they could try to work on their own account. This was an activity to which many were being called and in which very few thrived. In the 1990s 'business' became a ubiquitous pursuit among post-communist youth. In 1997 it was estimated that Russia had 10 million small traders many of whom were young people (Meek, 1998). In our qualitative, open-ended interviews in Armenia, 65 per cent of the males and 47 per cent of the females described some experience of 'doing business'.

Trading was the pivotal form of business. It could involve the street sale of personal or household possessions, or of garden produce, or of cigarettes or confectionery bought in small quantities. However, with sufficient capital traders could begin to buy in bulk. They could go on 'shopping tours' to countries (usually Middle Eastern states in the case of the young people in this study) where goods were cheaper than at home. All this was most likely to be done in partnership with friends or, less frequently, as a family venture. As they became better capitalized, traders could acquire fixed sites (shops or kiosks) or they could diversify into other kinds of business, sometimes using specialist skills in catering, medicine, teaching, architecture, house construction, car repairs or whatever.

Business was the only way in which most young people could hope to become rich. Working for someone else (except a Western organization) was never going to deliver affluence; hence the attractions of business. However, business was intensely competitive and the essential skills included being able to arrange self-protection and the co-operation of a variety of state officials. Business could be a useful sideline or a secondary source of income but was high risk as a main occupation. The young people who were most likely to succeed in business had 'connections', plus an entrepreneurial psychology (see Semenova, 1998).

In our surveys the young people who were self-employed or working in family businesses as their main occupations stood above-average chances of earning good money – over $100 a month – but for this they were working longer hours than most employees. And one in seven of the self-employed were earning less than $30 a month. They were more likely to be low paid than employees in large and medium-sized private companies but less likely than those employed in the public sector. As might have been expected, there were dramatic contrasts in how the young people's businesses were faring. As a group, the young self-employed were characterized by their chequered careers. There was rarely a link between their businesses and their educational backgrounds. Compared with other respondents, the self-employed were more likely to have experienced redundancy and other dismissals whereas previously they were less likely to change jobs of their own accord. It was obvious that there had been a great deal of 'push' as well as 'pull', the lure of becoming rich and independent, in many decisions to become self-employed. Another, predictable, feature of own-account working was that those concerned were more likely than other respondents to report differences between their official (declared) and their actual earnings.

Families would often spread their risks. Relying on just one family business was more likely to be a last resort than a first option. Families were more likely to encourage one member to concentrate on business while others held on to 'proper' jobs, preferably with stakes in both the public and private sectors.

PAY AND LIVING STANDARDS

Most of the public sector jobs held by the young people in our study paid between $30 and $100 a month, when the employees were paid, with earnings in Donetsk being more likely than elsewhere to be towards the upper end of this range. Private sector pay was neither higher nor lower overall but simply more varied and often partly 'off the record'. Approximately two-fifths of our respondents who had private sector jobs or who were self-employed reported that there was a difference between their official and their actual pay. Needless to say, there is likely to have been significant under-reporting in responses to this question. Reported discrepancies between official and actual pay were far from absent but were distinctly less common in the state sector, where just a quarter of the employees reported a difference.

Westerners always wonder how people in ex-communist countries manage when their incomes have sunk to levels of $50 a month and lower. The answer is that in many cases they have simply survived. In all the countries in this study there was general agreement that to live decently a household needed a monthly income of around $200 and preferably more. In some (a few) cases this could be provided by a single earner but more often the total would be generated through several income streams. Husbands and wives, grown-up children, and sometimes grandparents, could all contribute. The same individual might have two or even more jobs. In this study just 4 per cent of the young people in Donetsk, but 12 per cent in Lviv, 18 per cent in Armenia and 22 per cent in Tbilisi reported income from 'other' jobs. These incomes were often very low – earnings from second economy weekend, evening and holiday jobs, for example – but in some cases the earnings exceeded $200 a month, which was far more than most main jobs offered. And in addition to their own members' earnings some households received gifts from relatives who were abroad.

Of course, notwithstanding all these possible sources of income there were many households with incomes of far less than $200 a month. These were the families that were just surviving. If they already owned the dwellings and furniture they had no short-term housing costs. If they paid rent this could be allowed to fall into arrears. The old systems still operated in some places in so far as water, heating and electricity were in effect free (included in the rent) or very cheap. When the price of electricity was raised, as had happened in Armenia, families would wear coats and sweaters in their homes throughout the winter. Locally produced food was cheap, especially in the markets. Clothing could be recycled. People would make and mend and generally help each other. Daily life under communism was never as 'monetarized' as in the West (see Ashwin, 1996). Post-communism has shown that people can maintain basically modern lifestyles without most of the spending that the Western population has come to regard as essential. That said, life in many of the households in this study had become grim. Meanwhile, other families were prospering. There had been a rapid decomposition of the common ways of life that people had led under communism.

Western visitors have often found it incredible that rates of pay can be so low (well under $100 a month) when they pay twice this amount for a single night in a hotel. However, they are likely to observe that the hotels employ many staff in the reception areas, on the bedroom corridors, in the bars and restaurants and for security. They will also recognize that a hotel's business is public and cannot be mainly second economy. Much of its income is therefore likely to be syphoned off in government charges, both official and unofficial (bribes). Guests may or may not realize that a significant proportion of the business is most likely to go 'under the counter', some finding its way into the pockets of the various grades of staff, state officials and perhaps private 'security' businesses.

Cities that have attracted large numbers of Western visitors, most of whom spend hundreds of dollars a day, have prospered. Westerners' spending becomes income for the local populations through a variety of official and unofficial channels. Residents in Budapest, Moscow, Prague and Warsaw have benefited from this, as have people in non-capitals such as Gdansk (on Poland's Baltic coast) and Szambothley (in the west of Hungary, close to the Austrian border), two of the regions in Eastern and Central Europe investigated in our parallel studies in the 1990s. Lviv (close to Poland) was experiencing some such benefits but on a much lower scale, and Western visitors were much scarcer in Donetsk, Tbilisi and Armenia.

CAREER PREFERENCES AND ACHIEVEMENTS

Career preferences

The young people in this study were quite clear about the main advantages and disadvantages of public and private sector jobs and self-employment; and they were generally agreed on their ranking (see Table 2.1). Most felt that, on balance, it was preferable to work for a large private company (preferably Western-based or -linked) than for the state. But best of all was to be successful in business.

The samples were asked to rank the prestige of a set of occupations (see Table 2.2). Lawyers and businessmen were the top ranked. Lawyers were typically self-employed and in demand from individuals and corporations. Teachers and engineers were at the base of the ranking. Engineering was associated (indelibly it appeared) with declining state plants. Teaching was a low-paid public sector job in which there was little scope for supplementing one's official income. Since the 1980s the prestige of teachers and engineers had fallen drastically, while the prestige of bankers and businessmen had risen (Adibekian, 1985, 1992). Doctors, managers, politicians and ministers of religion were quite highly ranked occupations. Scientists, book-keepers and army officers were ranked as distinctly less prestigious but

Table 2.1   *Attitudes towards different kinds of jobs*

Percentage 'agreeing' or 'strongly agreeing' that:	Donetsk	Lviv	Tbilisi	Armenia	Poland '93
It is better to work for a private business than for a state firm	53	70	62	54	56
It is better to work in the public sector than for a private employer	29	16	22	33	25
I would rather work for a large company than on my own account	34	16	55	27	n.a.
I would like to have my own business	46	54	77	89	61

Note: n.a. = not available.

Table 2.2   *Prestige of occupations*

	Percentage saying 'high' or 'very high'		Percentage saying 'high' or 'very high'
Lawyer	87	Scientist	45
Businessman	83	Book-keeper	40
Doctor	72	Army officer	26
Manager	67	Engineer	17
Politician	60	Teacher	16
Minister of religion	60		

still superior to engineers and teachers. It followed that law and business studies had become the new prestige courses in higher education.

Main career flows

Most of the young people in this study had been unable to obtain jobs matching the career preferences described above. Table 2.3 gives an overview of the samples' career development. It gives the percentages in each area who were in various 'main positions' during selected years from 1991 onwards. The respondents were asked about their main positions during each year, but for simplicity's sake Table 2.3 gives this information for just four – 1991, 1993, 1995 and 1997. A caution must be appended to these figures: the 'main position' measurement is crude. Individuals had to choose just one main position for each year; so short-lived jobs, second or part-time jobs and brief spells of unemployment will not feature. Nevertheless, the table portrays the main career flow in all the areas from 1991 onwards, which was, predictably, out of full-time education and into employment.

Table 2.3 also portrays the rise in unemployment as the samples moved into their regions' labour markets. In Ukraine the unemployment levels (just 3 per cent of the sample in Lviv, and 9 per cent in Donetsk at the time of the interviews) would be regarded as very respectable nowadays in any Western country. This is another indication of how, in Ukraine, the old economic order was holding relatively firm or, at any rate, fraying rather than collapsing. Government policy in Ukraine had encouraged state firms (with exhortation and financial incentives) to hold on to their workers, and sometimes to continue recruitment, even when there was neither work to do nor cash to pay salaries. This was one way of containing 'open' unemployment and minimizing claims for unemployment benefit, but in a context where the managers of most state plants and departments were reluctant to dismiss 'their' workers unless there was absolutely no alternative. The management culture in Ukraine (as in Russia) was paternal. Separating workers from their jobs, incomes and all the associated welfare entitlements had never been a normal management prerogative. And, in any case, there was the prevalent expectation, or at least hope, that before long supplies, sales, workflows and everything else would return to normal levels.

Table 2.3   Career development: main positions (%)

	1991	1993	1995	1997
Donetsk				
Education	71	50	37	14
Full-time job	12	36	49	57
Part-time job	1	1	2	3
Educ. and work	3	3	2	3
Self-employed	—	1	1	3
Unemployed	2	1	2	9
National Service	8	5	2	1
Other	1	2	5	9
Lviv				
Education	81	60	49	9
Full-time job	4	16	33	57
Part-time job	1	6	7	19
Educ. and work	1	3	1	2
Self-employed	1	1	1	5
Unemployed	1	5	5	3
National Service	9	7	1	—
Other	2	1	2	5
Tbilisi				
Education	77	76	66	16
Full-time job	7	8	20	50
Part-time job	2	1	1	6
Educ. and work	—	4	1	2
Self-employed	1	3	4	6
Unemployed	11	7	7	19
National Service	1	1	—	—
Other	—	—	1	—
Armenia				
Education	92	76	50	40
Full-time job	2	6	3	10
Part-time job	—	2	1	6
Educ. and work	1	4	6	5
Self-employed	1	7	4	11
Unemployed	3	7	17	28
National Service	—	1	20	2
Other	—	—	—	—

Military service

Some smaller-scale ripples are also visible in Table 2.3. In all the countries young males were eligible for military service lasting from 12 to 24 months. Avoiding military service had been a preoccupation of many young males and their families under communism and has remained so under post-communism (see Vlachova and Stanek, 1992). However, in Armenia most of the males in our main sample had undergone this experience: unless they had genuine medical grounds it was difficult for young men who remained in Armenia to avoid conscription. Staying in education was usually no protection. Males became eligible before they started their university courses. Those who had not served were not free to leave Armenia, although many had obviously circumvented this restriction (147 out of the 551 names in our original Armenia sample could not be contacted because the individuals had left the country). Maintaining the army was a political priority in Armenia: it was actually engaged in protecting Armenians in Nagorny Karabakh and defending the narrow land corridor that linked this territory to Armenia proper. In Armenia military service involved real fighting rather than just training.

In Ukraine most males who had not entered higher education had been conscripted. There, as in Georgia, avoiding conscription was an incentive to remain in education for as long as possible. Young males in full-time education were not being conscripted at the time of our study. In Georgia there was a quite powerful incentive to avoid conscription because of the distinct possibility that fighting might resume in the regions that were seeking autonomy. In the early 1990s thousands of young Georgian males had obtained first-hand experience of combat without the kind of training, equipment, medical and other types of back-up which Western armies take for granted. By the mid-1990s Tbilisi (and Yerevan) had hundreds of physically injured and psycho-logically scarred young war veterans. Most of the young males in our Tbilisi sample (even those who had not entered higher education) had managed to avoid conscription. This is evidence of their own reluctance (the enthusiasm to enlist that arose in the initial years of Georgia's independence had evaporated) and of the general inefficiency of state administration in Georgia. It was not too difficult for young Georgian males or their families to purchase exemption from conscription. Their main problem was most likely to be the cost. Doctors would provide medical certificates (for a fee). These certificates would be accepted at the conscription offices on payment of a further fee (bribe), usually in the region of $1000. Without a medical certificate a buy-out was likely to be more expensive, at about $1500.

Maternity leave

A second ripple evident in Table 2.3 had been into and sometimes out of (official) maternity leave. Under communism maternity leave had been generous, and women with child care and other domestic responsibilities had usually been accommodated by their employers. In 1997 this system appeared to be surviving only in Ukraine. This was one reason why young women in Ukraine were remaining in low-paid state sector jobs. At the time of the survey 18 per cent of the females in Donetsk and 10 per cent in Lviv were on official maternity leave. In Georgia and Armenia, according to our evidence, by 1997 official maternity leave had ceased to operate.

Elsewhere under post-communism a polarization has been noted in women's labour market behaviour following childbirth. On the one hand, more women have been returning to employment rapidly; simultaneously, more mothers have been leaving employment (see Kurzynowski, 1997). Another response to the economic uncertainty and the loss of entitlement to maternity leave and associated benefits among young women has been to postpone fertility. Maybe in some cases fertility will be postponed indefinitely – it is still too early to tell. By the mid-1990s this had become a public issue throughout much of the former Soviet Union: the populations were not being reproduced. It was a public issue in Ukraine at the time of our research (see Chapter 4 for a fuller discussion). In Armenia and Georgia the main perceived threat to the populations was youth out-migration: the decline in the birth rates (no higher than in Donetsk and Lviv in our samples) was a subsidiary concern.

It is noteworthy that hardly any of the young women in any of the countries in this study described themselves as 'housewives'. Many were *de facto* housewives but they regarded themselves as either on official maternity leave or unemployed. According to this evidence, the role of the housewife, supported by a male breadwinner, had not won acceptance by 1997 among young women in any of the places in this study. In other former communist countries the youth unemployment figures appear to have been swollen by females who in practice, given their domestic commitments, have been unlikely to obtain employment (especially when what many have really wanted was maternity leave) but who have regarded themselves as unemployed rather than out of the workforce. In Poland approximately a half of all unemployed females under age 30 appear to have been in this kind of situation (Jung, 1997).

Employment and unemployment

One measure of the state of the labour markets that our samples entered is the levels of unemployment in their early careers. Rather than quoting percentages of the total samples, it is more meaningful here to calculate the unemployment rates among just those who had left full-time education. At the time of the interviews these rates were relatively low in Ukraine. In Tbilisi the unemployment rate was much higher, 23 per cent, and in Armenia it was higher still, a massive 45 per cent, an outcome of the breakdown of the old Soviet system coupled with Armenia's experience of war and economic blockade in the 1990s.

An alternative measure of the state of the local labour markets is the percentages of those who had left full-time education and were in full-time jobs. In Donetsk, Lviv and Tbilisi similar percentages (60–67 per cent) were in full-time employment at the time of the interviews compared with just 16 per cent in Armenia.

How dire economic conditions had become in Armenia can be glimpsed in the sample's responses to a question about what should be done about Chernobyl-type nuclear power generators. Between two-fifths and three-fifths of the samples in Donetsk, Lviv and Tbilisi argued that such plants should be closed immediately, and most of the remainder wanted them to be phased out gradually. In Armenia, in contrast, only 2 per cent favoured immediate closure while 80 per cent wanted the plants to remain in operation indefinitely. By the mid-1990s Armenia had endured several years of daily cuts in electricity and water supplies which operated for only a few hours each day. There had been similar problems, though on a lesser scale, in Tbilisi and Lviv. In Armenia the problems had been so acute and were still so severe in 1997 after Armenia's own nuclear power station had restarted that the overwhelming body of opinion preferred living with the risk of nuclear disaster to having their lives become even colder and darker.

In 1997 a significant proportion of the young people in the Armenia labour market (18 per cent) and an even higher proportion in Lviv (23 per cent) had part-time jobs as their main occupations. These part-time workers were as likely to be male as female. The prevalence of part-time employment appeared to depend mainly on whether full-time jobs were available and the strength of the private sectors, which was where most such jobs were based. As explained earlier, a problem with the expanding private sectors was that much of the new employment that was being generated was 'bitty jobs' rather than regular, full-time, permanent, decently paid occupations.

At the time of the interviews 4 per cent of the Donetsk sample who had completed their full-time education, 5 per cent in Lviv, 7 per cent in Tbilisi and 18 per cent in Armenia, had self-employment as their main occupations. In Armenia most employment was either part-time or self-employment. Where there were alternatives, as in Ukraine, where unemployment was lowest, the young people were likely to have been pulled into self-employment by the relative attractions, whereas elsewhere, and particularly in Armenia, they were more likely to have been pushed by the absence of alternatives. Their own businesses were not all flourishing. Self-employment was often a survival rather than an enrichment strategy. As explained earlier, the most typical form of business was trading – trying to sell goods to other poor people.

The public and private sectors

The relative contributions of the public and private sector economies to the demand for youth labour in the areas in this study can be gauged from where the respondents had been employed. The proportions of their last jobs that had been in the state sectors differed little from place to place – between 48 per cent and 58 per cent everywhere. The surveys among 22–24-year-olds in three regions of Poland in 1993 recorded a very similar split between public and private sector employment. Poland in 1993 might be considered as having reached the same stage in its transition in which the former Soviet countries remained in 1997. They had all experienced the shock of reform – the initial shake-out from public sector employment – but the private sector economies had yet to generate net growth in employment and incomes.

Table 2.4   Current or more recent occupations (%)

	Donetsk	Lviv	Tbilisi	Armenia
Management, professional, intellectual, artistic	46	63	61	31
Clerical, office	17	10	24	42
Manual, farm	39	27	15	27
n =	115	130	229	71

Occupational profiles

The distribution of our samples between different types of occupations may look unrealistically top-heavy (see Table 2.4). Everywhere there were white-collar majorities, and in Lviv and Tbilisi over three-fifths of all the young people's most recent jobs were in the management or professional grades. A point to bear in mind here is that the samples were not intended to be simple microcosms of the local populations. However, two additional points are pertinent. First, most of the research areas were major cities where one would have expected to find above-average proportions of administrative jobs in public authorities, central and local government, and company head offices. Donetsk, located in a region dominated by coal mining and other heavy industries, had the largest proportion of manual workers, as would have been expected, but Donetsk itself is the region's administrative, commercial and cultural centre. Second, factory closures and run-downs had slimmed the manual workforces and decimated young people's chances of entering these kinds of jobs. Employment had been de-industrialized not as a result of new technology maintaining or increasing output with fewer workers but because plants had lost supplies and orders. White-collar employment had been less vulnerable in the short term. However, the entire occupational structures were obviously resting on very shaky foundations. The local economies had ceased producing the types and quantities of goods that people in higher level occupations customarily expect, with the inevitable consequence that many of the apparently high status occupations that the samples had entered paid poverty salaries.

The respondents were asked for details about their first and most recent jobs. If they had not changed jobs they were asked about various features of their jobs in the early months of their working lives and currently. Table 2.5 divides the samples according to whether their first and their most recent jobs were management, professional, clerical or manual, then lists some of the features of, and the labour market experiences associated with these different grades of work.

Management and professional jobs were the most likely to correspond with the incumbents' education. However, in other respects

Table 2.5 Types of occupations (%)

	Management	Professional	Clerical	Manual
First job				
Corresponds with education	44	53	33	29
Had only one job	48	52	49	45
Been made redundant	6	10	18	19
Sacked	8	6	6	8
Left job of own accord	39	47	39	42
Been unemployed	42	43	51	56
Hours worked:				
20	18	24	24	22
40	60	61	43	46
Longer	23	15	32	32
Workload heavy	13	14	9	32
Difference: official and actual pay	29	34	33	33
n =	59	198	121	128
Most recent job				
Corresponds with education	44	57	26	24
Applied for no job in last 12 months	34	35	41	31
Hours worked:				
20	15	21	19	19
40	42	61	44	52
Longer	43	19	38	28
Workload heavy	26	15	15	38
Earnings from a second job	12	24	23	16
Earnings per month after deductions				
Under $30	15	23	14	9
Over $100	21	12	18	16
n =	75	189	96	92

it was not clear that management and professional jobs were particularly advantaged. There was a similar wide spread of weekly hours
of work and earnings within all the occupational groups. In all the
groups, about a quarter had worked for less than 20 hours per week
in their first job, and about a fifth were working less than 20 hours a
week in their present or most recent jobs. In terms of current earnings
there was, once again, a wide spread within all the occupational groups
but with no clear difference between the management, clerical and
manual grades, whereas the professional employees, who were mostly
women (see Chapter 4), were distinctly more likely to be low paid
(less than $30 a month) and less likely to be well-paid (over $100 a
month).

This is evidence of how the conventional (hitherto in all modern
societies) occupational structures had collapsed during the transition.
This is why so many young people argued that there was no longer an
obvious occupational hierarchy. Whether a professional engineer had a
better job than a taxi driver was a matter for debate among young
people themselves. This might prove to be a purely transitional
phenomenon, but by the mid-1990s it was already clear that the
transition was going to be a protracted process in the former Soviet
countries. In the meantime, conventional occupational groupings had
ceased to be an effective way of distinguishing young people's
experiences in the labour market and employment.

The Kalamari Union is the title of a Finnish film in which a group of
working-class men set out to ascend into the middle class, but none
reach this destination. *The Kalamari Union* is also the title of Markku
Kivinen's edited volume on the new middle classes of Eastern Europe
and the former Soviet Union. Communism had a 'holy working class'
but the reality was very different from the ideal. Kivinen (1998)
argues that the 'sacred middle class', supposedly being formed in ex-
communist countries, is a remarkably similar fiction. It is supposed to
be supplying the new market economies with entrepreneurial drive and
political stability. Individuals strive to enter the new middle class
hoping to find prosperity. But usually the destination turns out to be a
mirage. In our study the young people who reached nominally middle-
class employment were often discovering on entering the promised land
that their occupations had been seriously degraded.

CAREER DEVELOPMENT

Career stability

In all our research areas the economies were still in acute crisis in 1997 but the labour markets were not in complete turmoil. The main turmoil in employment had occurred earlier, at the end of the 1980s and the beginning of the 1990s alongside the 'shock' when entire segments of the planned economies had been eliminated or had contracted sharply and when private businesses first began to trade openly and develop. Since then there had been continuous 'churning' but mainly within segments of the labour markets. New businesses were being created constantly and were being killed off almost as rapidly, to be replaced by others but without, according to our evidence, any large-scale redistribution of employment between the public and private sectors or between different occupational grades.

The respondents in this study had begun flowing out of education and into the local workforces before 1991 (in a few cases) and, as already explained, it was possible to compare their first and most recent jobs. There had been quite a lot of job changing: 47 per cent of those with any experience of employment had held more than one job. However, the net redistribution between types of occupations and business sectors had been modest in scale. The proportion of employment in the state sectors had declined only slightly from 57 per cent to 51 per cent between first and most recent jobs. There had been a similar drift up the occupational structure with the proportion of jobs at the management and professional levels rising from 47 per cent to 55 per cent. These cannot be described as sea-changes. To some extent the overall picture of little change had been a product of compensating movements: some individuals switched from public to private sector jobs while others moved in the opposite direction, and so on. However, in practice most job mobility had been within, not between, broad sectors of the workforces. And 53 per cent of the respondents who had ever been employed had held only one main job. The beginning workers had tended to settle into one of several distinct labour market niches.

There were several indicators of the young people's tendency to have remained within distinct career groups. First, all respondents were asked if they had ever worked in the public sector, for a private firm, in a family business, and on their own accounts as a main occupation. A noteworthy feature of their answers (see Table 2.6) is that although it was possible for a single individual to have been in all these types of employment, in practice just 1 per cent of those who had ever been in any kind of employment had experienced all four types and only 9 per cent had experienced three or more.

Table 2.6   Number of sectors in which worked (%)

1	65
2	25
3	8
4	1
$n =$	606

Second, from the answers to the questions about their main positions during each year from 1991 onwards, it was possible to calculate the proportion of time that different groups had spent in different labour market situations. From this evidence it is clear that some had completed full-time education, had then become employees, and had remained more or less continuously in particular kinds of employment; that a much smaller number had been building long-term careers in self-employment; and that another minority was having difficulty in obtaining and holding on to any employment. The situations of the respondents at the time of the research in 1997 give a good indication of the sizes of each of these groups, and the group in which each person was located. Those in full-time employment when interviewed had in fact spent 78 per cent of their time since leaving full-time education in full-time jobs and only 7 per cent in unemployment. By contrast, those who were unemployed when interviewed had been unemployed for 57 per cent of their post-school careers and in full-time jobs for only 19 per cent. Nearly a half of the young people (49 per cent) had been unemployed for a month or longer on at least one occasion but many of these unemployment episodes had been brief or only one. Just 26 per cent had been unemployed as a main position for an entire year, and nearly all of these had been chronically unemployed.

Self-employment was even more concentrated. Just 10 per cent of all the respondents had ever been self-employed as a main occupation. The same proportion had spent one or more years with self-employment as their main position; and almost as many were developing long-term careers in business. Those who were self-employed when interviewed had spent exactly a half of their post-education careers in self-employment, 15 per cent as full-time employees and 22 per cent unemployed, while the remainder of their time was accounted for by part-time jobs, military service and maternity leave.

Table 2.7 describes the year-to-year continuities in the young people's labour market experience. Most of those who were in full-time jobs, self-employed or unemployed in any one year were most likely to be in exactly the same situation a year later. With full-time employment and unemployment the year-on-year continuity became stronger the further individuals progressed into their working lives. In other words, the young people were being divided into increasingly separate career groups.

Table 2.7   Employment in same position, year on year (%)

	1991–2	1992–3	1993–4	1994–5	1995–6	1996–7
Full-time employment	79	86	87	84	93	91
Self employment	38	78	88	52	48	75
Unemployed	46	59	61	68	75	69

CAREER GROUPS

In terms of their employment careers the young people were divisible into six main groups. One was the chronically unemployed (25 per cent of all those in the labour market when interviewed but with wide inter-area variations). The second group was composed of the self-employed (10 per cent of most recent jobs). Then, among those who had been in more or less continuous employment with an employer or employers, there was a division according to whether they were based in the public or the private sector (roughly a half of employees were in each of these sectors at the time of the fieldwork). Then there was a division cross-cutting all the employees and the self-employed according to whether they had obtained, held on to or developed regular work for themselves, or whether they were making do with 'bitty' jobs.

The distinctive characteristics of public sector employment were described earlier. These, and the corresponding characteristics of other types of jobs, are summarized in Table 2.8. Public sector jobs gave individuals official positions in their countries and tended to be consistent with the incumbents' education. Young people who had obtained such jobs had tended to remain. Those in these jobs at the time of our interviews were more likely than any other employees to have held only the one job. Entering public sector employment reduced individuals' risks of becoming unemployed. However, the downside was that public sector jobs were more likely than any other kind of work to pay less than $30 a month. During the 1990s swathes of such jobs had become 'bitty'.

Table 2.8   Characteristics of different types of employment

Public sector	Large private sector	Micro
Enter directly from education	Enter with experience gained elsewhere	Chequered careers; spells of unemployment
Low termination rate	Low termination rate	High mobility
Risk of job becoming marginal	Full-time employment	Jobs often part-time and/or casual
Work in speciality	Work in speciality	Work outside speciality
Official 'status' position	Quasi-official position	Low status
Relaxed work regimes	Heavy workloads	Variable workloads
Able to take time off and hold second job	Full-time commitment	Variable commitment
May receive bribes and unofficial payments	Official and unofficial fringe benefits possible	Work sometimes without contract, usually wholly or partly off-the-record

Large and medium-sized private sector firms were also tending to employ young people in jobs that corresponded with their educational backgrounds. These jobs were more likely than any others to pay more than $100 and were less likely than any others to pay less than $30 a month. However, relatively high levels of employment commitment were expected – long hours of work (relatively speaking) and no time for second jobs. Individuals tended to have moved into 'good' private sector jobs after starting their careers somewhere else and had usually left their previous jobs of their own accord. But once in their 'good jobs' in the private sector they were tending to stick; they were less likely than any other employees to have applied for other jobs during the previous 12 months. The peak of this labour market segment was composed of blue-chip jobs in Western-based or -linked businesses or projects. However, there was another, larger extremity to the private sector labour market composed of 'bitty' jobs, mostly in small businesses.

On the basis of interviews with 100 St Petersburg households, Piirainen (1998) has argued that a major 'class' division within the workforces in post-communist societies is between those still relying on the old system for their livelihoods and the 'new class' that has become integrated into the market economy. We agree that this is one major division but wish to add that integration into the private sector labour market can lead to many different outcomes.

Like employees, the self-employed could be divided into those with relatively substantial businesses or who were working in such family enterprises and those for whom working on their own account was basically a means of survival. Neither the self-employed nor private sector employees have all been winners from the reforms.

In our analysis we have adopted 20 hours per week and $30 per month as the baselines for describing jobs as regular, and beneath which they are classified as 'bitty' or marginal. Generally, if they had been more or less continuously in employment, our respondents had spent most of their working lives either developing their own businesses or in the state or in the private sector, and each of these groups could be further divided according to whether individuals had obtained and held on to regular work or had been unable to escape from 'bitty' jobs. Then, as explained above, there was another group whose careers had become stories of chronic unemployment.

The young people were being held within their particular career groups by normal labour market processes. The qualities that enabled some individuals to obtain good private sector jobs to begin with stood them in at least equally good stead if and when they returned to the labour market. Indeed, their career experience was likely to increase their apppeal to the relevant employers. Private firms in the new market economies have often been keen to recruit young people on account of their lack of experience of the old system (see Roberts *et al.*, 1997), but this advantage is surrendered if school-leavers start their working lives in public sector jobs. Individuals with the skills and contacts to start businesses of their own can soon enlarge these skills and contacts, thus increasing their likelihood of remaining in business.

Many individuals' working lives had been less tidy than these career groups may appear to imply. For example, some who had been mainly self-employed had experienced spells of unemployment. Nevertheless, the tendency was for individuals' working lives to approximate towards one or another of the above career types.

The proportions in the various career groups differed, but exactly the same basic career types and divisions were apparent in all the areas where our research was based. Table 2.9 gives probably the most realistic picture of all our statistics of how the samples had fared since entering the labour markets. In Armenia only 19 per cent of the respondents had established themselves in regular work of any kind and 47 per cent had been chronically unemployed. None of the areas had a majority of its young people in regular employment (44 per cent in Donetsk, 46 per cent in Tbilisi and 49 per cent in Lviv). Chronic unemployment was less common in Donetsk and Lviv than in Tbilisi but this was partly because more young people in the former areas had 'bitty' jobs (47 and 44 per cent against 39 per cent).

Table 2.9   Career groups (%)

	Donetsk	Lviv	Tbilisi	Armenia
Self-employment	7	10	3	10
State regular	22	19	25	3
Private regular	15	20	18	6
State marginal	20	13	15	6
Private marginal	22	34	14	27
Unemployed	14	4	24	47
n =	103	122	238	112

Our thresholds for describing jobs as regular are modest: 20 hours work a week and $30 a month. Of course, all the countries were in transition. If and when their private sector economies develop and/or the public sectors revive, labour demand will strengthen, 'bitty' jobs will become regular and the unemployed will be absorbed into the active workforces. However, there is no guarantee that the economies will develop and, if they do, the transition is likely to last a very long time. Up to 1997 the transition had created enormous slack in all the countries' youth labour markets. Even where the economies were growing strongly in 1997 this was from a very low baseline. On the basis of this evidence it would be difficult for anyone to describe the transition as a success.

HOPES AND EXPECTATIONS

Most respondents appeared to accept the description of their countries as in transition and believed that better times lay ahead. Most also believed that they themselves were still in transition towards what would be their main adult occupations. Very few wanted to believe that they had already reached their ultimate destinations. Most of those who were in employment wanted better jobs or at least much better pay. Those who were self-employed hoped to develop their businesses or switch into proper jobs.

Everyone was asked what he or she expected to be doing in five years time. Everywhere, except in Armenia, 69–74 per cent expected to be in full-time jobs. Armenia had the most pessimistic young people. Only 32 per cent expected to have obtained full-time employment in five years, 17 per cent expected to be in part-time jobs, 16 per cent self-employed, 5 per cent unemployed, another 5 per cent expected to be housewives and 4 per cent expected to have emigrated. A further 21 per cent expected to be still in or to have returned to full-time education.

Pessimism was most common in Armenia but everywhere there were some young people who believed that their best prospects would be realized by quitting the cities where they had been reared. Some thought it likely that they would move to other areas within their own countries: 7 per cent in Tbilisi and 17 or 18 per cent elsewhere. Except in Ukraine, where Kiev, the capital, was a magnet, these young people were rarely contemplating movement into areas with better job prospects. The most common intention was to move to the countryside or a smaller town, or back to their families or to where it would be easier to obtain housing or where the dwellings were more spacious.

About a fifth of the young people said that they were definitely or very likely to emigrate (23 per cent in Lviv and Armenia, 18 per cent in Tbilisi and 15 per cent in Donetsk). Georgia and Armenia had both lost around a fifth of their populations, mainly young people, in the early 1990s and the outflow seemed likely to continue unless conditions at home improved. They would go initially to study, to take temporary jobs or to visit friends or relatives, not necessarily with any intention of severing links with their own countries but with every likelihood that their permanent returns would be postponed if better jobs and lifestyles were discovered in Moscow, Warsaw, Prague or wherever. However, surveys in the early 1990s estimated that over 80 per cent of young people in Armenia were potential emigrants (Adibekian, 1991, 1992, 1995). According to our evidence, using this particular indicator, by 1997 pessimism about the country's prospects and the life chances of the people who remained had at least subsided. Conditions had been even worse in the early 1990s.

EXPERIENCES IN LATER LIFE

Young people were the age group most exposed to all the changes that were underway in the 1990s but their lives were not necessarily being damaged irrevocably. They had time to recover. Older people had often seen all their achievements obliterated. We interviewed some adults, sometimes because they were around in workplaces where we were interviewing young people, and in other cases they were the parents of our main subjects.

Grigory, aged 40, had studied physics at university and on graduating had gone to work at a research institute that was attached to a military project:

> I worked in radio electronics. We were well resourced by Moscow. Over 2000 engineers were employed. I was promoted and finished up in charge of a group of 20. Then Ukraine became independent. Ukraine just did not

have the resources to keep us going. The place has been run down. Now there are just 60 people there. I left of my own accord in 1992 because the programme on which I was working was closed. I moved to the university physics department but there was no money and no work. I was then unemployed for a year. So I decided to change profession. I came here when this business started. I'm called the technical director. This means that I am responsible for everything. I fix the electrics, windows, anything that needs attention. But in my mind I am still an engineer. I have had articles published and I have been to six or seven international conferences.

Occasionally I still receive invitations to present papers. I can feed my kids so I'm lucky. But my 1980s' salary was much higher than my present salary. I used to be able to visit Moscow just to have a drink with friends. This cost a fifth of a month's salary. I could do more things with my family. We used to have a car, but not now. We used to be able to go to the Black Sea for a holiday every year, but no longer. I was proud to be in the Soviet Union. It was good to me. Now my state can do nothing to defend me and my family. I voted for independence. I believed that Ukraine was the strongest republic in the Soviet Union. It does have the potential but our leaders have just run Ukraine for themselves. A lot of people as well-qualified as I am have emigrated. They work in Poland, anywhere, in agriculture, on building sites, because wherever they go and whatever they do they can earn more than in Ukraine.

Tania was aged 55 and had recently retired following a successful career. She was born in 1944 and shortly afterwards her father, who had been injured in the war, had been sent from Belarus to work in Lviv. Tania had lived there all her life. When younger she had played volleyball for Ukraine and had become a physical education teacher at the university. Her husband was also good at sport – basketball in his case. He had played for the army team:

So we qualified for a flat soon after we married. All the leading players were given flats, and subsequently we qualified for a three-bedroom flat. When I was a child, conditions were very difficult. We all lived in a one-room flat. My life has been better than my parents', but everything we have, we've earned.

Tania believed that her children's lives would be more difficult than her own:

We could buy fridges, TVs and so on. Now it's impossible. And we, the older generation, can't help them. We have very little money. My pension is $13 a month. The system has changed. Life is not good. In fact it's painful [*begins to cry*]. Our governments have never cared about the people. Child benefit payments are ridiculous - trivial. I'm worried about what will happen to the children. The government care only about their own pockets. They're all corrupt. We vote, and we hope that they'll do what they promise, but once they're elected they're just the same as all politicians. It seems that Ukraine cannot be both successful and independent.

3. Education and Life Chances

COMMUNIST EDUCATION

All the communist countries of Eastern and Central Europe and the Soviet Union organized their education in basically the same way and up to 1998 none had made wholesale planned changes in the structure of the systems. Education has not been a candidate for privatization. All Western countries have operated mass state education systems for decades (for some reason this ceased to be regarded as socialist ages ago). There was little distinctively communist about education in Eastern and Central Europe and the Soviet Union except the Marxism in the curriculum.

'Except' is probably the wrong word here. In practice Marxism occupied a pivotal postion. It was not just another school subject. The Communist Party youth organizations (Octobrists, Pioneers and Komsomol) were present in all schools. Communist ideology pervaded all subjects and marks were awarded for ideologically correct behaviour and ideas, not just for the academic quality of students' work. All this ceased as soon as communism formally ended. This alone was a big change: it made a considerable difference to the ethos and daily pattern of school life. But the overall structure of the school systems remained intact everywhere.

Elementary schools

Under communism all children attended elementary schools (which provided basic or foundation education) from age 7 to 14–16. Compulsory schooling did not commence until age 7 but was preceded by generous and heavily subsidized, if not completely free, provisions in nurseries and kindergartens and zero grade classes in the elementary schools themselves.

All children followed the same basic elementary school curriculum.

These schools were organized in grades – it was necessary to pass one grade in order to proceed to the next – but the system operated on the assumption that all pupils were capable of completing the full elementary course.

In most Western countries 'full' elementary education was abandoned when secondary education for all was introduced. For example, in the UK 'all age' schools were phased out when the 1944 Education Act was implemented. The main reasons why the communist countries never made similar reforms have less to do with communist doctrine than exactly when their mass education systems developed. In the initial decades of communism the main drive was to provide all children with complete elementary schooling. In much of the Soviet Union and, indeed, in Eastern and Central Europe, this was not achieved until the 1960s by when many Western countries were introducing common (comprehensive) secondary schooling up to age 14–16. So there was never a clear educational (let alone political) case for dividing the communist elementary courses and institutions into primary and early secondary levels. In 1998 Poland became the first ex-communist country to propose such a division: one of the many steps that Poland has been taking and planning so as to Westernize its institutions (often doing more than strictly necessary) to prepare for full EU membership.

Secondary schools

After elementary education young people in all the communist states transferred to secondary schools, where the courses usually lasted between 2 and 4 years (until students were aged 17–19). By the 1980s, certainly in most urban areas, secondary education had become more or less universal. At the secondary level there were different types of schools. The general (academic) secondary schools were the oldest and always the most prestigious. Their courses led to the qualifications normally required to enter university. Other types of secondary education were provided in a variety of professional, technical and vocational schools. Many of these schools were formally attached to state enterprises or departments, and the curricula usually included some work experience.

This secondary school system was, and still is, generically Germanic or Central European rather than distinctly communist in several respects: first, in separating pupils into an academic group, on the one hand, and, on the other, those following more practical, professional or vocational courses; second, in the combination of classroom instruction and work experience on the non-academic tracks resembling Germany's dual system of apprentice training.

There were some differences among the communist countries at the secondary school level. Generally speaking, the closer the countries were, and are, to Germany, the more firmly established their non-academic secondary schools became in terms of the proportions of children attending these institutions and their acceptance by parents, employers and young people as a genuine alternative route rather than distinctly second best. Alternatives to the traditional general or academic secondary education developed larger and, it has proved in the 1990s and subsequently, more resilient roles in countries such as Czechoslovakia, Hungary and Poland than in South-East Europe and the republics of the Soviet Union.

The communist regimes also created a variety of specialist schools. Some were for children with physical or mental handicaps, while others were for those with special talents in sports, the arts, languages, maths and science. Most of these schools were based in the main population centres. The schools for children with special talents were designed to produce, and largely succeeded in producing, future sporting, artistic and intellectual elites. They recruited disproportionately, but not exclusively, from elite families, but their role in reproducing the countries' elites should not be exaggerated. The special schools were not the sole or even the main route to privilege. Communist Party organizations and mainstream higher education were more important.

Higher education

Under communism higher education was provided in universities and a variety of mono- and poly-technical institutions at which the students became specialists in academic subjects or in the various professional fields. About a fifth of young people in most communist countries progressed directly from secondary schools into higher education. There were some differences between countries and within the Soviet Union, where Georgia and Armenia were among the best-educated republics.

Higher education was usually entered from general (academic) secondary schools and was the normal next step for young people who received this type of secondary education. However, they had the option of entering employment immediately or via shortened post-secondary professional or technical courses. Pupils from the non-academic secondary schools usually progressed immediately into employment though it was possible for them to top up their qualifications and thereby enter higher education. And some professional schools combined preparation for a specific career with a final qualification that was recognized for entry into higher education.

Equal opportunities?

Under communism all types of secondary education were supposed to have parity of esteem. It was considered unacceptable for manual work to be despised; hence the periodic campaigns (never with long-term success) requiring all students to gain practical work experience. There was also supposed to be equality of opportunity for pupils from all social backgrounds. In the early years of communism 'positive discrimination' in favour of young people from peasant and workers' families was practised in recruitment to higher education, but these practices did not endure. The schooling that young people received was in fact related very strongly to their parents' positions (see Gerber and Hout, 1995; Roberts and Jung, 1995).

It tended to be parents who had been through higher education themselves and then entered professional or management jobs who were keen for their children to attend general secondary schools and then to enter higher education. These parents valued education 'for its own sake' and for the 'way of life' with which it was associated. The occupations to which higher education led were not always highly paid. Some manual jobs, coal mining being a prime example, were much better paid than teaching or medicine. Higher education could be a route to high-rising careers in the Communist Party, politics and management, but these were not the usual outcomes. The normal rewards of academic attainment and professional status were cultural rather than financial: city centre flats, travel opportunities and the satisfaction of cultural appetites nurtured in intelligentsia families and in academic education.

Parents who were keen for their children to succeed academically made sure that they attended 'good' elementary schools, 'goodness' being judged in terms of the pupils' success in the entrance examinations for the general secondary schools. Parents would often pay for extra coaching in order to strengthen their children's chances. Eventual success would be an occasion for family celebration. There was a similar competition for entry to higher education. Selection was partly on the basis of secondary school records, but since the exams were marked by the pupils' own teachers the results were not considered entirely trustworthy so higher education institutions set their own entrance examinations. Once again, anxious parents would pay for their children to receive extra tuition. This was a way in which teachers could supplement their modest salaries. And there were constant rumours of parents in powerful positions using 'influence' to assist their children's pursuit of higher education at the institutions of their choice. In our qualitative interviews in Lviv we found that 85 per cent of the university graduates had received private tuition prior to entering university.

Applicants who succeeded in the selection process received their higher education free of charge. Others could be offered 'paid for' places. Maintenance allowances were paid to students, usually on some sort of selective basis with satisfactory academic performance being the main decider. However, families were expected to be among the students' main sources of support. This made it an advantage to live in a city with a choice of higher education institutions though subsidized dormitory accommodation was available for those who needed to live away from home.

School-to-work transitions

On graduating from higher education young adults could be directed into jobs. For the first three years of their careers they could be obliged to work where the planners required. This was said to be their obligation to the societies that had provided their education. Students could try to influence this allocation process, as could their parents (by pleading or by offering bribes, threats or other inducements, depending on the parents' positions), but not always successfully. This allocation system was used to direct labour to otherwise unpopular regions. And the higher education courses and places that were made available were governed by the planners' assessments of future labour needs.

In all the countries in this research the job allocation regime for university graduates had been scrapped in the initial wave of reforms. Some of our respondents had in fact been directed into jobs (in the early 1990s) and had not necessarily resented this. By 1997 they were grateful that they had been found jobs; even if the jobs had not lasted they were often appreciative of the work experience. However, there was little support for returning to the old system. In Ukraine in 1995 there was in fact a political debate on whether the old system should be reintroduced. This was at the time when we were conducting our qualitative interviews. All the young people who were asked about this issue were opposed to the return of the job allocation system. They argued that it was incompatible with the market, but the real basis for their opposition seemed to be a fear of being allocated to low-paid jobs in unattractive regions.

Under commmunism young people who sought jobs immediately following their secondary (or elementary) education were legally able to work for whichever employers would recruit them. The only exceptions were at times and in places where, in contexts of acute labour and skill shortages, the regime that operated for university graduates was applied to graduates from some professional and technical secondary schools. Employers had to operate within the parameters of the planners' assessments of their labour requirements and rates of pay were not negotiable by individuals or, in most cases, by trade unions at the plant level. But at least mild labour shortages were endemic and plants could sometimes offer inducements including the likelihood of bonuses and, even more enticing for many young people, tied accommodation.

In all except the general secondary schools young people were prepared for specific occupations. Supporting linked secondary schools was one of the main ways in which establishments tried to ensure that their labour requirements were satisfied. In the normal course of events young people were expected and able to work according to their specialities. Indeed, there were unlikely to be powerful reasons for individuals to try to alter the occupational destinations that the system had mapped for them. Links between education and initial training, on the one hand, and first jobs, on the other, were extremely tight – tighter in East than in West Germany, for example, where, in turn, the links have been tighter than in Britain (see Konietzka and Solga, 1995).

All this changed dramatically in the early stages of the reforms, when many of the careers for which young people were being prepared disappeared while they were in their secondary schools or completing higher education.

EDUCATION DURING THE REFORMS

Up to 1998 no former communist country's government made wholesale changes in the basic structure of the education inherited from the old system. There was no widespread dissatisfaction with the system, though many individuals may have been disappointed with their own achievements and, in some cases in the 1990s, alarmed by the underfunding of elementary and secondary schools. By 1997 Russia was listening to proposals to cut back the numbers of young people entering higher and secondary education and for privatizing entire segments of the school and higher education systems, but none of these ideas have yet become serious politics.

The main planned changes in all ex-communist countries have been within the inherited systems. For example, Marxism was ejected from syllabuses as soon as reforms commenced. The Communist Party and its youth organizations lost their former privileged positions. In some countries the youth organizations simply dissolved. In most new independent states there has been greater emphasis in school curricula on the national history, language and literature. Usually the national language was already the normal language of instruction. In some new independent states – where there are significant national minorities – the language of instruction has resurfaced as a contentious issue. For example, the majority populations in South Ossetia and Abkhazia have not wanted a Georgian curriculum. Russians in Ukraine have resisted and resented any changes that they have regarded as making them into second class citizens.

Another curriculum change has been greater attention to Western languages and information technology. These are widely seen as highly desirable springboards for success in the developing market economies. In so far as demand for these subjects has not been met in mainstream schools and colleges, private institutions have appeared to fill the gap.

There have been further unplanned changes in education, particularly in the proportions and numbers of young people attending the different types of schools and colleges. Most of these changes have in fact been a direct response to the developments in the surrounding economies that were described in Chapter 2. The most significant developments for education have been the downturn in school and college graduates' employment prospects and the crises in public finances that have occurred in all the ex-communist countries.

Crisis in non-academic secondary schools

By the early 1990s non-academic secondary schools were in crisis virtually everywhere. Many of the state firms with which they were linked either disappeared or faced crises of their own, which meant withdrawing the support that they formerly offered. Many state plants ceased to be able to provide cash and materials and, of even more basic importance, they were no longer able to supply work experience for the students or subsequent jobs. Needless to say, these trends have been uneven. Some state plants have fared better than others. Up to 1997 the mines close to Donetsk had not been closed or even run down. In Poland some professional and vocational secondary schools have been able to establish links with new private businesses (see Roberts and Szumlicz, 1995). However, many professional, technical and vocational schools throughout the ex-communist realm have faced a choice of either closing or transforming themselves into *de facto* general secondary schools. There has rarely been much resistance to the latter strategy from pupils, parents or governments. General secondary education was always the most prestigious and there has been a prevalent feeling that academic education and qualifications will carry greater weight than ever in the new market economies. In East Germany young people have responded to the new uncertainties by 'taking shelter' – remaining at school longer – and, in most cases, prolonging their general education (see Grunert and Lutz, 1996).

The spread of general secondary education has in fact been most sweeping in those countries where other types of secondary education were least secure under communism, and where the reforms created the deepest economic crises, that is, in the former Soviet Union rather than Central Europe (see Meshkova, 1998). As we shall see later, in the late 1980s and early 1990s general secondary education became the norm in our survey areas for young people from all kinds of family backgrounds.

Staying on

A second trend during the reforms has been for stay-on rates in education to rise. Once again, this trend has been strongest in the countries where the economic crisis has been deepest and longest. There has been no general flight from education under post-communism. Predictions that young people would quit schools in favour of well-paid unskilled jobs in private businesses have been confounded. Enrolments in higher education and on other post-secondary courses have risen virtually everywhere.

In some countries, including Georgia, it has been government policy to open the university and college doors. This policy, needless to say, has proved popular among parents and young people. Where the growth of free places has been restricted the numbers of students paying for their higher education have risen. Where there have been insufficient places in state higher education to satisfy demand, private institutions have filled the gap. This was the case in Armenia where, by 1996, there were more private than state universities. In Yerevan the government reduced the number of free higher education places from 60,000 to 15,000. This created scope for new private universities which, by 1995, had 20,000 students enrolled, paying fees ranging from $300 to $800 per year. Tbilisi also had new private colleges, but in a context where (free) state higher education remained available to virtually anyone who wished to enter, the annual fees at these private colleges were usually around just $200.

More young people have prolonged their education under post-communism basically because of the acute shortages of (decent) jobs for them to enter. As explained in Chapter 2, staying in education has enabled young people to shelter from the labour market until, they hope, economic conditions improve. There has been a prevalent feeling that qualifications will eventually be rewarded and, indeed, that in the new market economies it will be more important than ever to be well qualified. Qualification accumulation has therefore appeared to be a perfectly rational strategy. Nearly all the young people in this study (86–94 per cent in the different areas) said that it was 'very important' to be properly qualified for one's job. Surveys elsewhere have also noted young people's enthusiasm for extended education. Kharchenko (1998), for example, found that most young people in Western Siberia were keen to continue their education beyond high school.

The popularity of extended education was evident in the high proportions of our samples who had continued in education, even those who had attended non-academic secondary schools (see below). This trend has threatened to devalue both general secondary schooling and higher-level studies. However, some traditionally prestigious secondary schools and higher education institutions have been able to protect their positions by remaining highly selective and making entry even more competitive than formerly.

More young people have opted for extended education, and have thereby prolonged their dependence on their families. However, in most instances, this has been in a context where they would in any case have been unable to obtain jobs which would have made them financially independent. And some have been able to work while studying, typically in 'bitty' private sector jobs, own-account trading or freelance work using their professional skills. In our research, among those who were still basically students at the time of the interviews, 33 per cent reported incomes from 'main' and 12 per cent from 'other' jobs. Many students have hoped that their work experience will further strengthen their longer-term job prospects, though by 1997 there must have been many 25–30-year-olds who recognized the danger that they might become perpetual students or perpetual peripheral workers.

Underfunding

Another widespread 'reform' has been that state funds for education have declined in real value or, at any rate, have failed to keep pace with student numbers. This has been a consequence of the financial crises faced by governments in all the ex-communist countries. As state factories closed or ground to a halt, governments found their main source of income shrivelling. And all the governments have found it difficult to tax the new private sector economies since so much of this activity has remained 'grey'.

All public services have suffered. Welfare payments have declined in value. Hospitals have been unable to replace or repair equipment or to pay for medicines. Schools have had no cash for books, let alone PCs and other teaching aids. Extra-curricular activities – sports, arts clubs and excursions – have often been axed. In these senses education has been driven back to basics. Teachers' salaries have deteriorated: in 1995 school-teachers in Georgia were paid just $10 a month. Private work, coaching for example, has become more important than ever to impoverished teachers. Those with skills that are in demand, especially foreign (Western) languages and computing, have been best placed to earn additional incomes. Others have simply been impoverished. However, the schools have continued to operate even when there has been insufficient cash to keep the buildings properly repaired or to pay for heating, and even when teachers' salaries have lagged months in arrears.

In higher education class sizes have become larger than ever. Teaching was always primarily via lectures to large audiences. Students were expected to attend, take notes and obtain access to relevant text-books. Most examinations were oral, and remain so, though it was always necessary, and remains necessary, for students to produce some written work in order to graduate. However, with the enlarged enrol-ments in the 1990s there have inevitably been larger than ever question marks against, and wider than ever variations in, standards.

It has been impossible to conduct collaborative research in the new East without directly encountering the financial crises that have engulfed higher education and research institutes. The problems that hit the research reported here included E-mail being disconnected, shortages of paper and hold-ups in printing reports due to power failures. Research budgets have been at risk in currency and banking crises. The only safe tactic has been to transfer and hold funds in hard currency. It is surprising how quickly it becomes accepted as just normal, rather than incredibly risky, to be carrying more cash than ten local people earn in a year.

Private education

This was legalized and then began to flourish in most countries in the early stages of the reforms, partly to meet shortfalls in state provision relative to demand, and partly in response to the deterioration in the quality of the education in public schools and universities. In most countries new private secondary schools, colleges and universities have opened, some linked to churches and some supported by Western foundations. Others have simply been local entrepreneurial ventures.

Everywhere there has been a high birth rate of small colleges offering short courses in (Western) languages, computing and business subjects. Most private establishments have concentrated on subjects which, it has been believed, will be required in the new market economies. Law, business, management and computing quickly became the prestige specialities in the 1990s. The prestige of the Russian language has declined everywhere except where it is the population's mother tongue.

Private finance has become more important within state education. Most higher education institutions have increased their 'paid for' places and raised the fees. In elementary and secondary schools it has become increasingly common for schools to charge for anything additional to the basic curriculum (see Meshkova, 1998). Nowadays families expect to have to provide their children with food and reading and writing materials. The situation is similar in state hospitals, where families usually need to pay for patients' food and medicines.

SOCIAL ORIGINS, EDUCATION AND DESTINATIONS

Family backgrounds and education

Table 3.1 relates our respondents' family backgrounds to their types of education. Under communism this was never a major research topic. Intellectuals were not expected to challenge the official view of the class equality of the societies, that all types of education had equal status and that children from different home backgrounds had equal opportunities. Even in the 1990s local researchers have often hesitated

Table 3.1 Education and family background (%)

			Low		Family class		High
			0	1	2	3	4
	Low	1	45	32	25	14	5
		2	4	8	6	13	10
Education		3	38	36	19	11	3
		4	5	7	9	12	11
	High	5	8	17	41	50	72
n =			190	87	144	120	239

before classifying the local populations and types of education. Like other locals, given the turbulent conditions, intellectuals have often been genuinely puzzled as to which families are advantaged and which types of education are advantageous.

The Western partners in this research had no difficulty in constructing scales of family and educational backgrounds which prove so strongly interrelated as to be regarded as mutually validating. Family backgrounds are scored 0–4 with full marks awarded where a mother and father had both been through higher education and are employed in management or professional jobs. Under communism there had been tight links between higher education and these types of employment, and (as elsewhere) like had tended to marry like. So the largest family background groups are those with zero or the full four points. The family origins of these groups correspond closely to ideal typical elite and working-class backgrounds. They represent extreme but simultaneously typical family origins.

We shall see shortly that the largest educational groups were also at each end of our scale. The implication is that the countries had been, and remained, polarized: the middle ranks were sparsely populated rather than bulging. Under communism the distance between the bottom and top (in pay, for example) may have been less than in Western countries, but within their own parameters the Eastern systems of stratification were polarized.

Education is also scored on a linear 1–5 scale in Table 3.1. Groups 3, 4 and 5 had all received an academic secondary education at a general secondary school or one which specialized in a particular group of academic subjects. Groups 4 and 5 had then proceeded to higher education, and Group 5 had paid no fees and had received (invariably modest) maintenance allowances. Group 5 are therefore the educational elite, but an elite that had experienced a hitherto perfectly normal career of academic secondary followed by higher education. Group 4 is different in that this group's academic careers had been chequered in some way or another, resulting in them failing to gain free places or to qualify for maintenance allowances. Group 3 had been to general (academic) or to academically specialized secondary schools but had not progressed into higher education. Group 2 had entered higher education despite attending non-academic secondary schools, while Group 1 had completed its education in non-academic secondary schools or, in a few cases, at the elementary level. Group 1 is the other extreme group on our scale but, once again, represents a common, in fact the most common, educational career under communism. As explained above, Group 5 (226) and Group 1 (109) contained much larger numbers of respondents than Groups 2, 3 and 4 (52, 61 and 47 respondents respectively).

All the respondents had begun their education under communism and some had finished before communism ended. So it is unsurprising that the relationships between education and family backgrounds that existed under communism were present (very strongly present). The proportions following the top educational route (Group 5) rose from 8 per cent among those from 'solid' working class to 72 per cent among those from elite families. The proportions on the lowest-status education route (Group 1) rose from 5 per cent of young people from elite to 45 per cent of those from 'solid' working-class homes, although as many as 51 per cent with the latter background had in fact received an academic secondary education (Groups 3, 4 and 5), reflecting how other types of schooling had been contracting in the latter stages of communism and during the years of reform. However, only 17 per cent of the respondents from 'solid' working-class homes had entered higher education (Groups 2, 4 and 5). The proportions proceeding to higher education rose in a series of massive leaps, from 17 per cent to 32 per cent to 56 per cent to 75 per cent then to 93 per cent, with each step up our family background ladder. In the 1990s social inequalities were persisting in access, or at least in entry, to higher education. But expansion at this level was reflected in higher education having become normal for young people from intermediate as well as from elite families.

Education and employment

Was education being rewarded in the 1990s' labour markets? The samples' different educational backgrounds remained linked to traditionally commensurate occupations (see Table 3.2). So the proportions of respondents whose last jobs had been manual descended from 50 per cent to 8 per cent between the lowest and the highest educational groups. Conversely, the proportions whose last jobs had been professional or management rose from 14 per cent to 77 per cent. Saar and Helemae (1998), using survey data gathered in Estonia, have shown that in the early 1990s there were no significant changes in the volume or pattern of social mobility and stability, measuring attainments in the conventional way, that is, according to the status of the occupations that individuals entered. So far, so familiar: it has been business as usual in these respects. But all this rests on measuring occupational achievements in the conventional way, and we have seen in Chapter 2 that in the 1990s the old occupational hierarchies had collapsed. During the 1990s new career groups composed of the self-employed and the chronically unemployed had been created. And among young people in employment, divisions had arisen between those in the public and the private sectors and a cross-cutting split between those with regular employment and those confined to 'bitty' jobs.

Table 3.2 Education and types of jobs (%)

		Education				
		Low				High
		1	2	3	4	5
	Management	6	19	11	19	21
	Professional	8	44	26	43	56
Last job	Clerical	35	19	26	21	15
	Manual	50	15	33	17	8
	Farm	1	2	3	—	—
$n =$		109	52	61	47	226

Table 3.3 compares the labour market experiences of our respondents from different educational backgrounds using our typology of career routes. It can be seen in this table that education was making some, but not much, difference. Six per cent of the pure non-academic (Group 1) and 8 per cent of the academic high-fliers (Group 5) had become self-employed, and 23 per cent and 19 per cent respectively had become chronically unemployed. There was hardly any difference in the public–private sector split between these extreme educational groups. However, the academic high-fliers were the more likely to be in regular employment (39 per cent against 30 per cent) and the less likely to be getting by with 'bitty' jobs (35 per cent against 40 per cent). Educational backgrounds were making some, but not much, difference to the quality of our respondents' jobs, and interestingly all this difference was within the private sector.

Table 3.3   Education and career routes (%)

	Education				
	Low				High
	1	2	3	4	5
Self-employed	6	7	5	2	8
State, regular	20	23	10	15	22
Private, regular	10	23	9	28	17
State, marginal	14	16	11	15	14
Private, marginal	26	19	11	17	21
Unemployed	23	12	54	22	19
n =	125	43	99	46	219

In Table 3.3 there is an interesting peak in one of the intermediate educational groups. Unemployment was highest (a massive 54 per cent) in Group 3. This was the group with academic secondary schooling but no higher education. It seemed that unless it included higher-level studies academic education was proving a negative investment. This is confirmed in Table 3.4, which compares the earnings of the young people in the five educational groups who had 'main jobs' at the time of our survey. Groups 5 (the educational elite) and 2 (those with non-academic secondary schooling followed by higher education) were the best paid. The groups most likely to be earning less than $30 a month had been to academic secondary schools but had no subsequent higher education (Group 3), or had 'chequered' educational careers at the post-secondary level (Group 4). Academic success appeared to be yielding labour market returns only if individuals' records were un-blemished or if their academic achievements were combined with a professional speciality.

In Central Europe during the 1990s rates of return on 'investments' in education increased. In other words, the earnings differential between the well qualified and the poorly qualified widened (see Vecernik, 1995). This was despite the fact that the link between education and earnings remained weaker than in Western Europe (see Slomczynski, 1998). But in the countries of this study, unlike in Central Europe, private sector growth was too weak to create sufficient demand for well-qualified young people which would pull the earnings of most of them upwards.

Table 3.4 Education and earnings in main jobs

| | | Educational groups (%) | | | | |
| | | High | | | | Low |
		5	4	3	2	1
	Less than 30	20	30	34	24	21
	30–49	29	30	30	22	37
Earnings ($)	50–99	28	27	19	28	31
	100 and over	23	14	16	26	12
n =		207	44	73	46	101

If education was not governing labour market success and failure, then what was? Family origins were continuing to make a difference (see Table 3.5). The proportions who had become chronically unemployed rose from 18 per cent to 42 per cent from the top to the base of the family background scale. Young people from elite families (under the old system) were the better represented group on all the other career routes. However, a privileged background was certainly not guaranteeing career success in the 1990s. It was assisting individuals to obtain regular jobs in the private sector but only 'bitty' jobs in the public sector. Among the young people from elite families in this study, 56 per cent had careers composed mainly of 'bitty' jobs or unemployment.

Table 3.5 Family backgrounds and career routes

| | | Family background (%) | |
		Lowest	Highest
	Self-employment	5	6
	State, regular	18	22
Career route	Private, regular	4	17
	State, marginal	10	17
	Private, marginal	20	21
	Unemployment	42	18
n =		114	199

ELITE CIRCULATION OR REPRODUCTION?

Interest will run and run in whether the great transformation in the ex-communist countries is being accompanied by elite reproduction or circulation. Are the old elites being reborn in capitalist clothes? The answer does not need to be the same everywhere. Paradoxically perhaps, the old elites may have the best chances of successful rebirth where the reforms are most rapid and successful.

Most of the Central European countries replaced their old communist leaders as soon as the reforms commenced. The old elites have been more likely to hold on to their positions in the former Soviet Union than in Central Europe (see Bystrova, 1998; Slomczynski, 1998). However, the (relative) success of the reforms in Central Europe has created good jobs in the Western firms which have been attracted into these countries' new market economies and in successfully privatized businesses. In Central Europe government finances soon recovered, thus enabling state departments and services to restore professional-level salaries; so in these countries there have been good jobs for educationally successful children of the old elites to claim. Meanwhile, many non-elite children have been able to continue progressing through vocational and technical schools into acceptable, regular, non-elite jobs.

In CIS countries such as Ukraine, Armenia and Georgia, according to our evidence, elite families have continued to be able and willing to support their children through academic secondary and higher education. But they have often found that these routes are being devalued by the sheer weight of rising numbers of students and that the commensurate jobs awaiting on graduation have been degraded. Family connections have worked for some young people; but more often than not their cultural capital has proved useless in the new labour markets. Meanwhile, 'uncultured' individuals with enterprise and marketable skills, whether in plumbing, car repairs or computing, for example, have been able to prosper. People with skills and contacts initially acquired in the black (illegal) economies under communism have subsequently been able to flaunt their success.

Most of the young people we interviewed seemed to feel that they were growing up in times when nothing could be relied on. Everyone in each of the countries seemed to know someone who had been big before the reforms who had become even bigger, but they had also seen members of the old intelligentsia, university professors for example, sinking into poverty. They all knew, or knew of, children from formerly advantaged families who were struggling. They had good reason to believe that much depended on luck: being prepared for a job in a state sector that had fared reasonably well or joining a private firm that had thrived. They also had good reason to feel that much depended on each individual's own initiative (see Bruno, 1996). Few believed that they inhabited a 'just world' where riches normally followed effort and poverty was fair punishment for sloth. However, they also knew people who, largely through their own efforts, had obtained their good private sector jobs, or who were succeeding in self-employment. During the reforms, both success and failure had been privatized. The old social orders where everyone shared the ups and downs of their countries' fortunes had disappeared rapidly. The processes that were structuring career routes in the 1990s, governing entry, then holding individuals in place, had become opaque rather than transparent.

The young people who were interviewed knew full well, often from bitter personal experience, that in the short term at any rate educational backgrounds and qualifications counted for little. It is hard to square post-communist experience with the confidence that prevails in some Western quarters that investment in education will lead more or less automatically to more productive workforces, which will attract investment, which will create good, commensurate jobs. Nevertheless, in Ukraine, Armenia and Georgia most young people seemed to have remained confident that, in the long run, education would pay. This could be seen in the numbers (21 per cent of all respondents) who expected to return to education within five years, and in the overwhelming endorsement of the view that it was very important to be well qualified for one's occupation.

4. Family Transitions and Gender Divisions

HOUSING UNDER COMMUNISM

The housing problem

Communism left two housing problems. First, there was not enough. Communism systematically produced shortages of everything: there was too little labour, too few washing machines, too few dwellings, *ad infinitum* (all relative to manifest demand). There were fewer dwellings than families or, at any rate, units of people who wished to live independently. The proof of this was the length of the waiting lists (housing queues) and the number of young couples with their own children who were still living with one set of parents, and grandparents as well in some cases.

Second, the dwellings were too small and of poor quality relative, once again, to people's expressed needs. Most of the 'houses' that communism built were blocks of flats or apartments. The typical unit comprised one or two rooms, sometimes three, plus a kitchen and bathroom, though in some cases the latter facilities were shared with one or more other households. Squalid accommodation was the typical reward for spending years on a waiting list. Standards of accommodation left much to be desired, but people coped. Given the size of households, all the main rooms were normally used for both living and sleeping. This might be regarded as a sensible use of space, unlike in Western homes where much of the accommodation is left empty during the daytime and living rooms are unoccupied at night. However, under communism there were acute shortages of private space in most dwellings. Couples and sometimes other residents had to retire to bed simultaneously when the daytime lounge became a bedroom.

That said, another plain fact is that communism improved the

85

housing situation in all the relevant countries. Overcrowding was reduced everywhere. Communism may have left housing problems in its wake but these problems were much smaller than those that the regimes had inherited. Prior to communism many dwellings lacked basic amenities such as running water and electricity, and many contained just one main room. Three or four generations living under one roof, sometimes sharing just one main room, was common before communism which, for the most part, modernized what had formerly been rural, peasant, traditional societies. For as long as people's comparisons were with the past, the populations had reasons to be satisfied with communism's housing achievements. But as the pre-communist past receded into history, and as younger generations became more aware of and made comparisons with Western lifestyles, dissatisfaction with communism mounted.

All problems are relative to people's perceptions and standards, so the above sketch of the housing problem that communism bequeathed is not just a straightforward statement of the facts, even though few people (in the countries concerned or in the West) are likely to dissent from the judgement. The shape of the problem appeared much the same to Western observers, citizens of the communist states and even the authorities. The latter recognized that housing was a problem, and this problem was being tackled constantly – unremittingly. It was addressed (by the authorities) mainly with massive and sustained building programmes. New blocks of flats were always under construction, and the quality and amenities in the latest units were usually superior to the stock. There were always new towns and suburbs under construction to which visitors could be taken and which could be featured in newspapers and magazines. Yet the supply of accommodation never seemed to catch up with demand.

Housing strategies

Communism not only bred characteristic housing problems; it also bred characteristic coping strategies. One, as already indicated, was to build new, additional units. Production (building more and more) was the long-term strategy for solving the housing problem. In fact, production was supposed to solve all problems. It was by producing more and more that everyone's needs were to be met and the true communist society created. Most housing construction was by public authorities –

local governments, firms and co-operatives – the legal owners of the 'social housing' stock. Sometimes the dwellings became the property of the occupiers (owner-occupation was not regarded as unacceptable). Individuals and families could also build privately for their own use but generally this was practical only in the countryside (see Sik, 1988).

The main short- to medium-term coping strategies were by the families – both nuclear and extended families – which, in practice, not only lived in but managed and allocated dwellings. In the medium term most families sought to enlarge and improve their housing resources. For most practical purposes dwellings belonged to families rather than to individuals or the state (represented by the various legal social owners).

As explained above, dwellings could be privately owned in all the communist countries, the actual extent of private ownership varying considerably from one country to another, often between regions and between rural and urban areas. But privately owned dwellings were not assets that were normally bought and sold. This was legally possible, but exceptional. There were no housing markets in the Western sense. There were rarely purchasers with enough money to buy a dwelling outright, and in most communist countries there were no banks that would make loans for such a purpose. If anyone did have the required sum in cash there might have been grave doubts about how the money had been raised. In any case, the owners of dwellings did not normally want to exchange their properties for cash. What would they have done with so much money? It could not be invested within the communist countries in the hope of making a capital gain. Individuals were not legally able to export capital. Banks would not have been regarded as entirely trustworthy with such large sums. If people wanted to dispose of a dwelling in order to obtain another they would usually try to arrange an exchange which, needless to say, could be quite complicated since it required parties to identify one another and to agree that their properties were of equivalent value, or to agree on a means for compensating for any difference. Exchanges did occur, but generally dwellings remained within a family. Dwellings which were private property were passed on through families. They were family assets, held 'in trust', as it were, whichever individual or individuals were the legal owners or occupiers at any point in time. Individual owners were not expected and, in practice, were not easily able to dispose of dwellings and use the proceeds for their own private purposes, even if they wanted to do so.

Communism did not invent this system of allocating housing. It was the traditional method the world over. In this and other respects, communism did not overturn but reinforced long-standing practices. Capitalism has been at least as revolutionary.

Socially owned housing too, for most practical purposes, 'belonged' to families. Once a dwelling was occupied it would rarely be returned to the collectivity. Children, provided they were co-residents, were usually able to inherit their parents', grandparents' and even other relatives' tenancies. This was one reason why it made sense for grown-up children to remain living with older relatives. Sometimes they would move in with grandparents or with uncles and aunts. This could be a way of making the best use of space and also of maintaining a family's right to the use of a dwelling. Socially owned dwellings would be exchanged within families. A household that needed three rooms (because there were two or more young children, for example) might exchange its one-room flat for the larger dwelling of a one-person household (a widow for instance). In such cases both units would be regarded as continuing to belong to the same family group. Whoever had the current use of a dwelling held it 'in trust', in effect if not in law, on behalf of a larger family. Communism's housing system did not encourage people to identify with their societies at large so much as bind them into their particular families.

Families could increase their housing stock by building new accommodation or, more typically in urban areas, by having new units allocated to them by a collective. For this to happen one's name had to be placed on a waiting list, where it would stay for many years in the normal course of events. If the collective was a co-operative then the future tenant or owner, or someone on his or her behalf, would probably have to make regular payments in order to maintain the future entitlement. Young couples would often go on a waiting list in the expectation of being allocated their own homes by the time that their own children were teenagers. Parents would often place their children's names on a waiting list and make the necessary payments in the expectation that a dwelling would be allocated when the child had grown up.

Clearly, these methods of coping with communism's housing problems and managing the stock depended on, and helped to sustain or create, complicated systems of family relationships. Private life became extremely important to people under communism, in some ways compensating for the absence of civil society – institutions mediating between individuals and their primary groups on the one hand, and the state on the other (see Wedel, 1988, 1992). In the case of housing, family strategies (towards maintaining or increasing their assets and distributing these to family members) compensated for the absence of housing markets. Inevitably these processes sometimes triggered family tensions. Exactly who should have the use of a particular dwelling? Families had to try to achieve an equitable distribution of their housing resources, but there was no guarantee that all of a family's members would agree on what was equitable. These were problems of daily life and the life cycle with which people coped. Housing was a topic of constant concern and discussion between and within the generations.

HOUSING MARKETS

All the housing processes that developed under communism also operate in market economies. People can and do build houses for their own use. Children sometimes inherit and continue to live in their parents' dwellings. Families place their names on waiting lists for socially owned and managed properties. Exchanges of privately owned properties and tenancies are occasionally arranged within families and sometimes between strangers.

However, market economies have additional means, market mechanisms, for producing and allocating dwellings and through which housing problems are addressed. In market economies dwellings can be built for sale to make a profit. In fact, this is how and why most construction takes place. Dwellings can be bought as an investment in the hope of a capital gain at the time of sale, and to obtain a regular income from rent. If an individual or a couple want to acquire their own home they can make a purchase. If subsequently they wish to move to another area or into a larger dwelling, they will normally sell and buy. In market economies financial institutions have been created – banks which specialize in loans for house purchase, bridging loans and so on – to lubricate the housing markets.

Problems and strategies in housing markets

Market economies create their own characteristic housing problems. These are not usually experienced and defined in terms of shortages. The manifest problem is usually the price. Anyone can have a dwelling, as spacious as they wish, provided they are able and willing to meet the market price. So methods of coping with housing problems and discussions about these problems within families, among friends and in the public domain tend to focus on money. Young people complain about the price of houses – more than they can afford. They make housing plans based around saving towards the down-payment on a home, the size of loan that they will be able to obtain, and afford to service, and how these plans are likely to be affected by changes in interest rates. As individuals' incomes rise they may feel able to afford and may wish to move 'up' the housing market. In later life they may sell a larger and more expensive dwelling, move into cheaper accommodation and use the surplus to supplement their pensions. Parents and grandparents may help their children to buy into the housing market, usually with cash gifts. Support may flow up the generations, as when grown-up children provide homes for their ageing parents. However, the normal flow is down the generations (as it was under communism) because in the West it is older people who are most likely to own their homes outright without outstanding loans. And rather than inheriting the tenure, the 'use right', as under communism, in market economies children inherit capital assets (houses) which are normally sold and the proceeds used for whatever purposes the beneficiaries wish. The value of a dwelling is easily divided between several children or other beneficiaries: the property is simply sold and everyone receives a cash share of the proceeds.

Market systems facilitate and encourage the individual ownership of dwellings. It is possible for extended families to own dwellings collectively, in equal shares or in whatever portions they wish, irrespective of whether all, some or none of the owners occupy the dwelling, but this kind of arrangement is unlikely to have widespread appeal. It is also possible for individuals and couples to buy a dwelling upon which no one else has any legal or moral claim, and in practice this is the most common arrangement. Couples are often joint owners. Indeed, this particular joint venture is taken to indicate their special long-term commitment to one another; that the bond between them is closer than other family relationships. Other types of family ownership are far less common.

As under communism, in market economies parents often help their grown-up children to move into independent accommodation, and, as already indicated, the most common form of help is money. Parents can give exactly the same amounts to all their children; and once they have used the cash to help to buy their 'own' homes the individuals concerned are unlikely to regard the property as belonging to anyone other than themselves. Moral sentiment can be a base for law, but it is also the case that moral sentiments tend to reflect actual practices. The legal owners of a dwelling in a market economy are unlikely to feel morally obliged to allow a wider circle of kin to use their property. Markets tend to individualize house ownership and thereby weaken wider moral bonds. In all the former communist countries where we have conducted research, young people have often felt able to assume that they will be welcome to visit and stay in the home of virtually any relative. Those with family in other countries have taken it for granted that they will be welcome to visit for holidays. Families based abroad have been equally confident of being accommodated when visiting their former home towns. Young people have felt able to move to other towns and cities for jobs if they have had relatives in the area able to provide accommodation. Individuals from outlying villages have often been willing to stay in town until late evening, after public transport has ceased to operate, because there have been relatives in the towns with whom they have been able to stay overnight without any special prior arrangement.

Under both the communist and the market systems difficulties have arisen that individuals and families have needed to settle among themselves. On occasions tensions have inevitably been aroused and feelings injured. Everywhere housing processes are entwined with family relationships and the latter, and indeed the former, are usually charged with emotion. Under communism it was often necessary to decide which among several children or grandchildren would inherit the ownership or use of a particular flat. Would the individual concerned feel or be pressured to move out should another family member demonstrate an even greater need in the future? In market economies it may be easier for parents to treat all their children equally if they so wish, but families may have to decide, and in practice may be undecided, individually and collectively, whether assistance should be linked to need, which is likely to vary depending on the children's different occupations and incomes and on parental status.

Many equivalent difficulties arise under all housing systems, as when couples wish to separate or divorce. Under communism this was often felt to be impossible because someone would be left with nowhere to live (a consequence of the housing shortage). In a market economy the problem presents itself as neither individual being left with sufficient money to purchase a home when the assets of a marriage are divided, So under both systems couples may have felt that they had no choice but to stay together. Also, under both systems these problems have usually been solvable if one or other of the separating parties has been able to move into a new partner's home.

Young people's housing strategies

Broadly comparable problems have arisen under both systems, but the systems have required those concerned to seek solutions in rather different ways. This has applied to young people seeking their own places.

Under the communist system it was difficult for young people to do this except in and with the support of their families. So the problem of housing the younger generation was treated as a family responsibility. Parents would build new houses or add rooms or storeys to their existing dwellings, or they would place their children's names on waiting lists so that their responsibilities could be discharged. Before a young couple married their families would normally meet to try to agree on the best way of accommodating the new family.

In a market system, by contrast, it is possible for young couples or individuals to raise the cash by saving or borrowing to purchase their own accommodation. Families may or may not assist but if they do they will be regarded as helping the young people to resolve what is basically their own housing problem. Markets tend to individualize problems whereas under communism it was hardly possible to cope with the normal problems of daily life (to look after one's children, to obtain housing and to maintain a decent standard of living in old age) except as part of a larger group, namely, a family.

HOUSING AND FAMILY TRANSITIONS

Family transitions

At the time of our research the young people had recently made, or had reached the age at which they needed to plan, their life course transitions from dependence on their parents. They were doing this in societies which were themselves in transition in numerous respects, including the ways in which housing was owned and managed. In Armenia, where most of the young people in our study were aged 20–22, only 16 per cent were cohabiting or married and just 11 per cent had children. In all the other areas, between 27 per cent and 33 per cent of the young people were married or cohabiting, and between 22 per cent and 27 per cent had children. In Armenia, 2 per cent of the respondents were single parents (nearly all of them females), as were 4 or 5 per cent of the respondents in the other areas. Roughly a fifth of all the parents were single parents.

Couples who lived together were nearly always married. Unlike in many Western countries, cohabitation prior to marriage had not been normalized. In Georgia and Armenia this behaviour would have been considered outrageous. Single parenthood was simply not an acceptable option, but this did not stop it happening. In Ukraine cohabitation was morally acceptable but normally impractical on account of the housing situation. Families would not assist a couple to obtain their own place, or invite a child's partner to share the family home, unless the partner had become or was in the process of becoming a family member by marriage. In all the countries marriage was followed by parenthood quite rapidly. The separable (in principle) decisions to marry and to become parents were obviously being treated as parts of a single package.

Blocked transitions

The proportions of respondents who had their own dwellings were substantially lower than the proportions who were married: 21 per cent in Donetsk but only 17 per cent in Lviv, 14 per cent in Tbilisi and 11 per cent in Armenia. It was rare for single young people to have moved into independent accommodation: only 7 per cent had done so. Single parents were usually (88 per cent) living with their own parents. Families would not normally assist young people's housing transitions unless they were marrying. Among those who were married without children, just 32 per cent had independent accommodation, though another 14 per cent were in lodgings of some description. Only 44 per cent of those who were married with children had their own dwellings: 47 per cent were still living with one set of parents. So even when they had started their own families, most young couples' main housing problem – obtaining their own place – had not been solved. And most of the young people were still single, without children and living with their parents. Many of them felt unable to make normal family and housing transitions because of their countries' housing problems.

Differences within and between countries

There had always been differences – inequalities – in access to housing within communist countries. In some districts the housing problem was particularly acute. And within all districts some families had control over more accommodation than others, relative to their needs. So it had been possible for some of the young people in this study to take over a dwelling previously occupied by a grandparent or some other relative. In a few cases the families, and in even fewer cases the young people themselves, had been able to purchase flats. However, the majority were not in such privileged situations.

In Ukraine the young people's actual housing situations were rather different than in Armenia and Georgia. Households were larger in the latter countries, where the traditional practice had been for several generations to live together. The main family bond in Georgia and Armenia had not traditionally been between spouses but between parents and their children, and households had normally been patrilocal (the wife becoming a residing member of the husband's family). In Georgia 75 per cent and in Armenia 83 per cent of our respondents lived in households of four or more persons, compared with 40 per cent and 44 per cent in Donetsk and Lviv respectively. But there was not more overcrowding, in fact there was less overcrowding, in Georgia and Armenia than in Ukraine. In the former countries, dwellings tended to be larger because they had been constructed to accommodate the traditional family. In both Armenia and Georgia, three-quarters of the respondents had rooms of their own at home whereas only 30 per cent in Donetsk and 26 per cent in Lviv did so. It was easier in Georgia and Armenia than in Ukraine for young people to be accommodated in their own rooms in their parents', or some other relatives' dwellings. Youth out-migration and population decline had eased the housing problems in Georgia and Armenia. Overcrowding was no longer the main housing problem in these countries. The problem was that most of the young people did not really want to live as part of 'traditional' families. They and, by all accounts, the majority of their parents regarded the 'modern' nuclear family as the ideal domestic unit. And establishing such households was proving difficult for most of the young people in all three countries.

Housing in transition

Everywhere the housing systems were in transition. As explained earlier, private ownership had been possible under communism but in the 1990s it was fast becoming the norm everywhere. The housing stock was being privatized. This was usually accomplished by transforming tenants into owners, sometimes for no more than a nominal charge. The former social owners were thereby privatizing responsibility for maintaining and repairing the properties, servicing them with energy and so on. This was why the opportunity to become a property owner was not always being grasped gratefully and eagerly. In some places there were fears that home owners might be targeted with a property tax. Becoming an owner–occupier was not being accompanied by new feelings of independence and prosperity. Owner occupation was not new. It had never been regarded, and was not coming to be regarded, as particularly advantageous.

Privatization was accompanied by the creation of genuine housing markets in all the areas in this research. It had become possible for young (and older) people to buy their own places. The problem was, of course, that prices were far beyond most young people's means: from $6000 upwards for a two-room flat, depending on the area. Property prices were low by Western standards but unrealistically high for most people in places where typical earnings were less than $100 a month. In the short term the creation of housing markets was not expanding the quantity nor improving the quality of the housing stocks.

In 1997 housing markets were emergent rather than fully operational. There were still no estate agents or pages in local newspapers advertising homes for sale or financial institutions offering mortgages. Most of the housing had already been privatized, except in Donetsk, but social values had not changed overnight. Most legal owners were still acting as if they held their properties 'in trust' on behalf of a larger family group. Most privately owned dwellings were still being passed on through the family rather than through the market place. However, it had become possible to sell a flat that was surplus to a family's requirements in order, for example, to raise the capital to start a business, which was how some of the more substantial enterprises of the self-employed young people in our research had been created. In these cases an entire family whose property had been sold would regard itself as having a stake in and a rightful claim upon the business, but in the long term the market was likely to liquidate such sentiments and individualize property rights.

Nevertheless, a fact of the 1997 situation was that most young people were having to rely on old methods to solve their housing problems. The family was not just an institution but also a value. In the surveys 72 per cent to 85 per cent in the different areas (80 per cent overall) rated 'having a strong family' as 'very important'. 'Being happy' was considered equally important, but material security, becoming rich, serving one's country, and enjoying public status and recognition were ranked much lower. The young people's housing chances were dependent on their existing families and, in turn, they wanted to create strong families of their own.

But virtually everything in the societies in which they lived was changing. Young people trying to make housing transitions in the 1990s were often in a double bind: housing was becoming a marketable asset but few young people were earning enough to make house purchase a realistic proposition. In most cases they were relying on old methods, but these had not worked for them in the short term and all the time these methods were breaking down. In the past they would have gone on waiting lists, but this had become pointless. If market reforms succeeded, and if they obtained good jobs, house purchase would become possible, but by this time, if it ever arrived, it was unlikely that our respondents would still be young.

The state of the economy was an issue in all the countries and, as we have seen, it was a personal problem for most of the young people who had no jobs, 'bitty jobs', or even regular jobs that did not pay a living wage. However, the housing problem was the really emotive issue – a desperate issue for many of the young people who wanted to marry but felt that they were simply unable to marry and become parents, given their housing situations. Housing was an equally hot, painful issue for the parents of these young people because the former were unable to provide the assistance that families in their countries would customarily have offered.

Housing transitions in Lviv

Joint interviews (by Western and local interviewers) were conducted with 16 young men and women in Lviv to obtain their own accounts of their labour market and housing histories. These case studies illustrate the extent to which young people were still relying on old methods to solve their housing problems.

As in our main surveys, a good proportion of those interviewed who were in their late twenties were still single and living with their parents and could see no exit from this situation. Most of the young adults whose marriages had already collapsed were also living with their parents. If they had moved out previously, they had usually returned when their marriages ended and it had been necessary to leave the in-law's dwellings or impossible to continue to afford privately rented accommodation.

Most young couples who had their own places had inherited family dwellings. Maria, aged 29 and married but still childless, had inherited her flat from her deceased parents. Eva, also aged 29, married with a son aged 8, lived in a village outside Lviv in a flat which had originally belonged to her husband's parents. The son normally stayed in Lviv with Maria's parents during the week because this was most convenient for his schooling.

Ivanna was aged 30 and had a husband and a 9-year-old daughter. They lived in a two-bedroomed flat which had been vacated when Ivanna's parents had moved into their own (deceased) parents' flat. Ivanna expected to occupy this larger flat eventually. The dwelling in which they currently lived was actually owned jointly by Ivanna and her daughter (not the husband). The latter was the part-owner, with two siblings, of his own deceased parents' flat. He was not using the dwelling but had a financial and, depending on circumstances, a moral claim on the property. The expectation was that eventually Ivanna's daughter would have the sole use of her family's

current dwelling and, later on, presumably her own children would
live there.

Separation and divorce had become quite common in Ukraine.
Hence the strategy, illustrated by Ivanna, of transferring ownership
solely to one's own children (not their partners). It was different in
Poland in 1993 (see Roberts and Jung, 1995). Divorce had hitherto
been uncommon in Poland and parents appeared to have no qualms
when passing property into the joint ownership of their own children
and their partners.

In Lviv, Lilia, aged 28, and her husband had been living with both
of Lilia's parents until her father died. In 1999 they were still living
with Lilia's mother. Eventually Lilia and her husband expected to
become the owners of the property which had been constructed quite
recently in the grounds of an older dwelling, the former family home.

Tania was aged 27 and was married with a 5-year-old son. They
lived with the couple's parents, 'sometimes mine and sometimes his'.
This couple hoped eventually to have saved enough ($6000) to buy
their own flat. The husband earned most of his money abroad as a
construction worker. He would leave home for 4–6 months at a stretch
and earn enough to keep the family for another 6–12 months, which
he would spend at home. The need to draw on savings during these
periods was making it difficult to build up the sum required for a flat.
However, there was also the possibility that Tania's parents would sell
a small city centre flat which was suitable for conversion into office
accommodation, in which event Tania hoped that she and her husband
would be able to buy their own place with their share of the proceeds
combined with their own savings.

Olena, aged 30, had also continued to live with her parents when she
married, but her father had been 'queueing' with a co-operative and,
when his turn came to be allocated a flat, Olena and her husband had
moved in. Shortly afterwards, in the early 1990s, this flat had been
privatized. This had cost the couple three-fifths of the price of a new
(Russian) car. They were not sure whether they had gained or lost:
'The law is not clear. We are not sure what it means to say that we own
it.' Olena was certain that they could sell the flat if they wished (for
around $10,000), but they had no such plans. What would be the
point? They would have to use the proceeds to buy an equivalent place.

Vera and her husband were the only young couple interviewed who
had obtained and held on to their own place by moving out of the

parents' home and renting their own flat. Another young man who was interviewed, Myklos, had done this when he had married, but his marriage had not lasted. He attributed this to having lost his job and the difficulties that he and his wife then faced in keeping up the rent and other payments. At the time (when he was married) Myklos had been paying $25 a month in rent. Prices had subsequently risen. Vera and her husband were paying $60, which included all services (gas, electricity and water). Both Vera and her husband had good jobs. He was a computer programmer and she was the office manager for an international organization. This was why they could afford to rent. Simultaneously, they were saving to buy. It was impossible to obtain a commercial loan. Anyone who wished to buy a flat needed to save the entire sum beforehand.

THE DEMOGRAPHIC 'CRISIS'

There was a demographic crisis (at any rate, most people seemed to believe that there was such a crisis) in all the countries in our research: the populations were declining. One reason was that life expectancy had fallen – an indication of how conditions of life had become harsher. In Georgia and Armenia the main reason for population decline was out-migration, but reduced birth rates were also contributing. In Ukraine the decline in fertility was the main reason for the population decline. It was believed that economic uncertainty and cutbacks in welfare support for child-rearing families (maternity leave and kindergarten places, for example) were making young people unwilling to have children. And everywhere it was also widely believed that the housing situation was a contributory factor. Everywhere the harsh economic conditions, interacting with the housing problem, were believed to be placing young families under intolerable pressures, and the rise in single parenthood was believed to be a consequence.

In time much of the alarm may prove unfounded. In the 1990s rates of fertility among women in their twenties in Eastern Europe and the CIS have fallen sharply and the proportions of parents in lone-parent situations have risen, but in both cases only to present-day Western levels (see Silbereisen *et al.*, 1996). It is possible that many young people's child-bearing and -rearing are simply being postponed. Given time, the young people in this study are likely to solve their housing problems using either new or old methods. Housing markets could take off and adjust prices to would-be purchasers' means. Failing this, the young couples of the 1990s could fall back on old methods: waiting for a family property to become vacant or raising their children while still living with their own parents.

GENDER ROLES

During and after communism

There is now an orthodox Western (social science) view on gender relations under communism and its aftermath. Communism decreed sex equality. Men and women had equal legal and political rights and formally equal access to virtually all jobs. There were no blatant barriers based on sex. So there were no feminist movements: there was obviously (to the authorities) no need for such movements. Rather, women's organizations within or led by the Communist Parties enabled women to applaud the system's achievements. Some Western observers were impressed. Women were known to be well represented in some occupations which in the West have tended to be masculine enclaves. In the East most doctors were women, and there were plenty of women to be seen driving buses, working in construction and sweeping the roads.

In practice, however, as everyone has now conceded, men and women tended to have different occupations and, in their own countries just as in the West, under communism women's occupations tended to be of lower status and worse paid than men's. And as in the West, women in the East were expected (by men) to do most of the housework. This was officially acknowledged in so far as women were granted special welfare rights (maternity leave, for example, whereas fathers did not have paternity leave). All women did have genuine access to employment, so in most communist countries women amounted to 50 per cent of the workforces. They were also well represented in parliamentary assemblies though not in the politburos (the real power centres). The official (and popular) justification for the inequalities was the 'natural differences' between the sexes. Women's compensation for the double burden of having to balance paid jobs and housework was indulgent treatment in employment. Maternity leave and nursery and kindergarten provision were generous, by most Western standards. Moreover, (state) employers understood when women needed to take time off work to care for sick children or other relatives and when they needed to leave work early or take extended mid-shift breaks to stand in queues.

The now standard Western view is that since the reforms began the situations of women in Eastern and Central Europe and the CIS have become even more disadvantaged: that there has been a silent social revolution with distinctly regressive implications for women (see Watson, 1993). Women have been more likely than men to lose their jobs. Plant directors and trade unions have sometimes taken the view that kindness to families, and to women themselves (given their dual role), has required women's jobs to be the first to go (Bridger *et al.*, 1996). Unemployment rates have generally been higher among women than among men. Maternity leave and other welfare rights have been curtailed. Nurseries and kindergartens have closed or have become expensive. By 1995 in Tbilisi a nursery place cost approximately $20 per month plus food – usually a large slice out of either parent's income. Interruptions to basic services such as electricity and water have added to the normal burden of domestic work. And while some women have been eased out of the labour market, females have also been losing their positions in politics. In most ex-communist countries politics has become even more male dominated.

Women in the East, it has appeared from the West, have often been accomplices in their own oppression. Some are said to have welcomed the opportunity to lead 'normal lives' as full-time wives and mothers. Some are said to have welcomed their new freedom to be glamorous sex objects. Some have opposed any restriction on their right to be sex workers. Perhaps most perplexing of all to Western enquirers, there has often been resistance to opening private life to public scrutiny. Private life was treasured under communism. It was a haven that the authorities could not control, and a feeling has persisted that how men and women choose to arrange their domestic lives is no one's business but their own.

Gendered youth

To what extent is all this corroborated by our evidence? Generally the
picture is corroborated except that the young women in our study were
less acquiescent than might have been apparent from their outward
behaviour. In moving through education then into the labour market
the men had become the increasingly advantaged sex. The women had
been the more likely to complete their studies in a non-academic
secondary school (26 per cent against 20 per cent). When the sexes
proceeded into higher education the men were the more likely to have
remained in the high-flying elite stream (43 per cent of male and 39 per
cent of female respondents). Women's academic progress was more
likely to have been 'chequered' and it was taking them longer to
complete their education and enter employment. At the time of our
interviews 29 per cent of the females against 23 per cent of the males
were still in full-time education. When the young people studied
employment-related subjects, these tended to be geared to masculine or
to feminine occupations. So, for example, 90 per cent of the young
people who had studied medical-related subjects but only 8 per cent of
those who had studied welding in their secondary schools were women
(see Table 4.1).

*Table 4.1   Percentages of students with various specializations who
            were female*

Secondary school	
Clothing manufacture	94
Medical	90
Sales	72
Education	75
Electrician	21
Welding	8
University	
Book-keeping	82
Languages	80
Medical	80
Management	39
Engineering	31
Architecture	20

The young women were more likely than the men to have entered jobs wholly corresponding with their education (42 per cent against 33 per cent) but in all other respects they appeared to have encountered the greater difficulties in establishing themselves in employment. More were unemployed (21 per cent against 16 per cent at the time of our survey). The young women were far less likely than the young men to have become successfully self-employed and to have obtained regular private sector jobs (those offering more than 20 hours work per week and over $30 per month). The men were over-represented in the management and manual grades, and the women in professional and clerical jobs (see Table 4.2). Overall the men had the higher earnings. Among those in employment at the time of our survey, 26 per cent of the men but only 11 per cent of the women were earning over $100 a month; 31 per cent of the women against 19 per cent of the men were earning less than $30 a month.

Table 4.2   Labour market achievements of males and females (%)

	Males	Females
Most recent jobs		
Management	19	11
Professional	32	46
Clerical	19	24
Manual	30	17
Farm	2	1
Career routes		
Still in education	23	29
Not in labour market	1	6
Self-employed	7	1
Regular: state	14	13
private	15	7
Marginal: state	9	10
private	15	14
Unemployed	16	21

There were some, but only slight, differences in the sexes' value orientations. The women attached slightly more importance to being happy and building strong families and the men to becoming rich and earning public status and recognition (see Table 4.3).

Table 4.3   Life values: factors assessed as 'very important' (%)

	Males	Females
Being happy	77	86
Strong family	76	83
Material security	54	57
Status and recognition	37	26
Becoming rich	34	24
Serving country	27	27

Generally the men were having the more adventurous economic lives. They had made more job moves for all reasons – redundancy, other dismissals and of their own accord. They had held more jobs in total than the women and were more likely to have applied for different jobs during the previous 12 months. And it was the men who were more likely to expect to move within and beyond their own countries at some time in the future. The men were already more likely than the women to have been to some other country to earn money. Generally, the women were leading the more 'orderly' lives. When unemployed they had been more likely to register and to receive benefit and were less likely than the males to have worked unofficially. When in jobs the men were more likely to have received both official and unofficial payments (see Table 4.4).

Table 4.4   Career experiences (%)

	Males	Females
Been made redundant	12	9
Been sacked	7	3
Left job of own accord	37	26
Applied for job (last 12 months)	53	46
Earned money in another country	20	10
Definitely or very likely to:		
move within country	18	10
emigrate	27	13
Difference: official and actual pay	34	26
Been unemployed	52	47
Last occasion:		
registered	10	23
received benefit	8	19
earned money	36	21

This was the context wherein the sexes were becoming couples in which the man tended to be one or two years older than his partner. So the women in our study were more likely to be living as couples (27 per cent against 19 per cent) and to have children (28 per cent and 12 per cent). Generally, the men were becoming the main breadwinners.

However, the women were not relishing their opportunity to lead 'normal lives'. In our study hardly any of the young women in the East described themselves as housewives. If they were not in jobs at the time of our survey, they nearly all described themselves as either on maternity leave (mainly in Ukraine) or unemployed. The women were much more likely than the men to believe that housework ought to be equally shared (it rarely was in practice), and were much less likely than the men to believe that married women ought to stay at home. Sixty per cent of the men but only 20 per cent of the women thought that the man should be the principal family decision maker: the females were far more likely to favour shared responsibility (see Table 4.5).

Table 4.5   Attitudes of males and females (%)

	Males	Females
Agree or strongly agree:		
Married women should stay at home	52	31
Men and women should do equal housework	49	69
Who should make key family decisions?		
Husband	60	20
Wife	1	3
Both	27	52
Whole family	11	25

SEX

Sex, birth control and marriage

Ukraine experienced the Soviet version of the sexual revolution in the 1970s. In other words, premarital sex was normalized. Even unmarried active members of the Komsomol could have sexualized relationships without censure. However, unlike in the West, in the Soviet Union the sexual revolution in attitudes was not accompanied by the contraceptive pill. Abortion had been the standard method of birth control since the 1920s and remained so until communism ended. Premarital birth control was a mixture of withdrawal and restraint, as in the West until the 1960s. The Soviet solution to any problems that this created, and to unplanned pregnancies, was to marry or abort. Once again, this was not unlike the pre-1960s West, except that in most Western countries at that time abortion was usually illegal. Unless they entered higher education Soviet females usually married and became mothers in their early twenties. Abortion was then used to prevent unwanted additions.

In the 1990s the situation had become more complicated. 'Delayed' marriage and parenthood had become the norm in all social groups. In our survey there was no clear relationship between family and educational backgrounds and whether the respondents were married and/or had children. More young people were prolonging their education but, no matter at what age they completed their studies, the majority were unable to obtain the jobs and incomes needed to establish independent households. Rather than having a greater need to postpone their family transitions, young people from advantaged families who progressed through higher education were often better able (because of their family resources and connections) to embark on marriage and parenthood.

As in the West, most young people were delaying marriage and parenthood until long after they became sexually active. During the 1990s the contraceptive pill had become available in all the countries in this study. In fact, a wide range of contraceptive devices (and other sexual aids) were on sale in high street shops. But the price of the pill was a problem for most young women. In addition, there was no way of knowing whether the products were genuine or imitations and women had to proceed without medical advice and supervision. In our main survey the samples were not questioned about their own sex lives but these matters were explored in some of the qualitative interviews. In Tbilisi half of the women who were interviewed, typically aged 25, had experienced at least one abortion, and this experience was near universal among the mothers.

The double standard

In Georgia and Armenia young people's sex lives were further complicated because these countries had missed the sexual revolution. In
both countries there was still widespread support for the 'virginity
institution'. Most of the young people believed that they were expected
to remain chaste until they married. This was considered especially
important for women. In our main survey majorities of both the young
men and women in Georgia and Armenia endorsed the view that for
women premarital sex was always undesirable or usually unacceptable
(Table 4.6). Attitudes towards male sexual behaviour were rather more
relaxed. It was generally conceded that 'hot blooded' men had to have
their way. The double standard had not crumbled. In our survey the
males were the more tolerant towards their own sex's misdemeanours
but the less tolerant towards women's.

Table 4.6   Attitudes towards premarital sex (%)

	Ukraine		Armenia and Georgia			
			For men		For women	
	M	F	M	F	M	F
Desirable	41	28	57	43	11	19
Acceptable	40	39	32	44	23	33
Usually unacceptable	11	24	6	6	27	25
Always undesirable	8	10	4	7	39	23
n =	150	148	259	322	257	328

In Soviet times, Georgian and Armenian males had usually been
sexually initiated when in the army in a distant land. The normal way of
dealing with the virginity institution when men completed their army
service had been to marry quickly, but in the 1990s this had ceased to
be possible. Young couples were in fact entering into sexually active
relationships without marrying. However, they were unable to do this
openly; and any couple with an obviously close and continuing relationship was assumed to be en route to marriage. Serial relationships were
not acceptable, for women at any rate. Single parenthood was a social
calamity rather than a choice.

WESTERNIZATION?

In some respects the trends in the 1990s had led to a rapid convergence with Western patterns as regards the ages when young adults were most likely to marry and become parents and in their premarital sexual lives. In the ex-Soviet republics most young people were delaying marriage and parenthood until their mid or late twenties and even beyond. By their late twenties many were still unsure about when or, indeed, whether they would marry and become parents. Of course, this applies nowadays in most Western countries. However, in the East prolonged family transitions were being experienced differently – as enforced and abnormal.

Attitudes were changing. Young people in the East were aware of and generally admired Western ways of life. However, they were experiencing a prolongation of youth with very low incomes, which inhibited the development of active, independent lifestyles. Most young couples' joint incomes were too low for them to contemplate living independently. The majority still had no secure methods of contraception. And even if they were somehow to obtain good jobs and the women went 'on the pill', their best chances of gaining independent accommodation were still through their families, with whom, in the meantime, they had no alternative but to continue living. Their longer-term hopes of independence hinged on preserving and respecting relationships of family dependence.

5. Leisure and Lifestyles

CELEBRATION OR IMMISERATION?

Up to now there have been two entirely different and, indeed, contradictory types of commentary on young people's leisure under post-communism. One proclaims immiseration (see below). The other focuses on the Western-type youth cultures that spread under communism, initially in defiance of the authorities, and which in the 1990s filled much of the cultural space vacated by the old system. Western fashions, music and (apparently) the associated attitudes and ways of life did not simply move in following communism. They played a part in underming the old system by enabling young people to flaunt their disaffection. In the 1990s Western youth (and other) cultures manifestly triumphed.

Youth cultures under communism

Under communism there were two recurrent themes in official discourse about young people. On the one hand, they were said to be vulnerable: early on (in the communist period) to traditional or counter-revolutionary influences, then subsequently to the appeal of decadent Western culture. Simultaneously, idealistic young people reared under socialism were to make the communist vision a reality. For this to happen, it was argued, young people needed guidance, which the Komsomol provided. Communism had official young heroes and heroines. These were not just members but enthusiastic about the Party and its mission. They attended meetings and participated in discussions and propaganda campaigns. They joined work brigades in developing regions of the Soviet Union. They had healthy minds and healthy bodies. They were involved in both physically active recreation and approved cultural activities – orchestras, theatre groups and so on – as participants and in the audiences. The state and Party provided these and other opportunities including holidays and the chance to be part of delegations to other countries where the young people could cement friendships with other representatives of socialist youth.

Most young people grasped some of these opportunities, but officially approved recreation failed to ignite everyone's enthusiasm. Some young people clearly preferred their 'own' cultures which usually incorporated some Western cultural products – hairstyles, music or clothing (blue jeans, for example). Despite the alleged totalitarianism of communism the authorities were unable to prevent Western fashions and music seeping in. The authorities' first response was to try to stem the tide. Over time, though with variations between the different communist countries, the authorities became more tolerant. But even under these conditions young people were able to challenge the system by expressing affiliations with Western youth cultures through the fashions that they wore and the music that they played.

And subsequently

Eventually the Western youth cultures won. Alongside the rise of the reform movements in Eastern and Central Europe in the 1980s, young people drifted out of the Komsomol and opted for Western ways. Within the Soviet Union, under Gorbachev's *glasnost* (freedom of expression) policy, the Komsomol was urged to listen to young people and to follow their interests. Thus, by the end of the 1980s, many concert halls and official meeting places had been taken over by Western pop music and its followers.

Once the authorities ceased to resist, participating in these youth cultures ceased to be defiant. No music or clothing is inherently rebellious; they become so only when authorities – parents, teachers or governments – make their disapproval evident. So it is now many decades since the mere act of listening to rock made a Western teenager into a rebel. In recent times it has become necessary to do more than just play the music. Dancing at all-night events, perhaps combining the music with illegal drugs, or maybe body piercing, has been necessary to provoke parental or wider moral panics. In the West nowadays, the types of music that young people follow have more to do with defining their particular membership groups and differentiating themselves from other age peers than with inter-generation relationships.

Likewise in the East, once the governments became pro-market and pro-West, young people could no longer use Western culture to protest and resist, and began to use Western and local cultural products to express their similarities and differences from one another rather than to distance themselves from the surrounding political system. However, some of the styles that young people in the East adopted in the 1980s and subsequently have had some political significance. For example, in the 1980s 'patriotic' Russian skinheads who had fought in Afghanistan expressed contempt for decadent peers (see Riordan, 1988). In Moscow distinctive styles have sometimes been adopted by young people from particular suburbs and from other specific regions of Russia. In other cases the styles have simply reflected a preferred type of music and a (symbolically) related set of attitudes. On the streets of Moscow in the early 1990s Hilary Pilkington (1994) was able to distinguish *stilyagi* (mods), *rokery* (motor bikers), punks and rockabillies.

This has been one picture of post-communist youth at leisure: partying at the barricades and subsequently revelling in their new freedom to express themselves through their choices of places to meet, their music and dress. Elements of this picture could certainly be recognized in the lives of the young people whom we investigated in Armenia, Georgia and Ukraine. The music and the clothing were very evident. In the 1990s Western youth cultures had clearly swept in. However, our approach 'in the field', as in this book, was to reach the young people's leisure via their family, educational and labour market experiences. These in fact governed the young people's immediate leisure opportunities. Passive consumer forms of spending free time, mainly watching television, were dominant. As Ule (1998) has noted in Slovenia, most young people seemed indifferent to sub-cultural styles. They had more pressing day-to-day concerns and their main response was to withdraw into privacy within their families and circles of close friends rather than to identify with and participate in any wider political or cultural movements (see also Chapter 6).

Surface impressions and underlying realities

Moscow may well be different. It contains more rich parents who are able to indulge their children's tastes in music, clothing and so on than any of our research locations. However, there are always inherent dangers in drawing general inferences from young people who can be clearly located within specific youth cultures, because they are

contacted through their participation in these cultures. Western countries have spawned numerous youth styles and identities but most
young people have always distanced themselves from the lot and have
insisted that they are just 'normal' or 'ordinary' (see Brown, 1987;
Willis, 1990). Even 'on scene', young people often explain, when given
the opportunity, that their involvement in youth cultures is just Friday
and Saturday night fun rather than their real selves leading real lives
(see Eygendaal, 1992).

Perhaps Western journalists have sometimes been too eager to take
the 'new generation of cola-drinking, gum-chewing, liberated Russian
youth' at face value (Meek, 1998). Maybe even youth researchers in
the East have sometimes been only too willing to highlight 'shocking'
evidence. For example, in the study which led to James Meek's report,
based on interviews with 3839 17-, 24- and 30-year-olds from all
across Russia, 65 per cent said that they would marry for money (more
than the 57 per cent who said that money was the most important thing
in their lives), and 28 per cent said that they would consent to paid sex.
Maybe the young people did say all these things, but there is often a
difference between what people say and what they actually do. In any
case, we do not know how many young people in the West would find
paid sex acceptable. In the USA pornography is now a larger industry
than the 'mainstream' cinema (Sharkey, 1997). We do not know how
many Western young people would marry for money under certain
conditions. It will be clear from the evidence already presented that,
given the profile of incomes in the age group, very few of the Eastern
young people who we interviewed were likely to have the chance to
marry for money.

Immiseration

This has been the second recurrent theme in previous accounts of
leisure under post-communism. It contrasts starkly with the alleged
flowering of youth and other consumer cultures. These commentaries
use entirely different evidence: on income and spending levels, cultural
production and participation in free time activities. Inspection of such
evidence suggests that, up to now, post-communism has been bad for
leisure in all age groups. People's real incomes have fallen in most ex-
communist countries, certainly in those in the CIS, which means that
people simply cannot afford to do as much as formerly. Higher

proportions of households' incomes have been absorbed by food and other basics. There have been declines, often steep declines, in state spending on culture and sport. Young people's opportunities have been affected adversely by the disappearance of the Komsomol. Neither the market nor new non-governmental youth organizations have filled more than a small part of the gap. Even classical Russian culture has been at risk (see Council of Europe, 1996). It is claimed that there has been a 'mediatization' of day-to-day leisure, meaning that people are now spending more time watching the small screen. To add insult to injury, fewer of the films and other programmes are now local products and more are imports (see Gvozdeva, 1994; Jung, 1994, 1996, Poretzkina and Jyrkinen-Pakkasvirta, 1995).

All this is plausible. The previous chapters have contained much evidence of immiseration, and one might have expected the leisure of young people in Armenia, Georgia and Ukraine to have been devastated by the economic conditions amid which they lived: their difficulties in obtaining decent jobs and their low, in some cases pathetically low, incomes. Moreover, the Communist Party youth organization, the Komsomol, which had formerly organized cultural and sporting activities and holidays for young people, had simply disappeared. Alongside this, national and municipal authorities were no longer able to afford to maintain or, in some cases, even to operate cultural and recreation facilities such as swimming pools and opera houses. In the 1990s there was less to do free of charge. Young people could not afford the kinds of commercial leisure that flourish in the West. So the commercial provisions that had been introduced were mostly 'basic', and even these were too expensive for most young people to use them regularly. The young people in this study, especially those who were able to talk freely in open-ended interviews, complained about how their leisure had been impoverished. There were fewer newspapers, magazines and books published locally and the young people could rarely afford those that were available. The films at the cinemas were mostly 'yellow' (old productions) and, once again, admission prices were usually too high. The young people complained that holidays had become a luxury. Some also complained that they were deprived of regular television entertainment by the unreliable electricity supplies. When these failed, homes and streets became cold and dim. The young people explained how, if they had any spare money, they needed to use it not for recreation but for more basic items such as clothing. Yes, they did wear trainers and T-shirts with Western prints on the chests, but they could not afford to buy new clothes regularly. Yes, they did have favourite bands (usually Western) and tapes of the music but these were usually pirate copies or home made. They could not afford to buy all the latest releases of their preferred kinds of music.

These young people were using the past in their own countries as a base for appraising their own opportunities. They had no doubt that they were disadvantaged compared with people of their age in the 1970s and 1980s. Needless to say, they imagined that things were much, much better in the West.

The resilience of basic leisure patterns

For Westerners there was little to envy but plenty to admire in the ex-communist East. It is true that the young people in this study had less than and were doing less of some of the things that young people in the West enjoy. However, this research offers many reminders that Western ways of life have accumulated considerable flab which, if necessary, can be discarded without undermining the core features of modern lifestyles. In the West we have come to regard as necessities things which, when conditions dictate, are shown to be luxuries.

Two introductory points can help to make sense of some apparent contradictions between the low incomes and spending of the young people in Armenia, Georgia and Ukraine and the vitality of much of their leisure. First, leisure can be cost free. In the West we have become accustomed to paying more and more for types of entertainment that can be self-generated. Listening to music and watching and playing sport are examples of this. Under communism people never lost the art of passing time without spending money. Daily life was never as monetarized as in the West. Even if people had money the shops did not necessarily have the goods that they wanted to buy. Young teenagers never felt unable to go out without sufficient cash to purchase chocolate bars and cans of drink or, when a few years older, without a new item of fashionable clothing. As in communist times, in the 1990s young people were spending time together in their homes and, when the weather permitted, in the streets and parks. Peer relationships had not been threatened but if anything had been strengthened under the prevailing conditions of adversity. Our respondents explained how in the 1990s friends had become more inter-dependent.

Individuals relied on friends for information about jobs – usually vastly superior to what the Labour Offices could offer. Young men with common experience of military conflict and young women whose husbands or boyfriends were in the forces often became mutual psychotherapists. Those who had served in the army complained about the conditions and the exploitation of young servicemen by older soldiers, but they also stressed how they had made real friends. In civilian life family members and neighbours helped each other, if only because they had no alternative, to make and mend their cars, dwellings, furniture and clothing. If people lost their jobs and the greater part of their incomes they still had one another. So young people were continuing to form the social relationships characteristic of youth. They were becoming involved in circles or networks of friends, then, as they grew older, in couple relationships which, they usually hoped, would lead to marriage and parenthood.

A second general point which helps in understanding post-communist youth's leisure is that goods and services have to be priced within the means of consumers otherwise the manufacturers and service providers cannot achieve sales. In the countries in this study Western goods could be bought readily, but only by the (few) people who were able to afford Western prices. Western motor cars, Japanese televisions and genuine Benetton clothes were priced at much the same levels as in other parts of the world. However, goods produced in CIS countries were generally much cheaper and local produce was extremely cheap (very, very cheap to Westerners). Low salaries meant low costs of production and low prices to consumers. Local food, wine and clothing had to be priced within the means of people who worked in the relevant industries. In all the countries there was a polarization between shops selling expensive Western goods and those selling local produce, and between hotels and restaurants catering for foreigners and the local rich and those catering for ordinary locals.

Throughout the former communist world there has been extensive pirating of audio and video tapes, and branded footwear and clothing. The multinationals have made few efforts to eliminate this. They would gain little if they succeeded. The populations in countries such as Georgia would be unable to afford world prices. Allowing consumers to obtain pirated products in the short term could prove a sound long-term strategy for developing new consumer markets. The same has applied to satellite television channels and computer software. What do the source companies lose if people who could not afford to pay Western prices are drawn into an official or unofficial lower tier of the market? An upshot has been that young people in countries such as Georgia have been able to watch Western films (mainstream and pornography) on video, to follow the latest sounds and fashions, and have usually succeeded in appearing much the same as young people the world over but at a fraction of the costs in London and Paris.

SPENDING

The value of money

Money is as good an entry point as any for examining the leisure of the young people in this study. It would be the obvious entry point in Western societies where daily life is highly monetarized and popular culture and consumer culture are difficult to disentangle. And money became more important (though exactly how important is a matter of some dispute; see below) in all age groups when the former communist societies introduced market reforms which led quickly to virtually everything having a price and anything becoming obtainable by those with the necessary cash. In the early 1990s visitors to CIS countries were well advised to carry tea, coffee, chocolate and soap. By the mid-1990s all this had changed. It was necessary to carry only hard currency. Everything could be bought – literally guns or butter – in the shops and spontaneous markets that had opened. Tape recorders and computer hardware and software did not need to be transported to local researchers. Most items could be bought in the East at sub-Western prices.

Making as much money as possible was not the young people's main goal in life, but in our qualitative interviews they made it clear that pay had become a crucial consideration when evaluating different jobs. This has been stressed, probably overstressed, in previous studies of post-communist youth. Zuev's (1997) 2500 interviews in 12 regions of Russia suggest that in the 1990s young people's main work value had become 'earning a lot of money'. Magun's (1996) surveys among 16–17-year-olds in Kiev, Moscow, Oriel and Mtsensk, conducted at intervals between 1985 and 1995, chart the rise of consumer aspirations among young people in the East. The trend up to 1995 had been towards seeking upper-rank jobs that would supply the income to purchase cars and suchlike. Rather than 'going East' or even 'going West', by the mid-1990s most young people were seeking branches of the West in the East. Saarnit's (1998) research among young people in Estonia tells the same story: a strengthening of material and status values. Likewise, Kharchenko's (1998) studies of young people in Western Siberia reveal a rise in the importance attached to high salaries and a related growth in the prestige of occupations such as lawyer, economist and accountant. Dementieva (1998), too, found that her sample of Russian high school students wanted highly paid jobs.

Levels and patterns of spending

In our study we did not find that making as much money as possible had become the young people's main life goal. Nevertheless, they wanted decently paid jobs. They could not but be aware of the new value of money in their countries. Very few of the young people had found well-paid jobs, but despite their low incomes (by Western and even communist standards) the majority had some money that they were able to spend on themselves. In the main surveys the respondents were asked for details about their incomes (under several broad headings) and also about their spending (again under several headings). Chapter 2 explained that earnings from main jobs were usually between $30 and $100 a month. When parents were the young people's main source of income the amounts being given were sometimes lower but otherwise covered the same range as earned incomes. The amounts received as educational grants and welfare payments were nearly always minuscule. All the above figures will appear low in the West, but some of the young people had several streams of income from various combinations of main and other jobs, parents, educational grants and welfare. As regards spending, for most of the young people, mostly single and living with their parents, 'things for myself' was their main type of outlay. The amounts being spent under this heading ranged from virtually nil up to $100 a month and, in a few cases, even more. The other major items in some of the young people's budgets were living costs, travel and other expenses connected with work or study and, for just 10 per cent of the samples, saving or repaying loans.

Very few of the young people had significant savings or debts. When they were repaying loans these were usually from friends or family members. There were no banks or other financial institutions offering hire-purchase or other kinds of consumer credit. Unlike in Britain, the young people were not being besieged with invitations to take the waiting out of wanting. Regular saving was uncommon not just because the young people's incomes were low but also on account of the absence of reliable financial institutions. Banks were not considered trustworthy. Private banks could go bust. The more substantial state and privatized banks were also considered unreliable because money deposited would not necessarily be released without paying official or unofficial commission. Savings were most likely to be held in cash, preferably in 'hard' currency. Any savings were most likely to be accumulated irregularly, when a person had a second job for example, then drawn on in leaner times. Very few of the young people were in a position to save regularly, over the long term, to purchase a house or a car, for example. There was simply no way in which the majority could make plans and take initial steps towards such goals. When the young people saved enough to go on a holiday in another country this was most likely to be from a working trip abroad, a lucrative deal at home or an exceptionally remunerative short-lived job.

Many of the young people were able to live free in their parents' dwellings. As already explained, in 1997 most respondents were still single and living with their parents. The previous chapter emphasized that many were worried because they were unable even to plan transitions into their own accommodation. In Ukraine it was normal for young people with earned incomes to contribute to the living costs while they remained in their parents' homes, as they would in Britain. Just under a half of the Donetsk and Lviv samples were making such payments, of varying amounts but usually no higher than $50 a month. In contrast, in Tbilisi only 28 per cent, and in Armenia only 18 per cent were making any such payments. This is one reason why the higher average earnings of the Ukraine samples were not reflected in their personal spending. In Georgia and Armenia young people would contribute to living costs in their parents' homes only if they themselves had earned incomes and their parents really needed the money. In these countries the influence of traditional family values (see Chapter 4) meant that parents did not like to take money from their children. The cultural norm was for support to flow down, not up, the generations.

The young people who had moved into independent accommodation normally had living costs, but not necessarily: sometimes these costs were met by a partner. In some cases the independent accommodation was actually within the parents' house and the parents continued to take care of all basic expenses. The actual expenditures on living costs of the young people who were living independently ranged widely, from under $10 to over $100 a month. As explained in Chapter 3, households with low incomes were able to contain their expenditure. The housing might be owned outright; if not, the rent could fall into arrears. Basic services such as electricity might be virtually free or households would use little. Food and other basic household goods could be bought at low cost on the streets and at markets.

If the young people had jobs or were attending college they sometimes incurred costs (usually under $30 a month) in travelling to and from their workplaces. Some also spent money on food and drink at work (again, usually less than $30). Other young people spent nothing on these items because they walked to work and took refreshments with them.

A result of all this was that most of the young people had some money that they could spend on themselves. Exactly how much depended on whether they were earning and, if so, how much; but equally it depended on their parents' generosity: whether the individuals were living free or at very low cost or, in the cases of students and the unemployed, whether their parents could afford to provide spending money. As explained earlier, when spending money was being given by parents the sums covered roughly the same range as the earnings of the young people with jobs.

There were wide inequalities in how much money the young people were spending on themselves. Some were spending over $100 a month. A tiny proportion were spending over $200, equivalent to the entire living costs of some households that lived decently rather than in poverty. A hundred dollars a month will not appear a huge sum to young people or adults in the West (or in Moscow for that matter). A few years on from our fieldwork in 1997, $100 may have become a modest sum in our research locations; but in these former Soviet countries at the time of our research, given that locally produced leisure goods and services could be low priced and few jobs paid more than $100 a month, this represented a high level of personal consumption. The main things that young people bought for themselves were clothing, footwear, music and cosmetics (bought mainly by females). A minority spent significant amounts on tobacco products. The more affluent were able to purchase personal entertainment equipment (video and audio equipment, for example), meals in restaurants, holidays, substantial wardrobes of fashionable clothing and motor cars. Other young people had less than $10 a month to spend on themselves. Most, of course, were between these extremes, but with more towards the base rather than the summit: 47 per cent were spending less than $30 a month on themselves, 24 per cent were spending between $30 and $50, 18 per cent between $50 and $100, and just 11 per cent were spending more than $100 a month.

Privatism and individualization

Market reforms might not have succeeded in raising general living standards but they had broken up the old (largely cashless) common ways of life based on publicly provided leisure services. There had been a general trend towards private leisure, mostly based on television, but with a wider choice of programmes on the terrestrial channels and, for those with videos and satellite connections, a much wider choice. Among the better-off, leisure was becoming individualized. It was individuals, not entire neighbourhoods or even families, who were able to spend handsomely on their own leisure. There may have been very few such persons but in the 1990s they had rapidly become high-profile, high-status role models. Under communism people with money could not spend conspicuously because there was little to buy and, in any case, they would not have wanted to advertise their (probably illegally gained) wealth. Formerly the high-profile, high-status group had been the intelligentsia with lifestyles based on the consumption of publicly provided cultural services. In the 1990s many of these services disappeared, threatening the intelligentsia's lifestyles. Some members of this group were succeeding in the new market economies and displaying the new symbols of success, but their achievements were in fact evidence of how the old lifestyles and status hierarchies were being undermined. And these changes were especially glaring among young people because of the wide inequalities in the amounts that they were able to spend on themselves.

LEISURE EQUIPMENT

Trends in the West

Nowadays a good index of the leisure opportunities of any household or wider group, especially outside the Western world, is its access to items of leisure equipment that became normal, in some cases near-universal, possessions in the West as prosperity spread following the Second World War. First, people bought television sets. They did likewise in the East and by the 1980s television ownership was at a level where it had ceased to discriminate between advantaged and disadvantaged families. In the countries in this research the main complaints of television starvation were in Armenia, where the frequent power cuts up to 1996, not the non-availability of sets, had deprived families of reliable evening entertainment.

In the West ownership of televisions was followed by video recorders or players (now near-universal in many countries) and subsequently by satellite and cable connections (currently spreading rapidly). Home computers may one day become a key item of leisure equipment. Currently they appear to be still in the experimental stage in terms of leisure use. Some people have become avid Internet browsers; others have become dedicated games players. But as yet neither of these uses has as widespread appeal as watching television films, sport, soap operas and game shows.

Alongside the spread of these items of home leisure equipment, the populations in Western countries acquired motor cars. Most households have probably come to regard at least one car as a necessity. There are ceaseless arguments (on ecological and health grounds) for encouraging people to do more walking and cycling and to make more use of public transport. Most people seem to agree that it would be desirable to reduce road congestion by persuading others to make alternative transport arrangements without themselves dispensing with their cars or leaving them at home more often. The first generation of car owners in the West was probably the most appreciative of the benefits of private motor transport. It saves time and widens employment, leisure and shopping opportunities. Owning a car as soon as possible is a standard aspiration among young people. Once they are in employment it is unlikely to be long before they become motorized. Indeed, they are

likely to feel that they need cars in order to get to work. And once
equipped with cars individuals' leisure opportunities widen considerably. Car ownership has become one of the big leisure dividers in the
West. The car helps to privatize and individualize leisure. People with
cars can go out without risking social encounters with neighbours.

And in the East

The populations in Eastern countries have always had similar consumer
aspirations to their Western counterparts (or so it now appears) and
admire the Western way of life because, it appears from the East, this
makes the goods available to virtually everyone. In the East long-
standing consumer aspirations strengthened in the 1990s alongside
market reforms. In our surveys the young people were asked not
whether they owned, but whether they had the use of cars, videos and
satellite links. In most cases the 'use' was of household/family
equipment because most of the young people were still living with their
parents. And in terms of their own leisure opportunities young people
were advantaged if they lived in families with motor vehicles that they
could use and, since so much leisure time is spent at home in all
modern societies, whether the range of entertainment available was
widened by the presence of videos and satellite dishes.

In presenting our evidence on the items of leisure equipment to
which the young people in Armenia, Georgia and Ukraine had access,
and later on when considering their leisure activities, we can make
some direct comparisons with evidence from Eastern and Central European countries and also from the West. Some identical questions were
asked in our surveys of approximately 900 21–24-year-olds in three
regions of Poland (Gdańsk, Katowice and Suwałki) in 1993. Some of
the same questions were included in our 1997 surveys of 400 young
self-employed and 800 young unemployed people, aged up to 30, in
four Eastern and Central European countries (Bulgaria, Hungary,
Poland and Slovakia); and in 1987–9 surveys of representative samples
of 16–19-year-olds in several parts of Britain, from which we have
selected the evidence provided at age 18–19 by the sample of over
1000 young people in Liverpool in 1988. Obviously, the findings from
the several surveys are not directly comparable: the evidence was not
all collected in the same year; the samples were not of precisely the
same age. Nevertheless, the evidence from elsewhere can act as a set of

benchmarks in assessing just how deprived, if at all, young people in the ex-Soviet countries were in 1997.

These questions on leisure are actually the items which could be included in all the surveys in identical forms. Questions on education and work had to be tailored to country specificities. Moreover, having the use of a video and access to satellite television have much the same significance everywhere. This is not true to the same extent of education, for example, where different countries have different types of schools; or of politics, since the alternatives and issues vary from place to place; or of employment, because the main career routes and divisions are not constant. By contrast, leisure seems to have much the same shape everywhere. The main differences are simply quantitative.

Motor cars

Among the ex-Soviet countries access to cars was highest in Armenia (the poorest of the three countries and the one where the respondents were youngest). A third of the Armenia sample had the use of cars, 20 per cent in Tbilisi, and 13 per cent and 14 per cent in Donetsk and Lviv respectively (see Table 5.1). As a benchmark, 52 per cent of the 21–24-year-olds in three regions of Poland who were investigated in 1993 had the use of cars. By 1997 the same proportion, 52 per cent, of Eastern and Central Europe's young unemployed had the use of cars, as did 87 per cent of the young self-employed. In Liverpool in 1988 only 26 per cent of 18–19-year-olds had the use of a motor vehicle. In the former Soviet countries in 1997, most of the vehicles were old Eastern models which were being kept on the road through do-it-yourself repairs and maintenance. The above figures give an indication of the extent to which the ex-Soviet countries lagged behind Central Europe in their peoples' standards of living and also of the speed with which levels of car ownership in the East have been catching up with those in the West.

Home entertainment equipment

Videos had not become standard domestic equipment in the former Soviet countries in 1997. In Liverpool 82 per cent of 18–19-year-olds had the use of videos in 1988 as did 61 per cent of young Poles in 1993. This applied to only 55 per cent in Tbilisi, 47 per cent in Lviv, 40 per cent in Armenia and 23 per cent in Donetsk in 1997.

Table 5.1 Leisure equipment

| Percentages with the use of: | Lviv | Donetsk | Tbilisi | Armenia | Poland | Eastern and Central Europe | | Britain |
						Self-employed	Unemployed	
Car	14	13	20	33	52	87	52	26
Video	47	23	55	40	61	n.a.	n.a.	82
Satellite or cable	9	6	38	6	35	72	53	n.a.
PC	12	7	11	4	n.a.	48	21	n.a.
Own room	26	30	75	75	84	n.a.	n.a.	83

Note: n.a. = not available

124

In 1993, 35 per cent of the young Poles lived in homes with satellite or cable connections (more than in Britain at that time). By 1997, 53 per cent of Eastern and Central Europe's young unemployed had such connections as did 72 per cent of the self-employed. By 1997, Britain was seriously behind Eastern and Central Europe in the spread of satellite and cable links. Tbilisi in 1997 was at the Poland 1993 level (38 per cent) but in the other areas only 6–9 per cent of the samples had this item of leisure equipment.

Most of the young people and their homes were poorly equipped for leisure compared with their Western counterparts, but this was not among our respondents' grievances. They had not lost ground in domestic leisure equipment in the 1990s. In so far as their home-based leisure was threatened by the changes, this had been due to irregular electricity supplies and to the (upward) movement in energy prices to full-cost levels which was gradually happening everywhere.

Country differences and specificities

Except that the CIS countries lagged behind Central Europe, which was rapidly catching up with the West and overtaking the West in satellite and cable connections, it is difficult to explain some of the inter-country differences reported above. Ukraine's economy had been less devastated by the reforms than Armenia's and Georgia's but this was not reflected in higher rates of ownership of leisure equipment. A general point made earlier about local prices having to adjust to consumers' means will be relevant. However, the goods that households owned in the 1990s did not necessarily reflect their prosperity in the 1990s. Some items had been acquired earlier, especially the motor cars. Others had been purchased from savings. The Georgian and Armenian economies had been crippled in the 1990s but these had been among the Soviet Union's more prosperous republics. In the 1990s there had been considerable income mobility among the local populations. The rich were new to their wealth and the poor to their poverty. Moreover, families' circumstances could change from year to year and month to month depending on whether the members' workplaces were operating at near-full capacity, whether any of the individuals had second jobs, and so on. Bogomolova's (1998) Russian panel study, in which households were surveyed in 1994, 1995 and 1996, found that only 20 per cent had remained in the same income quintiles throughout this period; 42 per cent of the households had some experience in the bottom quintile, but only 5 per cent had remained in it throughout the three years. Given the much greater income mobility than in more stable Western economies and societies, one would not expect to find a close match between individuals' incomes and their households' possessions in CIS countries such as Armenia, Georgia and Ukraine in 1997.

Surveys always produce findings for which their evidence offers no clear explanations. Why, among the countries featured in this study, were young people most likely to have the use of cars in Armenia and why was Tbilisi the best 'wired' area? At least part of the explanation of the relatively high level of car use is that Armenia was the country where there was the greatest need. Public transport virtually disappeared with the oil shortages of the early 1990s and was not back to normal in 1997. Hence Armenia was the place where there was the greatest incentive to keep private vehicles running. Needless to say, having the use of a vehicle did not always mean that the young people could afford to pay for fuel which, like most other things, was available in all the countries by 1995, provided customers could pay the market price.

In Georgia public transport was back to normal by 1996 and, prior to that, Tbilisi was well served by fleets of private minibuses. Ukraine's public transport was maintained throughout the 1990s. Tbilisi, Lviv and Donetsk also had plenty of official private taxis and a great deal of unofficial taxi transport – people wanting a lift could flag a passing motorist. People without cars were not gravely disadvantaged. They will become so in the main cities of Ukraine and Georgia only if and when car ownership reaches the threshold above which public transport begins to deteriorate through loss of custom, and shopping and leisure facilities begin to move out of town.

Up to 1997 Armenia had the most regulated private sector economy and relatively little visible private enterprise road passenger transport. It was not that private enterprise was illegal; it was rather a case that any private business needed official permission and had to comply with numerous regulations. In the course of obtaining all the necessary permissions to run a business, numerous official and unofficial charges were likely to be levied, and this would continue as long as the business operated. This was tending to inhibit some (publicly visible) types of private enterprise such as minibuses and taxis.

Georgia had the least regulated economy, so by 1997 the poverty of the population had not prevented Tbilisi becoming crowded with a wide variety of shops, bars and restaurants. This is also likely to be part of the explanation of why, by 1997, Tbilisi had become the best endowed of our locations in terms of video-players and satellite connections. Many of the latter were communal facilities: neighbours or co-residents in a block of flats would share the costs. There was a high level of pirating in the video and satellite industries. None of the governments seemed particularly interested in suppressing pirating itself, and in Georgia the relevant businesses did not seem to attract an above-normal level of harassment (and charges) from the authorities. In the other countries the survival of similar businesses was likely to depend on the proprietors being able and willing to pay regular, and relatively high, unofficial charges (bribes).

LEISURE ACTIVITIES

When asked how the reforms have changed their own lives, most citizens of CIS countries explain how conditions have become more difficult. The next chapter will examine young people's feelings about the reforms more thoroughly. If asked how the reforms have affected their leisure many CIS citizens will mention the upside: the wider range of television entertainment, even for households with just terrestrial channels, and the greater variety of shops with a wider range of goods, most of which, unfortunately, they themselves cannot afford. Enquiries about the downside for young people are likely to lead to descriptions of how recreation formerly organized for them by the Komsomol, schools and colleges, employers, trade unions and municipalities has disappeared. The Komsomol itself simply disappeared at the very start of the reforms. Cash starvation of schools and colleges cut education to basics. Cash-strapped local authorities ceased to be able to maintain and operate leisure facilities. There is a widespread, probably accurate, perception that young people's opportunities to take holidays away from home, to play sport and to attend film shows, theatres, concerts and theatrical performances have all been cut back and that young people under post-communism are doing less of all these things than their predecessors.

Our qualitative interviews with young artists in Tbilisi illustrate what had happened. Many of these young people had been trained at state academies and, under communism, would have progressed into careers as writers, musicians, painters, film makers, actors, stage designers and so on. Many of these careers in state cultural institutions had simply vanished. If state posts still existed the salaries had typically sunk to minuscule levels. So painters were trying to sell their art on the streets. Musicians were performing in restaurants, bars and on the street. They were discovering that, in the absence of visitors from abroad, culture had ceased to be a base for a livelihood. Local film production had ended. The films being shown in the local cinemas were imports, generally old, since the cinemas and their customers could not afford the latest releases. Some concerts were being organized. Rock was no longer underground. But everything was depressed by the poverty of the population.

Our evidence does not dispute the young people's own perception that their leisure had been degraded but enables the trends to be viewed from a different, comparative perspective. This suggests that, yes, in the 1990s post-communist youth were deprived of holidays relative to what they would have had under communism and also relative to the opportunities enjoyed by their Western counterparts. However, levels of sports participation, attendances at out-of-home entertainment and memberships of leisure-based clubs appeared to have simply fallen to Western levels. The main leisure activities in which Western youth are much more involved, so far, apart from holidays, are drinking and eating out.

Out-of-home eating and drinking

The surveys in Britain (1988), Poland (1993) and the CIS countries (1997) all enquired how frequently the samples participated in a list of leisure activities. In the presentation of the results (see Table 5.2) we shall focus on the proportions who participated regularly, at least once a week. In the CIS countries between 14 per cent and 32 per cent and in Poland 20 per cent of the young people said that they went to cafés, bars or restaurants at least once a week. In Liverpool in 1988 the proportion of 18–19-year-olds going to pubs at least once a week was 56 per cent and the proportion of young people who consumed alcohol at least once a week was roughly the same as the proportion visiting

Table 5.2 *Leisure activities: percentages taking part at least once a week*

	Lviv	Donetsk	Tbilisi	Armenia	Poland	Eastern and Central Europe		Britain
						Self-employed	Unemployed	
Playing sport	44	27	22	27	38	45	n.a.	n.a.
Watching sport	3	3	5	1	2	24	n.a.	n.a.
Cinema, concerts, etc.	5	1	6	5	3	4	n.a.	n.a.
Pubs, restaurants, etc.	22	14	18	32	20	56	n.a.	n.a.
Drinking alcohol	17	16	25	18	10	55	n.a.	n.a.
Smoking	36	34	50	29	34	28	n.a.	n.a.
Church	9	7	9	13	30	14	n.a.	n.a.
Holiday previous year:								
1	54	40	40	26	32	n.a.	46	5
2 or more	25	14	22	18	34	n.a.	17	34
Belong to recreation-based club	18	5	11	6	n.a.	n.a.	10	9

Note: n.a. = not available

pubs this often, whereas in most of the ex-communist countries the regular drinkers were smaller proportions of the samples than those who visited bars, restaurants and cafés. This appears to be the main difference in the day-to-day and week-to-week leisure of Western youth (or British youth at any rate, though Britain is below the EU average in its level of alcohol consumption). 'Nights out' in pubs and clubs have never been, and are still not, normal parts of Eastern youth scenes.

Smoking, by contrast with drinking, appears from our evidence to be more or less equally common among young people in the East and the West: 50 per cent of the Tbilisi sample smoked while in all the other CIS countries, in Poland and in the British research, between 28 per cent and 36 per cent of the samples were cigarette smokers.

Out-of-home entertainment

In the CIS countries the proportions of young people who were going regularly (at least once a weeek) to cinemas, theatres and concerts were between 1 per cent and 6 per cent. These are among the figures that in the East are taken as evidence of young people's leisure having been impoverished. The perception in the East is that attendances were much higher under communism, and this perception is probably accurate because the state and the Communist Party provided regular opportunities to do all these things either free of charge or at very low cost. However, the equivalent participation rate in Poland in 1993 was 3 per cent, and among 18–19-year-olds in Liverpool in 1988 it was 4 per cent. In the West television has been the populations' staple source of regular entertainment for over a generation. Home is where young people (and adults) are most likely to watch films and listen to music. What appears to have happened under post-communism is that young people's styles and levels of cultural consumption have been (partly) Westernized and this has involved their relocation from the public to the private domain.

Sport

In Lviv 44 per cent of the young people were playing sport regularly (at least once a week). Elsewhere in the CIS countries the regular participation rates in sport were between 22 per cent and 27 per cent. In the

Polish research the equivalent rate was 38 per cent and among Liverpool's 18–19-year-olds 45 per cent. Everywhere the likelihood of young people playing sport depends heavily on whether or not they are attending schools or colleges. The Lviv sport participation rate of 44 per cent among 25–26-year-olds, only a small minority of whom were still in full-time education, is extremely respectable by international standards. Precise like-with-like comparisons are not possible with our data which nevertheless suggest strongly that if the sport participation levels in CIS countries have fallen (as is quite likely, given the reduction in opportunities) the drop has been into, rather than far beneath, the Western range.

It was not playing sport but watching sport that was distinctly less common among young people in the East than in the West. No more than 5 per cent of the young people in any of the CIS countries watched sport regularly (except on television) whereas 24 per cent of Liverpool 18–19-year-olds did so in 1988. Watching professional (or top amateur) sport had not been a normal part of young people's leisure under communism and had not become so in the CIS countries in the 1990s.

Clubs

In the CIS countries 24 per cent of the Lviv sample and between 7 and 17 per cent elsewhere belonged to clubs which catered for leisure activities. These figures would have been much higher under communism because, whatever young people's political orientations, involvement in recreation organized by the Komsomol was near universal, certainly among those still in education. Memberships (and sport participation) had held up in Lviv better than elsewhere because nationalist parties and the (Uniate) church were filling part of the gap left by the demise of the Komsomol. Within the CIS countries young people's low level of involvement in formally organized recreation was perceived as further evidence of the general decline in their leisure opportunities, but in the West young people's leisure activities are far more likely to be informal or commercial than based on memberships of voluntary associations. In Britain the clubs that young people are most likely to visit are in fact night clubs.

All this suggests that the leisure of the young people in the CIS countries was not as deprived (relatively) and not as different from the leisure of young people in the West as might have been expected from the former's much lower incomes. To a large extent Western youth pay much more to do much the same things as Eastern young people.

Holidays and travel

Holidays are rather different. In Lviv 80 per cent of the sample had been away on holiday during the previous year, more than in Poland in 1993 (66 per cent), and among Eastern and Central Europe's young self-employed in 1997 (63 per cent), and the region's young unemployed (39 per cent). However, in the other CIS areas only 44 per cent to 62 per cent had been away on holiday. In Poland in 1993, 34 per cent had been away on two or more holidays during the previous year compared with only 14 per cent to 25 per cent in the CIS countries. There can be little doubt that these figures would have been higher under communism, which adopted holidays as a need and an entitlement and ensured that children and young people had opportunities to go away.

There were some interesting contrasts among the CIS countries in the extent to which the young people had travelled internationally to different destinations, and for different purposes (see Table 5.3). In Tbilisi 70 per cent of the young people had been to another country for at least one holiday (Poland 69 per cent) but only between 23 per cent and 29 per cent in all the other CIS areas. In the CIS countries holidays were most likely to have been spent in the local countryside with

Table 5.3   International travel

	Lviv	Donetsk	Tbilisi	Armenia	Poland
Percentages who had been to another country to:					
Visit relatives, friends	35	29	14	19	31
Earn money	25	10	19	8	30
Holiday	29	28	70	23	69
Percentages who had visited:					
Western Europe	33	5	31	8	60 [a]
USSR	38	53	72	54	39
Eastern Europe	34	8	20	5	25
North America	8	1	3	2	3

Note: [a] Germany only

relatives or in family dachas. The proportions in the CIS areas who had been to some other country or countries to visit relatives or friends ranged from 14 per cent to 35 per cent, with the Ukrainian areas scoring highest (Poland 31 per cent). According to this evidence, the Ukrainians were the most likely to have relatives abroad whom they visited. The Armenian diaspora seemed to operate more as a source of cash aid than a travel network. The proportions who had been to other countries to earn money ranged from 8 per cent to 25 per cent with Lviv heading this list (Poland 30 per cent) which is explicable in terms of Lviv's proximity to Central European countries that the young people could visit without visas, and where better paid work than at home was available.

In terms of destinations visited for all reasons, very few young people in any of the CIS countries, no higher than 8 per cent in Lviv, had been to North America. Only 38 per cent in Lviv (39 per cent in Poland) had been to another CIS country, whereas in the other CIS areas between 53 per cent and 72 per cent had done so. All this is evidence of the West Ukraine population's stronger orientation towards, and associations with Europe, than with other (ex) Soviet areas. The proportions who had visited at least one West European country were 5 per cent in Donetsk, 8 per cent in Armenia, but approximately a third in both Lviv and Tbilisi. In Poland in 1993 60 per cent of the young people had visited (West) Germany alone. The proportions who had visited at least one East European country were again higher in Lviv (34 per cent) and Tbilisi (20 per cent) than in Donetsk and Armenia (8 per cent and 5 per cent). In Poland just 25 per cent of the 21–24-year-olds had visited another East European country (far fewer than had been to Western Europe).

The frequency (relative to the other CIS areas) with which the young people in Lviv had visited Eastern and Western Europe can be explained in terms of geographical proximity and history. The relatively high level of youth travel from Tbilisi does not have such an obvious explanation. Our guess is that one reason is the number of low-cost flights from Tbilisi to Eastern and Western Europe that were introduced early in the 1990s and continued up to 1997. Georgia did not make its share of Aeroflot into a single publicly owned national airline; nor did it create one private national carrier. Several private airlines were formed which competed against one another as well as against other countries' carriers. A result was more and cheaper flights between Tbilisi and

Eastern and Western Europe than from Ukraine or Armenia (or any other CIS country beyond the Baltic). The Georgian airlines were cheapest for travellers from outside the CIS and even cheaper for citizens of these countries, and young people in Tbilisi were able to take advantage of this.

Religion

Our surveys gathered information about two additional aspects of the young people's lifestyles that look less startling when set against comparative evidence. In all the CIS countries there were supposed to have been religious revivals following independence. The view everywhere was that by the mid-1990s much of the earlier enthusiasm had subsided but it was still believed that the end of communism had permitted an upsurge of a previously suppressed religiosity. Religious fervour was supposed to be particularly intense in Lviv and also in Armenia, where the entire population was supposed to be relishing its freedom to celebrate its national faith openly. Actually the proportions of the young people who were going to church regularly (at least once a week) were between 7 per cent and 13 per cent everywhere, and the figure for 18–19-year-olds in Liverpool in 1988 was within this range. Religiosity among young people in the CIS countries appeared to have simply risen to Western levels.

In Poland in the 1990s there was much discussion about young people deserting the (Catholic) church. The church is believed to have been weakened by the loss of its monopoly role in expressing a national consciousness and resisting the hegemony of atheistic communism. Among young people the church's appeal is supposed to have been imperilled by its meddling in politics and its reactionary stance on issues such as abortion. The proportion of young people in Poland who were attending church at least once a week in 1993 was actually 30 per cent, much higher than in any of the other areas investigated, though many members of older generations in Poland regard 30 per cent as an appallingly low figure.

Personal safety

Another common perception in all the former communist countries in Eastern and Central Europe as well as the CIS is that crime rates have risen and that people and their property are now at greater risk. In 1987 three-quarters of Poles felt that their country was safe, whereas by 1997 three-quarters regarded Poland as an unsafe place to live (Oljasz, 1998). We suspect that these common perceptions, corroborated by official crime statistics, are indeed true. Universities keep their computers in rooms with security doors and grilled windows. Residents whose homes contain anything equally valuable act similarly. Vehicles are sometimes left overnight in guarded car parks. Banks in many places feel that they need armed doorkeepers.

Omel'chenko (1996) has described how, in a provincial Russian city, gangs of young males would extort money and valuables from other young people. She reports that some of these groups were linked to adult criminal organizations. The core members of street gangs in CIS countries have often used skills and hardware 'liberated' from the armed forces. The break-up of the Soviet army released a flood of military hardware into the second economies of Eastern and Central Europe and the CIS.

Just how dangerous is the new East? Our experience has been that for foreigners the East is no more dangerous than our own countries. Our combined experience as victims throughout the 1990s has been, first, losing $300, probably during a customs check at Kiev airport, and second, being pickpocketed in the main street of Bratislava (Slovakia) by young male refugees from Kosovo. The risks are different from those in the West but probably no greater. Of course, when first visiting Lviv, Donetsk, Tbilisi and Yerevan one is circumspect about taking the taxi offered by a leather-jacket-clad male at the airport, rail or bus station. In practice he is extremely unlikely to intend any greater harm than overcharging. The local mafia, if there is one, will wish to protect, not threaten, foreigners. If Westerners are injured, killed or robbed the outcome will be trouble. Kidnapping is a risk only in the few places where there is no single mafia, either official or unofficial. Hotels are concerned for the safety of their guests because they believe that foreigners may act foolishly. Hotels are aware that the risks of crime have risen since Soviet times and are anxious to avoid trouble that could blight their reputations. The main Lviv hotel catering for foreigners offers a bodyguard service for guests who wish to walk out after dark. The main hotel in Yerevan insisted on escorting us across the main square to the post office: it was evening, and pitch black at the time because Yerevan had no electricity. Guests are better protected

than in Western hotels. In Lviv a Western visitor who mislaid his passport and air tickets during a late-night casino session had everything
returned to him the next morning by the hotel staff. Everywhere one is
advised not to walk out alone at night except in the main lighted streets
and squares. The main difference between East and West in the 1990s
has been that in the former countries the risks have been new and
warnings have been issued.

In the CIS surveys the young people were asked whether they felt
unsafe during the daytime and at night in their local city centres and in
the districts where they lived. From the answers to these questions (see
Table 5.4) the Ukraine cities appeared to be the most dangerous places:

Table 5.4   Personal security (%)

	Lviv	Donetsk	Tbilisi	Armenia	Liverpool
Feel threatened during daytime:					
City centre	10	31	5	1	7
Where live	13	37	3	1	5
Feel threatened at night:					
City centre	50	50	15	12	53
Where live	44	54	6	10	21

approximately half of the Donetsk and Lviv respondents said that they
felt unsafe at night in their city centres and in the districts where they
lived. In Donetsk a third said that they also felt unsafe in the daytime in
these places. In the other CIS locations no more than 15 per cent
claimed to feel unsafe anywhere at any time. The sheer volume of
commerce and street life in Tbilisi appeared to be maintaining feelings
of security. In Armenia police surveillance was more likely to have
been responsible. And a different perspective on the Ukraine situation
is provided by the comparable findings from Liverpool, where in 1988
just over half of the young people said that they felt unsafe in the city
centre at night. Fewer felt unsafe in the districts where they lived than
those in the Ukrainian cities, and fewer felt unsafe during the daytime
than those in Donetsk. Nevertheless, it would appear from this evidence that concern for public safety in Ukraine had simply risen to a
Western level, while Georgia and Armenia remained more secure for
their inhabitants than many parts of the West.

WHAT DOES WESTERNIZATION OFFER?

People in CIS countries do not really believe that everyone in the West lives as in Dallas. They have always had other sources of information about the West apart from television. There are variations between Eastern countries, but since the 1980s, in the European parts of the East, most young people will have known someone who has visited the West even if they have not been personally. However, even people who live permanently in a country can have blurred and distorted views on the conditions faced by and the lifestyles of, groups other than their own.

Most Eastern impressions of what the Western way of life will be like, if it can be created in their own countries, are accurate. For young people it will mean more holidays, and especially commercial holidays in other countries rather than vacations spent with relatives or in a family dacha in the countryside. In CIS countries it will mean more young people having the use of cars and more households becoming equipped with videos and satellite connections. But it will not mean higher levels of membership in leisure-related or any other kinds of voluntary associations. It will not mean more church-going or attendances at cinemas, theatres or concerts. Nor will it mean much higher rates of participation in sport.

The main difference, in terms of day-to-day and week-to-week out-of-home leisure, will be that young people will go out to drink, and sometimes to eat, more frequently and overall levels of alcohol consumption will rise. Drug use will also spread if present-day Western youth's leisure practices are implanted in the East. There were already recognized drugs problems in 1997 in all the CIS countries in this study but their problems were minuscule compared with levels of drug use among Western youth. In Georgia soft drugs were being grown in Svanetia (a mountain region) and poppy (from which opium could be derived) was grown in Marneuly (in the south-east). Opium was also being imported from Azerbaijan and other Middle Asian countries (via Russia). Morphine was being systematically pilfered from clinics. But imported drugs were generally far too expensive for local youth. The Eastern problem has been as much one of the manufacture and transport as of the local use of drugs. Frantisek's (1998) study of secondary school students in Prague and in a small Czech town found that a quarter had some personal experience of drugs, but only 6.5 per cent of the males and 3.6 per cent of the females were using marihuana or hashish regularly. Hilary Pilkington (1996) reports that by the mid-1990s drugs were widely available (which we do not doubt) and were being widely used (about which we are not convinced) by young people in Moscow. The sources were probably similar to those in Georgia. The local populations in Armenia, Georgia and Ukraine were simply too poor to attract the main transnational suppliers.

In the West it tends to be the East that is regarded as having the chronic alcohol problem. There is such a problem, especially in the vodka-drinking countries, of which Ukraine is an example from this study. In Armenia and Georgia the staple alcoholic beverages are the local wines and brandies. None of the countries has a tradition of beer drinking. Regular (daily) drinking has always been a minority problem in the vodka cultures. Nowadays very few young people are involved. Many do not drink alcohol: they associate it with drunkenness and alcoholism, and explain that they have no need for the substance.

In Suwałki (north-east Poland) in 1993 we accompanied a group of young nurses from the local hospital to a bar when their shift ended. The young people were shocked when we ordered second glasses of beer. One of us was driving, and the legal alcohol limit on Poland's roads was zero. Mind you, this was at the time when lorry drivers could be seen drinking vodka at roadside cafés. The point is that this behaviour was regarded as a problem, albeit a minority problem, and very few young people were part of it.

Most young people in Poland do drink, and likewise in the CIS countries, but up to now their drinking has most likely been confined to special occasions such as family celebrations, and not (yet) on regular nights out with friends. There have been no equivalents (for local young people as opposed to visitors) to the music and drinking all-night clubs that are found in Western cities. In Frantisek's (1998) study of Czech youth, only a third of the males and a quarter of the females consumed alcohol regularly. This is likely to be the main change in their week-to-week ways of life that will occur if and when the youth of the East gain Western standards of living. As in the West, they will hang about in cafés and bars rather than in the streets and parks, and venues will appear which combine young people's music with the kinds of drinks (and probably other substances) that in the West have become the staple ingredients of a good night out.

SOCIAL DIVISIONS

What about leisure differences among the young people within each of our countries? Which other divisions, rooted in the past or the present, were patterning the young people's lifestyles? Were their family and educational backgrounds or their achievements in the new labour markets acting as bases for the reproduction or replacement of old status groups or social classes? Young people's uses of free time are matters of concern that extend beyond leisure and youth experts. It is of no minor political significance whether economic divisions act as the base for the formation of social classes whose members share characteristic day-to-day lifestyles and therefore tend to interact with one another and become more likely than otherwise, in the long run, to develop a similar consciousness. Alternatively, lifestyles with other bases may become the bedrock of status groups which subsequently acquire a broader social and political significance (see Veal, 1989).

Gender

This division cross-cut all the others. The manner in which the young men had pushed slightly ahead and progressed faster in education, then fared considerably better in the new labour markets, was reflected in the sexes' leisure (see Table 5.5). The men were spending more on themselves, but only slightly more. Rather more women were spending less than $30 per month on themselves, and more men were spending $30–$50, but very similar proportions of the two sexes were spending more than this. The women were more likely to be living with husbands or boyfriends and to have children, but family circumstances were making a clear (negative) difference to the amounts of money available for personal spending only among the (female) lone parents. Gender differences in personal spending were narrower than in their earned incomes. This is just one example (more follow) of how differences in earned incomes were being blurred during their conversion into leisure spending. How much the young people were able to spend on themselves depended not only on their own earnings (if any) but also on whether they received money from other sources, such as their parents, and if so, how much, and whether they were contributing towards household expenses and, once again, if so, how

Table 5.5   Gender and leisure (%)

	Male	Female
Spending on self per month ($):		
<30	43	52
30–50	27	21
50–100	19	17
>100	11	11
Use of:		
Car	30	16
PC	10	7
Video	46	41
Satellite or cable	19	15
Participation (at least weekly):		
Play sport	38	19
Pubs, restaurants, cafés	27	19
Cinema, etc.	5	4
Watch sport	5	1
Smoke	57	21
Alcohol	32	10
Church	10	10
Member of recreational club	12	7
Holidays last year:		
0	46	39
1	34	41
More	20	19
Holiday abroad (ever)	43	38
Feel threatened:		
Daytime		
City centre	7	10
Where live	8	11
Night		
City centre	15	34
Where live	14	27

much. These other cash flows were tending to counterbalance and to blur what would otherwise have been the wider leisure inequalities arising from differences in earned incomes.

The women were spending only slightly less on themselves on average and were just as likely as the men to be going regularly (at least once a week) to the cinema, theatres and other places of entertainment. The sexes were also equally likely to be regular church-goers, and neither was clearly advantaged in terms of holidays; in fact, it was the men who were slightly more likely to have taken no holiday away from home during the previous year. However, the men were by far the more likely to play and watch sport, to smoke, to visit bars and restaurants, to consume alcohol and to belong to recreation-based clubs.

If the men were doing more of all these things, then what were the women doing with their almost equal spending money? We did not gather sufficient detailed evidence to answer this question definitively but it is likely that the young women were spending more than the men on clothing and cosmetics.

There had been little, if any, of the blurring that has been noted within Western countries in the young men's and the young women's uses of free time as a result of unaccompanied (by men) females asserting their presence and claiming public space in bars, sports facilities and on the streets (see Roberts, 1996, 1997). The young women in our study were much more likely than the young men to experience their city centres and the districts where they lived as threatening at night. Nowadays in the West it is often young men who lead narrower leisure lives, doing little except drink, play, watch and talk about sport (and women), while young women have escaped from the 'bedroom culture' to develop broader leisure interests, relationships and skills (see Roberts *et al.*, 1990). The gender divisions revealed in our research would have arisen under, or preceded, communism but they were continuing rather than being overturned in the 1990s.

The reasons are not self-evident, but the women in our study were less likely than the men to have rooms of their own at home or the use of all the items of leisure equipment about which the samples were questioned – cars, videos, satellite and cable connections and PCs. Maybe households benefiting from the young males' higher earnings were better resourced overall. It will be relevant that more of the females had left their parents' home and were living in lodgings or their own places. However, in the case of cars, it is likely that the young men were being given more access to family vehicles.

Education and family backgrounds

Chapter 3 explained that the young people's experiences in education were very closely related to their family backgrounds. The educational elite who had progressed through academic secondary then into higher education with free places and living allowances were mainly from elite families. Those who attended non-academic secondary schools and who did not proceed to higher education were overwhelmingly from working-class homes. For practical purposes, family origins and educational backgrounds divided the young people into the same elite and non-elite groups.

Table 5.6 compares the leisure of these two extreme but typical

Table 5.6   Education and leisure (%)

	Academic	Vocational
Have use of:		
Car	20	23
PC	13	4
Video	51	30
Satellite or cable	24	5
Participate at least weekly:		
Play sport	34	19
Pubs, bars, etc.	28	13
Cinema, etc.	6	2
Watch sport	3	3
Smoke	36	41
Alcohol	21	16
Church	9	8
Recreational club	16	9
Holidays (last year):		
0	34	54
1	41	34
More	25	12
Holiday abroad (ever)	54	20
Earned money abroad	17	7
Visited:		
Western Europe	32	6
USSR (country of)	65	36
Eastern Europe	23	10
North America	4	1
Spending on self per month ($):		
< 30	46	60
30–50	24	23
> 50	29	17

groups. There are differences on virtually all the leisure indicators and some of the differences are extremely wide – generally wider than the gender differences. The educational elite were more likely to have the use of all the items of leisure equipment (PCs, videos, and cable or satellite connections) except motor cars. It appears from this evidence that the private motor car was signalling a different kind of status – money – rather than a generally cultured background and way of life. The elite group had taken more holidays in the last 12 months, were more likely to have been on holidays abroad at some time or another, and to have visited all the groups of countries about which the samples were questioned. They were also more likely to belong to leisure-based clubs, to play (but not to watch) sport, to consume alcohol and to visit bars, restaurants, cinemas and other places of entertainment regularly (at least once a week). The other exceptions to the elite doing and having more, apart from the use of cars and watching sport, were smoking and church-going.

Some of these differences were huge. One in four among the educational elite had cable or satellite connections compared with just one in twenty among the lower status group. Just over half of the educational elite had been on holidays in another country or countries compared with just one in four of the other young people. This evidence is not exactly what we had expected, given all the talk, on the one hand, about the disappearance or impoverishment of the intelligentsia stratum in former communist countries and, on the other, about Western-type youth cultures obliterating other divisions. The division between elite and non-elite leisure recorded in our research had been a feature of the old system and it was flourishing under post-communism. Exactly the same contrast was recorded in Poland in 1993 (Roberts and Jung, 1995). The persistence of this division is obviously not peculiar to any one ex-communist country. And our 1997 evidence from Armenia, Georgia and Ukraine does not suggest that the division is slowly being obliterated.

Jobs and money

We do not believe that we would have provoked much surprise inside or outside the transition countries if we were able to report clear and strong links between types of employment, income and spending levels and uses of leisure. The career groups that our evidence distinguishes –

the self-employed, those with regular jobs, those confined to 'bitty jobs' and the unemployed – differed not only in their typical earnings (if any) but also in their time rhythms. And as explained in Chapter 2, the young people were tending to stick within one or another of these groups.

There is a widespread perception within all the transition countries that money has become much more important than it was in the past. We have referred to this already on several occasions and have corroborated the perception. It is manifestly true in so far as the cities and shops are now full of things to do and buy for those who can afford what is on display. Everywhere the 'new rich' have become a high-profile group with their motor cars, newly built homes and expensive furnishings, and night life centred around expensive bars and restaurants. Surveys prior to our own (for example, Kharchenko, 1998; Magun, 1996; Saarnit, 1998; Zuev, 1997) consistently found that young people attached more and more importance to money in their career values and planning.

However, our own evidence shows that matters have really become a little more complicated than surface appearances may suggest. First, 'becoming rich' was not the top life goal of the young people in our survey. In fact it was low ranked (see Chapter 2). What the young people really yearned for was security: a way of life that was not constantly in jeopardy – basically what the old system had delivered.

Second, immediate earnings had obviously not been the overriding consideration when our respondents had faced a choice of career options. The young people had attached as much importance to being able to use their qualifications and skills. In doing so they were probably taking account of future (when things had returned to normal) as well as immediate income prospects. And even in the short term the normal official pay in a main job had to be set alongside the possibility of engaging in other remunerative activities. So the young people from the most advantaged family and educational backgrounds, who should have had the greatest scope for choice, were not monopolizing the better-paid jobs. On average they were the better paid, but there was a wide spread of earnings within all the educational groups (see Chapter 3, Table 3.4, p. 82).

Well-educated young people were spending more on themselves (and generally doing more) than non-elite youth but this was only partly because on average they were earning more, because links between personal earnings and what the young people were spending on themselves were being mediated, and typically blurred, by the varying amounts of money that they received from other sources and spent in other ways. Those with the highest earned incomes from their main jobs were as likely as the lower paid to also have earned incomes from second jobs, but were receiving much less from their families. And the high earners were spending more on virtually everything else as well as themselves, including household expenses. Families were obviously compensating, when they were able to do so, for young people's relatively low earned incomes. This happens in Britain, usually in covert ways, since parents do not wish their children to feel that they are not reaping the full benefits when they move from unemployment into jobs or from low paid to better paid employment (see Hutson and Cheung, 1991). That said, the highest earners in the CIS countries were in fact spending the most on themselves. Inequalities in earned incomes were so wide that they were making a substantial difference to what the young people were able to spend, own and do despite all the blurring.

However, individuals with unusually high incomes, such as the very successfully self-employed, were not necessarily adopting flamboyant lifestyles. Their behaviour suggested the presence of a protestant work ethic, except that in the countries concerned it could not have been based on protestantism. Their ways of life tended to be work dominated rather than leisure centred. They were investing in their businesses and saving towards long-term projects such as house purchase rather than going regularly to restaurants and taking frequent holidays abroad. Indeed, business success depended on forgoing such short-term indulgences.

The amounts of money that they could spend, and were spending, on themselves (which depended on their earnings and also on the generosity of their families) were making very clear differences to the young people's leisure. Things could hardly have been otherwise. In general, those with the most cash at their disposal were the most likely to have the use of all types of leisure equipment and facilities (cars, videos, satellite connections, PCs and their own rooms). They were taking more holidays overall, more holidays abroad and were the most likely to have travelled to all the destinations about which the samples were questioned. They were also the most likely to belong to recreation-based clubs, to visit bars and restaurants, and to drink alcohol regularly (though interestingly the top spending group lagged behind the second highest spenders in frequency of alcohol consumption). The leisure activities that appeared completely unresponsive to spending levels were playing and watching sport, visiting cinemas and other places of entertainment, smoking and church-going.

Spending levels were making a difference to uses of leisure, but not to all uses of leisure, and how much they could spend on themselves did not depend solely on the young people's personal earnings. In the light of all the above it should not be a total surprise that although there were some differences, there was no clear hierarchy in terms of leisure advantage and disadvantage among the career groups that we identified. Nor did any of the groups except the self-employed have a distinctive overall leisure pattern, a characteristic lifestyle. There were some differences, as there always are in survey analysis, but not the kind that were likely to lead to the members of each of the career groups regarding themselves as particular kinds of people.

The (reasonably successful) young self-employed came the closest to being a distinctive and advantaged status group. They were well ahead of the others in the frequency with which they were visiting cinemas and other places of entertainment, bars and restaurants, and consuming alcohol. However, they were not particularly advantaged in terms of the leisure equipment at their disposal (this depended more on family circumstances than the individuals' own earnings) or in their holiday-making or other experiences of foreign travel (the self-employed lacked the time, and the money as well in some cases, for such ventures).

Those employed in regular as opposed to 'bitty' jobs were more likely to have satellite or cable television but none of the other kinds of leisure equipment about which the young people were questioned. The regularly employed were more likely to be regular church-goers, but this was the sole clear difference in the two groups' day-to-day and week-to-week leisure behaviour. The regularly employed were slightly less likely than those with 'bitty' jobs to have been on more than one holiday, and slightly *more* likely to have been on no holiday during the previous 12 months.

The leisure of the unemployed was perhaps surprisingly buoyant. They were less likely than any of the other career groups to belong to recreation-based clubs, and to have visited Eastern and Western Europe and North America. They were also the least likely to play sport regularly, but here they lagged only slightly behind state sector employees and likewise in never having been abroad for a holiday. Despite this, the unemployed were actually the career group most likely to have taken two or more holidays during the previous year. Frequency of holiday-making appeared to be as responsive to time availability as to income. The unemployed were not disadvantaged in terms of their leisure spending. In fact, they were the career group that was most likely to be spending in excess of $50 a month on themselves (they were either working and earning in the shadow economy or being treated generously by their families) though there was little evidence of this in their actual leisure behaviour apart from their holiday-making.

MUCH PERSISTENCE AND LITTLE CHANGE

It is not an original observation that political constitutions can be changed in a matter of months, that transforming centrally planned state owned economies into private enterprise market systems takes years, while changing social relationships and the associated cultures is most likely to take generations. The main differences – all very clear differences – in the lifestyles of the young people in this study were by gender, educational and family backgrounds (which were very closely entwined), and levels of personal spending (which depended as much on family circumstances as on individuals' own earnings). Differences in spending levels were partly responsible for and were tending to reinforce and accentuate rather than obliterate the differences associated with family and educational backgrounds and with gender. However, money was not wholly responsible for these other differences. The lifestyles of males, and the academic elite, were distinguished by some features that were not responsive to money – sport participation, for example.

The career groups distinguished by their labour market experiences had different mean incomes from employment, but they were not arranged in a corresponding hierarchy according to their types or levels of leisure participation. The leisure of the career groups was also being affected by the proportions of males and females and the proportions from various educational and family backgrounds in each. The career groups could, in time, each develop characteristic lifestyles. This is most likely to happen if individuals spend their entire working lives within these groups, but this had not had time to happen by the mid-1990s.

The main lifestyle divisions were in fact traditional, vestiges from the old system: between the elite and the rest, with each group divided by gender. These long-standing divisions had not been overturned by the new market economies. They had not been obliterated as young people became involved in their various youth sub-cultures. They had not been buried by all-round economic immiseration or by the new importance of money. In fact, there were fewer leisure differences between the young people in Armenia, Georgia and Ukraine, on the one hand, and Western youth, on the other, than East–West disparities in earned incomes would have led anyone to expect.

The traditional status divisions will be threatened, and will almost certainly topple in the longer term, if the children from elite family and educational backgrounds whom we surveyed in 1997 are unable in time – meaning here by the time that they have reared a further generation of children – to gravitate into their countries' good jobs with higher than average financial rewards. Otherwise they will lack the resources to maintain and to transmit the lifestyles in question. New lifestyle status groups are most likely to be formed if the new career group divisions that had been created by the mid-1990s prove enduring rather than transitional. However, in the 1990s, among the rising generation of adults, traditional lifestyle divisions remained sovereign. Paradoxically, these divisions passed down from the old system are most likely to endure if market reforms succeed, as in Central Europe. The lifestyles and the associated status of traditional elite groups will be at greatest risk if the transformations of the political and economic systems in which the elites' advantages were originally rooted fail to deliver better jobs and living standards for all and especially for young people from elite family and educational backgrounds.

6. Politics

POST-COMMUNIST POLITICS

New parties

Everywhere, from Central Europe to the east of the former Soviet Union, post-communist politics has possessed some distinctive features. First, in all the countries dozens of new parties were formed when the Communist Party disappeared or shrank drastically. At first, inevitably, most of the new parties were little more than groups of professional politicians gathered around national leaders with no mass organizations and, in most cases, little public support. The only exceptions were the parties that inherited the old Communist Party's organization, where there were successors.

Many members of the public soon became disillusioned and angry about the new democratic politics. This was evident everywhere. In the early stages of reform national assemblies appeared to be mere 'talking shops' where politicians squabbled instead of tackling their country's problems. Dozens of small parties operating in systems of proportional representation meant that elections were unlikely to be decisive. Whoever people voted for, it appeared that the same politicians remained in office and squabbled endlessly. Then, in some countries, in Central Europe for example, there were mergers between smaller parties or the development of blocs which adopted policies which appealed to broad sections of the electorates within which reasonably reliable support could be based. Western-type democratic party politics thereby commenced. However, in most CIS countries, normal (in a Western sense) party politics, like the promised dynamic market economies, remained embryonic into and beyond the mid-1990s.

Demobilization and reform agendas

Second, the high levels of mass political activity that erupted everywhere at the end of the 1980s soon ebbed. During the final break-down of communism most young people, certainly most students, were involved in more or less constant meetings and rallies. In Yerevan, Armenia's capital, a mass meeting in the main Opera Square continued almost without interruption for several months. Everywhere there was not just very visible mass support, but mass enthusiasm for change. What was formerly latent became manifest. Once change became a real possibility there was no problem in mobilizing mass support. It turned out that communism had won precious little genuine affection.

The specific changes that were hoped for varied from place to place. Everywhere the people hoped for greater political freedom lead-ing to governments becoming more representative of, and responsive to, the public. In many places environmental issues were high on the agendas (following Chernobyl). Market reforms were not necessarily part of the agendas though there was always some longing for Western standards and styles of living.

Within the republics of the Soviet Union there was popular support for 'independence' everywhere, at the time when it was delivered, but the meaning of independence was then unclear. In Georgia and western Ukraine people hoped for an escape from Russian domination, but in 1991 no one was sure what would replace the USSR. One view, or hope, was that the CIS would be a similar grouping. but with greater equality among the republics. Even in 1998 passport and customs checks were not consistently applied at the borders between CIS countries. In 1995 we entered Georgia from Ukraine, and in 1998 we entered Armenia from Georgia, and Kazakhstan from Russia, without passport checks. All these journeys were by air. Throughout this period there were double customs and passport checks on the main road between Tbilisi and Yerevan. How the CIS would link its member countries was still unclear even in the mid-1990s. Armenia never wanted to break its links with Russia even though, in 1991–2, greater independence to settle the Karabakh issue was welcomed. The mainly Russian population in the east of Ukraine hoped to exert more leverage through Kiev than had been possible when economic planning flowed downwards and outwards from Moscow. The miners in Donbass did not want separation from Russia so much as greater control over their own enterprises and their own lives more generally (see Siegelbaum and Walkowitz, 1995). The ethnic Russians in Donbass were certainly not expecting to have to show passports and submit to (Soviet-style) customs checks when they visited relatives in Russia. Some sections of the Ukraine population, mainly in the west, were hoping for their own passports and currency, but these aspirations were not universal in Ukraine. Independent Ukraine's first government expected to stay within a rouble zone and created its own temporary currency, the coupon, only when the supply of roubles dried up amid a wave of hyperinflation.

People's aims and hopes varied, but everywhere there was not mass acquiescence but enthusiasm for change, which was demonstrated on the streets and in referendums. The populations for a time were highly politicized. There were simultaneous religious revivals in some places. Then, within a few years, the mass activity evaporated. Politics left the streets. Governments changed according to the results of elections or as a result of shifting alliances among politicians, rather than in response to mass demonstrations. In 1997 in Bulgaria disenchantment with the government's economic policies led to blockades of the main highways, which forced elections and a change of government. Elsewhere, although there were, of course, spasmodic marches and demonstrations, none had results remotely resembling the events of 1989–91.

In the CIS countries the political demobilization of the masses occurred against a backcloth of persistent economic crisis and falling living standards. Disillusionment with democratic politics spread rapidly. People did not mobilize for a return to authoritarian government or a restoration of the past but tended to withdraw from public into private life to seek solutions to their problems individually or just with close friends and family members. Politics was discussed by informal (usually male) groups on the streets and in the squares of Lviv, Tbilisi and elsewhere, but this grassroots political activity was separate from parties and other formal political structures. This, of course, is what normally happens in Western democracies; and in Central Europe as the new market economies began to grow many people were probably content to leave politics to the politicians. In the CIS, in contrast, overt political passivity was more likely to overlay mass disenchantment than mass contentment.

The actual reforms

Third, in all the ex-communist countries the governments, whether from inclination or force of circumstances, began to implement market reforms. In Central Europe the main driving forces included the opposition movements that had developed in the 1980s and assumed power in some countries when communism ended. Another driving force in Central Europe was international capital, which began to flow in and demonstrate how Western enterprises operated. In the CIS it was more a case of reform being implemented from above. In most CIS countries many of the old politicians remained in power. There was no loose capital within the countries nor any substantial inflows from outside. Before long, actually or potentially profitable enterprises, or potentially profitable parts of such businesses, were being privatized into the ownership of politicians and plant directors. Loss-making state enterprises sometimes developed shadow existences where they operated profitably for the benefit of the top managers and their protectors in politics and state departments. Individuals who had somehow accumulated wealth under the old system, and who had assets in the West, were able to purchase (potentially) profitable businesses or emerge as legitimate traders and brokers.

It has seemed to many members of the public in these countries that the reforms have been orchestrated by and in the interests of groups generally referred to as 'the mafia', partly due to their need to organize self-protection (see Eberwein and Tholen, 1997; Varese, 1994). Corruption was common under communism but many members of the public have felt that under post-communism it has risen to unprecedented levels. In some countries commentators have published tariffs of the bribes that normally need to be paid for interviews with tax and other public officials (see Isakova, 1997). Bribery has come to be regarded as a normal business method in much of the former Soviet Union. Police officers routinely stop cars and, if any offence can be alleged, give the drivers the option of an on-the-spot (unofficial) fine as an alternative to filling in forms and visiting the police station. This has happened to cars in which we were travelling (not driving) in Bulgaria, Georgia and Russia. Many politicians and officials in state departments have obviously developed mysterious means of supplementing their abysmal official salaries. Against this background, cynicism towards all politicians has become pervasive.

CAPITALISM VERSUS SOCIALISM

From our evidence we could, if we wished, extract statistics demonstrating that most young people in all the countries were pro-reform, rejected socialism, preferred capitalism and the market economy, and wanted their countries to press ahead with the reforms at maximum speed. Alternatively, we could choose to highlight findings suggesting that the majority believed that socialism was a superior system. The answers recorded in surveys always depend to some extent on the types of questions asked, but in this case the most likely explanation of the apparent contradictions in our evidence is that many of the young people really were split-minded.

Support for the market

When asked whether they preferred a market economy or the old system, three-quarters of the respondents in Armenia and Donetsk, and over 90 per cent in Lviv and Tbilisi, opted for the market (see Figure 6.1). But our qualitative interviews found that the young people did not equate a 'real' market economy with what existed in their own countries in the mid-1990s. 'Real' market economies, in the young people's eyes, were what existed in the West, and very few distinguished between different kinds of Western market economies: the North American, the European and the Far East types, for example. By

Life more difficult	66%	20%	Life better
Important industries should remain the public sector	66%		
Reforms a mistake	50%	50%	Like to work in the West
Enterprises should not be sold to foreigners	37%	75%	Want closer ties with the West
Prefer old system	10%	80%	Prefer market economy

Figure 6.1   Political opinions

contrast, they regarded their own countries as having moved into mixed economies, a transitional state in which neither part was working well. Many were cynical about the market systems that had developed in their own countries. As explained earlier, privatization was being implemented 'from above'. In all the countries everyone seemed to know about someone who had been prominent in the old system and who had benefited from a profitable privatization. Only a quarter of our respondents believed that becoming rich in their countries required hard work. A common view was that everything was controlled by 'the mafia'. This term was in constant use in all three countries: 'Everything is corrupt. The mafia are everywhere. The ordinary person is unprotected.' Only a fifth believed that poor people were to blame for their own poverty. The young people did not believe that rewards followed ability and effort which, in their view, would happen in a 'real' market system. Most of the young people were enthusiastic about the Western way of life. Their visions were not grossly rose-tinted, athough it is true that they knew much more about consumption than about work regimes and politics in the West. Three-quarters of the respondents, with little variation between the areas, wanted their countries to develop closer ties with the West.

Disillusion and nostalgia

Yet there was equally overwhelming endorsement of the view that life in the countries had become more difficult since the reforms. Two-thirds believed this, roughly the same proportion as in our surveys in Poland in 1993, and only a fifth believed that on balance life had become better. In this sense, the majority believed that communism had been superior. These views were based on the young people's first-hand experiences. Smaller proportions, only a fifth in Tbilisi (as in Poland in 1993) but roughly half in Armenia and Ukraine, argued that the reforms had been a mistake.

Some believed that, although daily life had become more difficult, the old system had so many detestable features, or any chance of gaining the Western way of life was so enticing that the reforms were justified. Many people in the East have been willing to pay an extremely high price to free themselves from communist 'oppression' (see Clarke, 1993). Whatever their shortcomings, the new regimes have often been welcomed simply because they are not the old system. However, there were those who, if they had been able to re-run history, would have written entirely different scripts. They included individuals who had been among the overwhelming majorities in all three countries that had not merely voted but actively campaigned for independence and reform at the beginning of the 1990s.

There was widespread disappointment over the course of the reforms. Some of those who felt, with the benefit of hindsight, that it would have been preferable to persevere with the old system often added that its restoration was no longer an option. But some did want to restore the past: 'We must return to the rouble zone. We must restore the old system and rejoin Russia.' This was an extreme, minority viewpoint, but there were many more who wanted to slow down the reforms and to reverse some of them. The young peasants who were questioned in Armenia during our qualitative, open-ended interviews all wanted the collective farms to be restored. In Armenia most of the land had been privatized in 1992, leaving most of the new independent farmers without the right equipment to tend their soil and without the skills or organization to market their produce. As in much of Bulgaria, reform had meant a return to pre-modern methods, such as tilling the fields by hand. In all the countries our main surveys recorded majority support (52 per cent to 84 per cent) for retaining basic industries in public ownership. Very few wanted to risk throwing everything into the market. Substantial minorities, between 29 per cent and 46 per cent in the CIS countries (and a similar proportion, 45 per cent, in Poland in 1993), were against selling any of their countries' enterprises to foreigners (see Figure 6.1).

There was some nostalgia everywhere for at least some features of the old system which had guaranteed jobs and a basic way of life. At a Moscow university in 1998 we attended a concert organized to celebrate the eightieth anniversary of the Komsomol. Most of the teachers had been Komsomol members. They recalled how they had participated in work projects and social events, and had thereby felt part of a wider national project. They regretted that their present students had no similar opportunities. At least some of the 1998 students must have shared these sentiments because the concert was well attended, and was led by student singers and musicians.

Split-mindedness

The ideologies of socialism and capitalism, the two systems – the market and state planning – were still competing for young people's loyalties in 1997. Neither had won. However, it is a mistake to imagine that this controversy was dividing the countries into hostile camps. Minorities were consistently pro- and anti-reform, but the main division was not between groups of people but within the same individuals' minds and hearts. Debates about which industries should be retained in public ownership and which might be sold to overseas investors had only recently begun, and opinion had not solidified. The young people's answers to our questions on specific issues often appeared spontaneous rather than carefully considered and rooted in coherent ideologies. There were some differences in the young people's views by gender, family and educational backgrounds and labour market experience, but within all these groups there was the same majority split-mindedness. It appeared that, ideally, most would have liked to combine the advantages of the old and new systems – the security and social services of socialism and the consumer choice and productivity of the market – had this been possible. Most young people (and probably adults) were simultaneously in some senses in favour of and in other senses hostile to the reforms.

Claire Wallace (1997) has shown, using the results from over 10,000 interviews in ten former communist countries, that it is possible to divide the populations according to their attitudes into macro-marketeers, individualists, collectivists, pessimists and the depressed. Computer programs will reveal such divisions, if they exist. This is what the programs are designed to do. But in doing this, their proper job, they are always liable to exaggerate both the neatness and the depth of the divisions that they discover. Ruchkin (1998) has claimed, on the basis of surveys conducted in Russia, that roughly half of the country's young people want to continue market reforms while a third want to go back to the communist system.

We did not find that our samples could be divided so neatly. In all the countries in our study public opinion apeared to be poised, and fluid, capable of swinging either way. It was likely to become firmly pro-reform if people could be convinced that the reforms would succeed eventually (in delivering Western standards and styles of living). Opinion was likely to swing the other way if the people were offered a

convincing vision of a socialist future without the disadvantages
(the low living standards and the authoritarianism) of the earlier
communism.

In 1997 there were no signs of the populations dividing into pro-
and anti-reform blocs according to their personal experiences of the
changes. Although there were some differences, there were no clear
and coherent differences in socio-political orientations between any
of the main socio-demographic groups. We had suspected that the
career groups that had been chronically unemployed and confined to
'bitty jobs' would be the most embittered, but in practice this was not
the case. The self-employed and those in regular private sector jobs
were more likely than the other career groups to want military
conscription to end. This was the only respect in which these groups
had distinctive political attitudes. Public sector employees were the
most hostile to the idea of selling their countries' enterprises to
foreigners and they were the keenest to work in public sector jobs.
There may well have been an element of choice in the direction that
these young people's careers had taken. The unemployed and private
sector workers (regular and marginal) were the groups who were the
most keen to start their own businesses, more so than those who were
actually self-employed who were aware of all the problems. And, as
explained in Chapter 2, there had been a great deal of push (due to
the absence of alternatives) in many of the young self-employed's
early careers.

There were in fact few differences in the samples' political outlooks
according to their labour market experiences or their educational and
family backgrounds. The educated elite were the least likely to support
compulsory military service (and the most likely to have avoided it).
They were also the least likely to believe that the reforms had been a
mistake. However, there were not the consistently higher levels of
support for private enterprise and the market economy among the
highly educated that were found in Poland in 1993. In Poland the pro-
reform orientations of the educationally successful were reflected in
their party choices. This difference between Central Europe and the
CIS is likely to be linked to the fact that in the latter countries the
educationally successful were not deriving greater benefits from the
changes than other members of their age group. In fact they were
bearing a full share of the pain.

Males were more likely than females to be politically active and interested in politics, but otherwise there were no clear differences in the sexes' political views.

The absence of ideological cleavages based on the young peoples's different experiences and positions in their countries would have been making it difficult for any parties to develop an appeal to, and to build 'solid' support within, particular sections of the populations.

NATIONS AND HOMELANDS

What to do about the reforms – whether to press ahead as quickly as possible or to bolster and build upon the remnants of the old system – was a contentious issue everywhere, but it was not a deeply divisive, explosive issue. It was a troublesome issue for all socio-demographic groups and for most individuals, but it was not setting one group against another except when it intersected with national, nationalist or patriotic feelings. The really 'hot' issue everywhere was how to protect 'the homeland' and 'the people', however these were identified. Often the 'nationalities question' was closely linked to people's feelings about Russia.

Armenia

Within Armenia these were extremely 'hot' issues but they were not internally divisive. Over 90 per cent of Armenia's population is Armenian. There was no significant opposition to the view that the rights of Armenians in Karabakh had to be protected, and Russia was generally regarded as a dependable ally. One of the new (in 1997) expensive private enterprise restaurants in Yerevan was called *The Moscow*, a title that would certainly not have been chosen in Tbilisi or Lviv.

The samples in all three countries were asked two questions about Russia. The first was simply whether they wanted closer ties between Russia and their own countries. The second was how they felt about the disappearance of the USSR. In Armenia approximately 90 per cent of the young people wanted closer ties with Russia. Many would have liked to resurrect the USSR or, more realistically, to develop the CIS into a confederation or even a federation. There were more young people in Armenia who felt that the disintegration of the USSR had too many disadvantages than who regarded the break-up as a good thing. Few of the young people in any of the countries had expected independence to lead to a descent to Third World status. By the mid-1990s there was widespread resentment about how the countries had become dependent on the World Bank and the International Monetary Fund. There was also resentment at how the countries' intellectuals had become dependent on Western-funded and -led research projects. People everywhere had fond recollections of the time when they were citizens of a world power. In Armenia (and also in Donetsk) there was a general sense of loss. Russia had been Armenia's covert ally (despite its official neutrality) in the dispute with Azerbaijan. Russia had maintained air links and trading relationships throughout the period of economic blockade. Russian was a quite widely used language within Armenia. It was the language of instruction in many schools in Yerevan and it remained the principal language of trade throughout the CIS.

Ukraine

In Donetsk the views of the young people were very similar to those expressed in Armenia on the desirability of closer ties with Russia and the ending of the USSR having too many disadvantages. There was a Russian majority in the Donetsk region. These families were from Russia and, as explained earlier, on voting for independence they had not expected this to lead to passport controls and customs checks at the Russia–Ukraine border. Donbass had voted for independence basically from a belief that the region would gain greater autonomy and that its economic importance would be better appreciated in Kiev than in Moscow.

In Ukraine, as in Armenia, many young people were not just concerned but deeply distressed at their country's condition: 'This country is in deep crisis. Everything is going to the bottom. We seem to live in worse conditions than Third World countries.' This feeling was expressed in both Donetsk and Lviv but different conclusions were being drawn. Closer relationships with Russia appeared obviously advantageous to most young people in Ukraine's east (most of whom were of Russian origin). In the west, to the majority of young people, this idea was anathema. Russia was a divisive issue within Ukraine because opinion in the west was diametrically opposed to opinion in the east. In Lviv most young people thought that the end of the USSR had been a good thing and only two-fifths wanted closer ties between Russia and Ukraine. Lviv had become a centre of Ukrainian nationalism in the 1990s. Indeed, the region had possessed dissident nationalist groups throughout the 1960s and 1970s when they had been crushed by Soviet power. Russia had been the Ukrainian partisans' enemy against whom they had fought in the 1920s and 1930s, during the Second World War and into the 1950s. When, prior to communism, Russia had been Ukraine's supposed ally and protector by treaty (from the seventeenth century until the First World War) the population in west Ukraine believed that Russia had been treacherous. This betrayal was part of the present since every Ukrainian school-child was being taught the story. In the west (of Ukraine) most young people favoured their country remaining as independent from Russia as possible. They wanted Ukraine to be able to defend itself – the people and their homeland. As far as they were concerned, there was no price to pay for independence from Russia. They believed that a revival even of trading relationships was more likely to act as a millstone than a stimulant.

Up to 1997 the various regions of Ukraine had remained united in wanting to hold the country together. There was a widespread fear that the nationalities issue and the Russia question might some day tear the country apart. Preventing this, which meant enabling every region to feel adequately represented in national political processes, ensuring that no region felt that it was bearing a disproportionate share of the pain and seeing too few of the benefits of the reforms, had to be the country's political priorities.

Georgia

The young people in Tbilisi had very similar views on their country's relationships with Russia to their Lviv counterparts. More felt that the disintegration of the USSR had been a good thing than that it entailed too many disadvantages. This was not a divisive issue among Georgians (by nationality). However, it had split Georgians (just 70 per cent of the country's population) from the majority populations in the region of Abkhazia, who historically had always felt closer to Russia than to Georgia, and in South Ossetia, where the people felt closest to a national group most of whom were inside the Russian Federation. How to resolve its regional problem was Georgia's hot issue. It was an issue in which Russia was generally considered to be both a source of the problem and a necessary partner in any solution.

Russian language

We mentioned in Chapter 3 how, in some former communist countries, the 'nationalization' of school syllabuses has led to the ejection of Russian as a taught language. As a result, Russian has been losing ground as an international language, certainly in Eastern and Central Europe. A generation on, throughout much of this region, Russian language will have been lost, except to experts in the field. This is unlikely to happen in the CIS, where so many countries contain Russian-speaking minorities. Moreover, Russian is similar to some of the other national languages, to Ukrainian for example, and Russian television is popular in many places – it has better news and films than on local Georgian and Armenian television, for instance. Russian is continuing to act as the language of international commerce in the region. So for the foreseeable future there may well be many people in Georgia, west Ukraine and elsewhere in the CIS who prefer not to use Russian, but there are unlikely to be many who do not understand it. The world region will remain integrated, if not harmonious; and separate from the rest of the world in having Russian as the common language.

Homelands

We must make it clear at this point that in none of the interviews did any young people express hatred towards any other nationality. Indeed, the young people were mostly exemplars of national and religious tolerance. The Armenians did not hate Azerbaijanis. Georgians did not hate Abkhazians. Ukrainians did not hate Russians. However, all the national groups felt, very strongly, that they had a right to self-determination in what they regarded as their homelands.

People may not always be conscious of this, but everywhere the populations have very similar feelings about 'their' land and property. In the Caucasus and in Ukraine, as the populations themselves see their situations, history has created conditions in which perfectly normal loyalties can turn different national groups into enemies. This, of course, was the case in Europe during the historical period when the continent became divided into its modern nation states. In much of the communist world, including the Balkans, the comparable processes of nation building were set in abeyance throughout the period of Soviet domination. Once Soviet power evaporated the old issues resurfaced immediately.

POLITICAL INTEREST AND PARTISANSHIP

Parties and votes

In 1997 political parties were still embryonic in the three countries in this study with a few notable exceptions, all in Ukraine, namely the main nationalist parties in the west and the socialists and communists. Otherwise the state of party politics in the CIS countries resembled that which the Central European countries began to leave behind in the early 1990s. Most parties represented in the CIS countries' national assemblies were still little more than groups gathered around national leaders, with no mass organizations and little mass support. There were no parties in any of the countries that were likely to win an election outright. Governments were formed through deals between the parties following elections – deals in which the countries' presidents were key figures. In Central Europe the main political parties soon moved out of this embryonic stage. By the mid-1990s there had been mergers and the formation of blocs, always pivoting around a left–right axis, but also in some countries highlighting other social divisions: between regions, between urban and rural areas, or between nationalists and others, for example. By the mid-1990s the main party blocs in Central Europe had attracted substantial phalanxes of fairly reliable electoral support. In contrast, in 1997 party politics in the CIS countries was still transfixed in the embryonic stage.

In our surveys the young people were asked whether they would vote in the next national elections and, if so, who for. There was little variation between the countries except in the parties that were named (a large number everywhere). Overall, however, only 11 per cent intended to vote for a named party. Up to 3 per cent said that they would vote but were not sure who they would support. The remainder said either that they were uncertain whether they would vote for anyone or were sure that they would not vote. In Armenia 57 per cent said that they would definitely not vote for anyone. Most of the young people in Armenia were dissatisfied with their present government but had no confidence in any of the opposition parties achieving power through elections or of their making a better job of running the country if they were to do so. In all the countries the main interest groups among the populations at large were still unclear. It was difficult for individuals to decide who to ally themselves to and to support a political party representing the group in question (see Kolarska-Bobinska, 1994).

Attitudes towards politicians

There was a great deal of disenchantment with so-called democratic politics. In all countries, in the East and in the West, substantial propor-tions of young people expressed no firm party loyalties and many were cynical about the motives of all politicians and the operations of political processes. However, in the CIS countries the level of cynicism was much higher than in countries such as Britain. Across our three CIS countries, two-fifths of the young people claimed that it made no difference which party was in power. In Britain in 1988 and in Poland in 1993, just one-fifth of the samples felt similarly. In the CIS countries the young people's experience was that whoever they voted for the same politicians reappeared in the national assemblies and redistributed offices among themselves. The view of most of the young people was that their elected representatives were ineffective, maybe because the problems faced by the countries were so overwhelming, but also, many believed, because of the politicians' own failings. Four-fifths overall endorsed the view that politicians were more interested in gaining power for themselves than in the good of their countries. There was a similar level of cynicism among the young people in Poland in 1993, whereas in Britain in 1988 'only' two-fifths agreed with the statement.

In our qualitative interviews many of the young people expressed impatience with multiparty politics. They criticized politicians for their petty squabbling and for just talking:

> Politics is a theatre with its own company of actors but the actors are not professional. They should be professional in politics the same as everywhere else.

> Politics is nothing more than a talking shop. There is no hope of changing anything. All the politicians want power just to become rich. They pay no

heed to other people's needs, interests and hopes, and do not represent them effectively.

Some of the young people favoured the installation of some type of dictatorship which would really get things done. This was a minority preference, but no more so than all the political parties, and one survey of young people in Russia has recorded two-thirds endorsing the need for dictatorship by a strong leader (Ruchkin, 1998).

In 1997 popular politics throughout the former Soviet Union was still in the fluid state where it was possible for a new leader or party to emerge from nowhere and outperform all the bettter-known politicians and parties. This happened in Latvia in 1998 when the presidential election was won by a recently returned émigré following a long-term career as a US government employee.

The young people's jaundiced views about politicians and their parties did not necessarily indicate total disinterest in politics. In open-ended interviews many of the young people expressed clear and strong political views. It was difficult to be disinterested in the issues, given what had happened in the countries during the preceding decade. Many spoke at length about what had gone wrong, and about how they wanted their countries to position themselves internationally. Some had very strong feelings about the old system and its leaders: 'The former communists have camouflaged themselves and returned to power as democrats. They must be ousted.' Some had strong feelings about their countries' independence:

> We do not need external help. We will revive through our own efforts. Everything is born in pain. We must tell the world, 'Don't help us but don't hinder us.' It is better to die of hunger than to live on our knees as before.

Disengagement

However, the reforms had created the option of being politically completely disengaged. When independence arrived and the reforms commenced there had been a widespread misconception that democratization would lead to sustained upsurges in politically active citizenship. Even the countries' own political scientists often assumed that political participation would be boosted once there was a genuine choice of political parties. Advocates of Western democracy often give the impression that the right to be active is used more widely in the West than is really the case. At the time of independence there was a feeling that communism had suppressed political activity and that under post-communism these levels would rise. As mentioned previously, people in the old Soviet Union knew far more about consumption than about work in the West, and their knowledge of the reality (as opposed to the theory) of democratic party politics was typically shaky.

Communist societies were in fact highly politicized by twentieth-century world standards. Politics affected all areas of people's lives. Political education was an educational priority. All young people were expected to know the names of leading local and national politicians. There were inducements (career rewards) for political activity (in the one legitimate party) and activity levels were in fact high by Western standards. With the reforms all this changed. Disengagement became a respectable position. Explicit indifference and non-involvement ceased to be symbolically defiant and challenging. Young people were able to decide to seek private solutions to their problems (as they had under communism) and to ignore politics (which had previously been more difficult). And, as in the West, the majority began to do exactly this. This has been confirmed in surveys of young people in numerous ex-communist countries. Few young people in Slovenia have remained interested in big historical, social and political issues. Their main concerns now are their relationships with their families and friends (see Ule, 1998). In Russia most young people see no possibility of influencing conditions in their communities. Only a fifth trust the government. Only one in ten trust political parties and movements (see Aleshonok, 1998). So most young people have retreated into private life.

In our main surveys the young people were asked to rate a set of life goals. 'Being happy' and 'having a strong family' were the most highly rated ahead of 'material security', which in turn was more highly rated than 'achieving public status and recognition' and 'serving or maintaining the security of my country'. Young people's ratings of service to one's country had declined since the heady days of the late 1980s as such service had become more of a necessity than a choice (see Adibekian, 1995). Interestingly, the lowest-rated life goal in our survey was 'becoming rich'.

In a late twentieth-century global context, post-communist youth have probably been just normal in terms of the priorities described above. Even so, substantial numbers were interested in politics (as is the case in the West). In the main surveys, two-fifths in Ukraine described themselves as 'very interested' or 'quite interested', the same proportion as in the comparable survey of young people in Britain. In Armenia and Tbilisi only a fifth described themselves as 'very' or 'quite' interested in politics, and the comparable proportion in Poland in 1993 was just 13 per cent.

Against international yardsticks the young people in the CIS countries were not particularly indifferent or apathetic about politics. They were different mainly in the very high proportions who did not feel that any parties or politicians represented their own views, or had no confidence in such a party achieving power and implementing its policies.

POLITICAL ACTIVITY

Activity levels

Levels of political activity were quite low, but not abnormally low by Western standards, in some of the places that we investigated and rather high in others. In Donetsk, Tbilisi and Armenia 3 per cent or fewer of our respondents actually belonged to a political party, but in Lviv 7 per cent did so. In Donetsk 8 per cent and in Tbilisi 7 per cent had been to a political meeting, rally or demonstration during the previous year, and in Armenia 17 per cent and in Lviv 24 per cent had done this. The latter figure would not have been considered high under communism when the Communist Party and its youth organization, the Komsomol, constantly tried to mobilize the age group. And political activity among young people, especially students, had been much higher at the time when communism ended and the countries became independent. At that time virtually all students were involved in meetings and rallies. By 1997 levels of political activity had fallen but, in Armenia and Lviv, remained quite high by Western yardsticks.

In Armenia the political meetings and rallies that the young people attended had mostly preceded the 1996 general election. Most of these events were anti-government rallies. Some had been disrupted by the police and army. The election itself was won by pro-government parties and candidates amid complaints of opposition parties and candidates being intimidated and disqualified and of voting irregularities.

In Lviv the political activists were mostly involved in the region's nationalist parties. The parties themselves did not have majority electoral support even in the region, though nationalist sentiments were near-universal among the region's Ukrainian population (as opposed to its Russians, Poles and other minorities). Some of the young activists in Lviv who were interviewed during our qualitative fieldwork belonged to the political parties that were holding military-style rallies. Their most popular demands were for Ukrainian to be adopted as the one official national language, to have the national flag and other symbols on prominent display, and for a Ukrainianization of school curricula. However, some of the parties had armed militia, some of which had experience of military action, in Abkhazia and Chechnia for instance, acting on the assumption that any enemy of Russia was their ally. Most young people regarded these nationalist groups as dangerous – liable to deepen divisions and even split the country: 'The nationalists are sick people. They must be kept under control. These people have guns and they're ready to use them.' Young Russians in the west of Ukraine felt intimidated and resented being made to feel strangers in what, having been born there, they had always considered their homeland.

None of the countries could be described as firmly on course towards becoming a Western-style democracy. They contained heady mixtures of strong political convictions, quite widespread interest in politics and high levels of activity in some places, alongside low levels of party identification and a low regard for all politicians and their parties.

Careers in politics

As explained above, most of the young people distrusted their countries' politicians: they were regarded as self-interested, apparently incapable of addressing let alone solving the countries' problems. Nevertheless, the job of politician was rated quite highly. It was ranked in prestige beneath lawyer, businessman and manager, but level-pegging with minister of religion, and distinctly higher than army officer, scientist, engineer and teacher. Politicians had to be respected because they had power. The young people might have been cynical about how this power was being used (for the politicians' own betterment, the majority believed) but they recognized that politicians could bestow patronage and enjoy the personal rewards of success. In the CIS countries all this was regarded as simply normal if not ideal politics. Reform was being implemented from above. There had been an expectation in some quarters that democratic politicians would be different but this was not how things were turning out. There had been corruption under communism but the general view was that during the reforms it had risen to unprecedented levels.

Most of the young political activists (party members who were active and who usually held some office in their local parties) who were interviewed in Ukraine and Georgia during our qualitative fieldwork were interested in building careers in politics. They were not just active supporters. They sought not just influence but office. The young people who had remained politically active after 1991 had moved from the streets into parties and some expected politics to be an important part of their adult lives. Most intended to qualify for or to continue to work in some other profession in the short term. Unless they were otherwise unemployed, the young activists thought that it would be unwise to stake their entire futures on successful careers as politicians. However, some had decided to gain qualifications relevant to politics, if they had not already done so. This usually meant taking university courses in politics or other social sciences, philosophy or law. Nearly all the party activists were university educated.

Some complained about the current weakness of their parties which meant that they were not being paid for their political work. Being unpaid was regarded as abnormal and, they hoped, temporary. For many politics had already become a quite heavy commitment. They were regularly devoting up to 12 hours each week to political work. They knew that politics could be a rewarding career but in countries where there were many parties everything depended on their own gaining at least a share of power. If this happened the young activists expected there to be personal benefits. Success for any party was not guaranteed, but a degree of success was quite likely, given the systems of proportional representation and the opportunities at local as well as national levels. Some of the party activists were hoping for elected office and, eventually, to become members of their countries' governments. In fact a few had already achieved elected office. In countries where the parties themselves were new, rapid promotion was possible. Politics was similar to business in this respect. If they did not become elected politicians the activists expected to be appointed to positions in state administration or in state, semi-privatized or shortly to be privatized enterprises. All this was regarded as normal political life. The prospect of such rewards was among the ways in which political leaders and parties attracted active supporters. The young people who were part of and who were publicly recognized as holding positions in parties with a share of power were already being shown respect by the police and staff in state offices, and were being asked for assistance by people who wished to register non-governmental organizations (NGOs) or private businesses, for example. The young activists were discovering that the ability to 'open doors' was appreciated by members of the public. And there were additional benefits, such as the opportunity to be part of delegations to meetings within their own countries and abroad. The activists we interviewed were not just careerists. They all had definite, typically strong ideological commitments. It was simply the case that, just like other people, the activists knew that politics could be a rewarding career.

The political views of activists

It was possible to gain more information about the countries' young political activists from our main survey. There were too few party members to justify a quantitative analysis but it was possible to identify a somewhat larger group of 'politicals' who were both very or quite interested in politics and had been to at least one political event during the previous year (a meeting, rally or demonstration, for example). Out of the 900 respondents only 54 were 'politicals' on these criteria: 25 of these individuals were in Lviv, where they amounted to one in six of the sample; another 16 were in Armenia (5 per cent of the sample); whereas there were only eight in Tbilisi and five in Donetsk. The extent to which young people were politicized varied from place to place though the levels never approached the peaks of the early 1990s, or what had been normal under communism. In Lviv the relatively high level of politicization was continuing whereas in Armenia it was more likely to have been a temporary upsurge connected with the national elections in 1996. Donetsk and Tbilisi appear quiescent in our data, but the underlying conditions were such that this situation could change almost overnight.

In terms of social backgrounds the politicals' distinctive features mirrored those of the party activists who had been interviewed earlier in our qualitative fieldwork. The politicals in the main survey were better educated than the sample in general. In fact 65 per cent of the politicals had followed the elite educational route. Their family backgrounds had a similar upward skew (see Table 6.1). However, the politicals were not being particularly successful in the labour market. In fact 56 per cent of those in the labour market at the time of the survey were either unemployed or doing 'bitty jobs'. They shared some of the general problems of well-educated young people in their countries: in

Table 6.1   'Politicals' and other young people (%)

	Politicals	All
Educational groups		
1 (Bottom)	10	20
2	8	7
3	10	17
4	6	18
5 (Top)	65	37
Family backgrounds		
1 (Bottom)	11	23
2	6	12
3	17	19
4	26	15
5 (Top)	41	30
Career groups		
Self-employed	9	6
State	18	19
Private sector	18	15
State (marginal)	12	14
Private (marginal)	29	22
Unemployed	15	23
Occupations		
Management	18	15
Professional	50	40
Clerical	12	21
Manual	21	24
Sex		
Male	67	46
Female	33	54

the 1990s conventional educational success was not being rewarded in the labour markets. In terms of their occupations (if they had any) the politicals were more likely than other respondents to have management or professional and less likely to have clerical or manual jobs. Two-thirds of the politicals were males.

In terms of beliefs and attitudes there were four main differences between the politicals and the rest of their age group. First, unsur-prisingly, the politicals were the more likely to believe that which party held power in their countries did make a difference (see Table 6.2). Second, as personal life goals they attached less importance to becom-ing rich and more to serving their countries and earning public status and recognition. Third, the politicals were more patriotic. They were less likely to want to work in the West, more willing than other young people to fight to defend their countries if necessary, to welcome the disintegration of the USSR, and not to want closer relationships with Russia (though 54 per cent did in fact want closer relationships com-pared with 63 per cent in the entire samples). Fourth, the politicals were the more pro-reform: the more likely to prefer a market economy, to want to work in the private sector, and to believe that life had become better, not worse, during the 1990s (though 59 per cent, against 70 per cent across the full samples, believed that life had in fact become more difficult). The values of these young political activists should be of wider interest. They are their countries' probable future rulers.

POLITICAL CONTINUITIES

In many respects politics in the CIS countries was continuing much as before the reforms except that politicians had splintered into different parties, although there had been cliques and factions and patron–client relationships within the old communist system. Many of the new party leaders and elected representatives had been politically active under communism. The old factions and cliques had simply become separate parties, all with their own 'clients' (see Kovaleva, 1997). Reform had not led to purges. The German Democratic Republic and the Czech Republic are the only countries where individuals who had been part of the old system were systematically expelled from office. Elsewhere this was considered pointless and, in any case, there were simply too many

Table 6.2 Beliefs and attitudes (%)

	Politicals	All
Personal life goals (very important)		
Being happy	87	82
Serving country	39	27
State and public recognition	44	31
Strong family	91	80
Becoming rich	13	28
Material security	57	56
Strongly agree or agree		
Better to work for private firm	71	59
Better to work for large firm than for oneself	32	36
Basic industries should not be sold to foreigners	41	38
Prepared to fight for country	76	60
Important to be well-educated and qualified for one's occupation	98	92
Like to work in the West	47	55
Compulsory military service for men: retained	57	58
Life more difficult since the reforms	57	70
Basic industries: remain in public ownership	69	73
Reforms were a mistake	35	39
Makes little difference which party is in power	24	37
Life better since the reforms	33	17
Politicians: more interested in themselves	74	80
Better to work in public sector	28	26
Poor people to blame for poverty	23	27
Becoming rich means hard work	24	32
Like to have own business	72	72
Feelings about break-up of USSR		
Very good	52	25
Mixed	26	29
Disadvantages	20	25
Don't know	2	22
Want closer ties with Russia	54	63
Prefer free market	91	83
$n =$	54	900

people with too much to lose. After all, everyone had been part of the old system to some extent. If people had wanted to influence events under communism they had no choice but to operate through the Party structures.

Following independence the old politicians splintered into numerous parties where they were joined by newcomers, including the young activists in this study. The co-existence of numerous parties and proportional representation meant that power had to be shared, and all career politicians had vested interests in a system that depressed the risk of any group being totally stripped of power, especially the ability to make or influence appointments and to exercise patronage. Ex-communists did not threaten these arrangements. The only threats were from outside politics – the risk of an outsider such as Latvia's new president in 1998 or perhaps someone such as General Lebed in Russia winning a crucial election (most likely a presidential election). All the parties had vested interests in excluding or incorporating such challengers. This was why, to the politically inactive majority, all politicians appeared much the same (part of 'the mafia') and why it seemed to make little difference which party gained or lost seats in the national assembly in an election and who was actually in a government. It appeared to anyone on the outside that the top priority of the entire political class was its own betterment. In other words, it was political business as usual.

7. Precarious Transitions

SURVIVING IN LIMBO

To repeat, there are no experts on post-communism and the so-called transition countries have no known futures; hence commentators' uncertainty over whether to describe them as in transition, transformation or crisis. Limbo seems as good a description as any, certainly of former Soviet countries. By the mid-1990s all the countries had made decisive breaks with the past. By then the countries of Central Europe could see where they were heading – into NATO, the EU, becoming part of the West all the time. The futures of former Soviet republics, with the possible exception of the Baltic states, were still indeterminate.

Their young people, including the subjects in our research, have been in a double limbo. Our respondents were attempting to make their own life stage transitions: into jobs and careers, marriage, parenthood and independent households. They had left childhood behind, for ever, but most of the twenty-somethings had not yet established themselves in adult roles. It was not just that they could not know which of the awaiting adult roles each of them would occupy. The societies into which they would have become integrated, had communism lasted, had disintegrated. The countries' destinations were still unclear. These young people's predicaments were not basically the same as those of young adults the world over, including those in Western countries which, if they are changing, are doing so gradually. In the limbo countries it has not only been disadvantaged young people – excluded groups and those who have failed to match the standards required by employers and so on – who have been at risk of marginalization. In fact 'marginalization' may be an inappropriate term. Can a majority be marginalized? All groups of young people have been and remain vulnerable. The kinds of societies in which they will spend their adult lives are still matters for conjecture.

We are aware that a post-modern condition, which some claim to be spreading throughout the Western world, means looser, more fragile social structures and roles for everyone. The literature on youth in the West is full of metaphors such as individuals embarking on the life course with no reliable maps of what lies ahead (see, for example, Furlong and Cartmel, 1997; Roberts, 1995). However, in the limbo countries the conditions surrounding young people are far less reliable. At any rate, the young people hope, often desperately, that the prevailing conditions will not last, but they cannot be sure. Moreover, unlike most Western youth, the majority lack the resources from either their own earnings or their families to select and construct preferred (temporary or otherwise) independent lifestyles.

A possibility that few will entertain, yet, is that their countries' transitions might be over – that by the late 1990s they had already reached their post-communist destinations. Yet this is in fact possible. All the countries experienced rapid, turbulent change in the early 1990s. Since then the pace of change has been normal by Western standards. By the late 1990s market reforms had been implemented everywhere, meaning that private businesses were legitimate and could set their own prices. Most enterprises that could be privatized were already in private hands. Monetary stabilization, meaning reasonably low inflation, was at least in sight. The private sector economies were consolidating. There were hotels, restaurants and shops with full ranges of consumer goods catering for wealthy locals and foreigners. The rest of the populations had learnt to live, when necessary, without proper salaries, reliable electricity and water supplies, and sometimes almost without money. Non-payment of rent and energy charges by families that were simply unable to pay was being tolerated. Much of the infrastructure – houses, roads and pavements – was crumbling, even in capital cities. Third World conditions were taking over. Everyone hoped that all this would be temporary. The alternative might be unthinkable, but it is still a possibility.

By the end of the 1990s even some of the direct beneficiaries had become aware of how Western assistance had consolidated their own and their countries' limbo status. The cases with which we are most familiar are, of course, academics who have participated on Western-funded projects. Like other forms of Western aid, this funding has normally been channelled to individuals and NGOs, usually 'shells' created specifically to receive the grants, rather than mainstream universities and research institutes. The West has been reluctant to pump money into any of the old, often unreformed, structures. A problem, needless to say, has been that all this funding has been short-term. Initially it was welcomed; so was the way in which the funds were distributed (to individuals). But by the late 1990s the disadvantages were transparent: no new, alternative institutions were being created; mainline institutions remained weak, indeed, they had been further weakened by their marginality to new developments; new equipment had ended-up with NGOs, or in private individuals' hands.

Young researchers who participated enthusiastically in the initial waves of projects were finding by the late 1990s, contrary to their earlier hopes, that they had no prospect of research careers. Under communism such careers were possible in the universities and research institutes but since the end of communism these have been unable to offer proper jobs, let alone careers. Western funding has not created new local research institutions, networks and journals through which national reputations might be built. Participating in a series of Western-funded projects has not built a stable position. Those concerned have been able to attempt to break into international (English language) networks, but this is incredibly difficult because of the language proficiency that is required and the need to prioritize travel and conferences over one's family's more basic needs. Aspirant academics have been able to try to emigrate, usually to North America, where they have been most likely to flounder as small fish in a large pond; in any event, this private solution has drained talent from their own countries. Western institutions and careers have benefited from the new East–West links. In the East the old institutions have been disempowered, though not destroyed, and nothing has been built in their place.

Claire Wallace and Siyka Kovatcheva (1998) argue that in the East youth has been 'deconstructed'. They are right, but the deconstruction concept blurs as much as it reveals. Under communism youth was firmly constructed. The age group was defined precisely by its eligibility for Komsomol membership. There were special provisions for the age group's leisure. Transitions from education into employment were planned by the system. There was an official ideology that further defined young people's situations. They were said to be vulnerable to Western propaganda and other temptations, yet simultaneously, under the leadership of the Communist Party, capable of rejuvenating their societies and leading the next stage in the construction of communism. By the mid-1990s everything that communism had constructed had gone. But 'deconstruction' implies a more deliberate dis-assembly than has really occurred. 'Destruction' seems to fit the facts more comfortably. Talk of 'deconstruction' makes it possible to identify close parallels with the situations of Western youth, whose life stage transitions have become longer and generally messier. Young people may perceive advantages in a loosening of constraints, but this will depend on there being a range of attractive opportunities from which they can choose. In our study the general view was that life had become more difficult.

Yet it is possible to over-play the downbeat. The young people whom we studied were surviving socially, psychologically and materially. Our evidence offers as much fuel for alarm as the results of Julia Zubok's (1998) surveys of up to 12,000 young people in 12 regions of Russia in 1990, 1994 and 1997. She draws attention, lucidly, to the rise in crime, use of alcohol and other drugs, suicides, and young people running away from their parents' homes. She describes how, by 1997, the optimism of the early 1990s had given way to indifference and even alarm. The young people in otherwise satisfactory jobs were scared and nervous about losing them. The majority were not in jobs corresponding with their qualifications; and the numbers in this marginal state, as Zubok describes it, had risen between 1990 and 1997. By then fewer young people than in the early 1990s wanted to become entrepreneurs, to work for foreign companies or for privatized enterprises. In other words, they seemed to be losing confidence in their own and their country's future. Ruchkin (1998) also quotes survey evidence suggesting that by the mid-1990s most young people in Russia had lost confidence in their own and their country's prospects.

This was simply not the case in Armenia, Georgia and Ukraine. Moreover, some of the problems faced by youth in the limbo countries' labour markets, like some features of their leisure, are treated as just normal life stage phenomena in the West. In all market economies young (and older) workers are at risk of dismissal. Firms are often liquidated. These are not specifically post-communist problems. Likewise in market economies, workers have to be flexible: they cannot always expect to obtain jobs which correspond with their initial education and training. Youth crime, drug use and suicide are issues in most Western countries. Moreover, limbo conditions are not necessarily disastrous. Most young people are able to cope with uncertainty. An open future can be more attractive than knowing just how limited one's prospects are. This is why, even though most felt that life had become more difficult during the reforms (they could hardly have failed to recognize this), the young people in our study did not necessarily regret the passing of the old system. Even those who regretted the break with the past did not necessarily want their countries to step backwards. For many it was sufficient, for the time being at any rate, to believe that a better way of life was possible. And such a future was, still is, a possibility. Things can change rapidly in the new East. Look at how Prague and Warsaw have changed since 1990.

When the reforms began, few outside commentators expected the transformation to be anything other than protracted and messy. These initial expectations have proved correct. If the countries make successful transitions into the global market economy they are likely to exhibit a set of very pronounced late development effects – current global trends taking hold with exceptional intensity. These include shrunken states (compared with their size and responsibilities in the era of 'Fordism' or organized capitalism), individualization, and risk and uncertainty. If these are to be destination features of successful transitions, the young people in the relevant countries who have stumbled around in the 1990s and their own and their countries' futures may be precarious, but they are not necessarily wholly off-course.

HOPES AND PREDICTIONS: RIGHT FIRST TIME

When communism ended there were celebrations in most of the countries. Students in secondary schools and universities were nearly all involved in movements or demonstrations of some description. They were excited at the prospect of becoming founder members of their societies' new social orders. There was relief in the West that the Cold War was over, that a peace dividend could be drawn and, in the longer term, that there would be opportunities to trade with the new market economies. Nevertheless, much of the enthusiasm in the West was restrained. A common prediction in 1989 was that it was likely to take 15 years or so to reunite Germany thoroughly, and that the Eastern and Central European countries would take somewhat longer to become part of the West. At that time the expectation was that communism would be reformed slowly rather than suddenly replaced in the USSR.

The latter expectation was wrong. Everthing else was spot-on. Yet by 1991 all forecasts were being shortened. The USSR was disappearing. By then it was plain that the peoples of the ex-communist countries expected quick benefits. They had endured the rise and, in the 1980s, the decline of communism (and in their living standards). There was an expectation, certainly in Central Europe, that the West would reward the peoples and movements that had overturned the 'evil empire' and that the Western way of life would flood in.

Explaining the death of communism

There are now so many explanations of why communism collapsed that its demise appears overdetermined. This is despite the fact that, well into the 1980s, much authoritative Western opinion regarded communism as an alternative, perfectly viable way of organizing a modern industrial society. The system appeared to have proved its durability by raising successive generations of at least acquiescent citizens. It is only subsequently that we have been authoritatively informed that communism was always doomed on account of its internal contradictions: between the equality and democracy that were promised and what was actually delivered, for example (see Holmes, 1993; Marshall, 1996). It has subsequently become crystal clear, or so we are told, that as the people gained more knowledge of the West, as telecommunications breached the iron curtain and as the gap between Eastern and Western living standards widened, it became impossible for the communist rulers to sustain the illusion that their countries were catching up and that what the people lacked in private consumption they gained in public welfare services. It was always inevitable, we are now told, that the people would eventually realize that their schools and hospitals were not really the envy of the world. In the 1980s attempts to reform communism simply reduced the system's effectiveness, with the result, clear enough with hindsight, that its downfall then became inevitable (see Misztal, 1993). It has also been argued that communism became unsustainable as people's appetites for consumption, personal choice and self-expression were whetted. Communism is said to have been a system that took the values of rational production to an ultimate extreme and became out of tune with, and unable to adjust to, late twentieth-century aspirations (Bauman, 1992).

Especially if some combination of these explanations is correct, one would expect the populations of the ex-communist countries to judge the reforms by the speed with which their consumption aspirations are satisfied and greater equality and democracy delivered. All of these have generally been taken, in the East, to be (attractive) features of the Western way of life. Needless to say, popular conceptions of the West in the East have often been just as inaccurate as the Western public's understanding of life under communism. Since the 1980s many people in the East have regarded the widening inequalities in their own countries as distortions rather than normal outcomes of market economics.

Be that as it may, the peoples of the East have looked for quick benefits. Reform politicians have needed quick results. Their failure to deliver has resulted in a rapid evaporation of the support that they attracted in the early 1990s and, in many countries, the return to office of (ex-) communists. The latter have shown that they are no threat to reform. Few would organize a wholesale restoration of the old system even if they were able to do so. Communism had many ideologically uncommitted cadres.

Western policies

Perhaps it was less inevitable that Western politicians would adopt the rapid-transition, big-bang, shock-therapy vocabulary. On the other hand, they soon recognized the need to lay out a clear transition path, with a visible destination, in order to preserve any influence in and trust from the East. Whatever their private thoughts, they have been quick to adopt projects such as an enlarged and unified Europe and a new world order in which the old First and Second World countries become partners for peace, capable of dousing any trouble spots whether in Africa, the Middle East or the Balkans. Virtually everyone who matters has had a vested interest in believing that shock therapy and big bangs will work. But it is now equally clear that the earlier, sober forecasts were basically sound. Communism built factories of a (typically huge) size, located them in places and created a demand for the products that was always most unlikely to be sustained by the global market economy. The transition, if that is what is happening, was always going to involve massive re-investment and restructuring over a great many years.

PRESERVING HOPE

Up to now all the great world systems have eventually run their course. No one can know whether capitalism and its market economy will prove different. Communism has already proved true to type. Its coming and going were great world events of the twentieth century. When such grand designs collapse the societies sometimes experience regression. For some CIS countries this is just as possible as transition. In most of the countries this is what has actually happened up to now. The direction that the latest grand transformation will take in the twenty-first century is the twentieth century's big unanswered question.

There are pessimists who claim that communism systematically failed to nurture the values and motivations required for successful market economies and, therefore, that mounting frustration leading to a backlash of some description is virtually preordained (Bauman, 1992). This seems unnecessarily pessimistic, given the mixed track records of the ex-communist countries. World systems theory is probably a better source of predictions than close inspection of the so-called post-communist mind. Some countries are simply better placed than others by history and geography to make successful transitions into the global market economy and the West. Georgia would probably flourish if it could relocate to Switzerland.

That said, it was not just the young people whom we studied but also the countries in which they lived that were experiencing difficulties in the mid and late 1990s. The old system had shrunk and was probably beyond repair. The countries were peripheral in the world market economy. Balkanization, bandit or mafia capitalism or perpetual underdevelopment were, and remain, as likely destinations as Westernization.

Another reminder of how communism ended in these countries may be useful. There were reform movements with mass support in the late 1980s and early 1990s but it was not these that toppled the Soviet system. Reform became a necessity rather than just an option when the Soviet Union ended. The old elites did not subsequently retire and write their own obituaries: they set about introducing reforms and, in the process, they sought to transform themselves into the new elites. That so many of their children have floundered in the 1990s is a sign of the extent to which the old system collapsed and the modest, if any, pace of recovery. Some young people have succeeded. They either have good jobs in strong private sector businesses, are in business on their own accounts, or are forging careers in politics. Needless to say, there are very few such young people. Most are still simply surviving. In some respects the countries already resemble Third World states in which elites control wealth and power and use both, with no effective checks and balances, to maintain their own positions.

Yet the hoped-for future of most of the young people in our study is still possible. They had abandoned neither hope nor optimism. Some were growing angry and frustrated. Some were resigned, for the time being. Most were simply becoming more realistic about the timescale and how difficult the transition was going to be. We must bear in mind, of course, that these young people were relatively privileged. Most lived in major cities. They had better chances in education and the labour market than young people from small towns and rural villages, though perhaps the latter had the compensation that it was easier for them to fall back into traditional ways of life. It is a sobering thought that our quantitative surveys did not cover young people (and families) who were war refugees or those who had fled from the dire economic conditions or the prospect of military service. If we had wished to do so, we could have discovered much more suffering. Equally to the present point, the optimism of the young people whom we studied was unlikely to last for ever. It is better regarded as a loan extended to those with power but with the expectation of repayment.

POLICIES FOR YOUTH

How might young people's hopes be kept alive? What should governments and NGOs do for the young people? Our advice is deliberately restrained. Empowerment is probably what the countries need above all else. They need effective governments and economies so that they can take charge of their own destinies. Their own citizens are better placed than any outsiders to decide what needs to be done and what is practical. Enough damage has already been inflicted by encouraging, sometimes requiring, the ex-communist countries to act on Western advice, mostly from experts with economic theories to peddle. Our recommendations are therefore explicitly non-authoritative suggestions for the countries to consider.

Even with this in mind, we see little point in constructing a wish list. Of course, what the countries' young people would like above all else would be good jobs and decent salaries which would give them access to independent housing and the kinds of lifestyles that they associate with the West. Our research has revealed the need, but it does not allow us to pontificate authoritatively on how all this should be brought about. We have no doubt that all the governments would create thriving industries, able to employ well-paid workforces, if that was within their power. But this does not mean that, in the meantime, there is absolutely nothing that governments (and NGOs) can do for the countries' young people. Certain measures, which would be zero cost or low cost to the public purse and within some externally funded NGOs' means would make a considerable difference to young people's quality of life and confidence in their own and their countries' futures.

Free education

We hope that the spread of fee charging will be resisted. This applies in higher education and at the secondary level. The disadvantages to young people from poor families are so blatant that feelings of unfairness are inevitable. In countries where educational enrolments have risen largely because young people are unable to obtain decent jobs, paid-for education is tantamount to a tax on the jobless. Opportunities in education enable young people to equip themselves for what they hope will be their futures. Maintaining these opportunities is a way of preserving hope.

Housing markets

Their development will give hope to young people from families which are neither cash wealthy nor well endowed with accommodation. There is a need to attract dwellings on to the market. Property taxes and rents pitched at realistic levels will discourage hoarding. Any subsidies and tax or rent relief should go to types of people, not indiscriminately to property. An increase in the number of sellers will lead to the price of dwellings adjusting to market conditions, that is, what local purchasers are able to afford. Owners need to be educated out of the idea that their own properties are worth what foreigners will pay for city centre flats and whatever the construction costs might have been in the past.

Fertility control

Sex education should be part of the curriculum in all elementary and secondary schools. Contraceptives should be available through the public health services, or on sale if cost would otherwise be an obstacle. Young (and older) users should be confident that the products are reliable, and authoritative advice and information should be available at the point of distribution.

Consumer markets

Commerce should be set free everywhere to open shops, cafés, bars, clubs (of various types) and places of entertainment. Competition is the best form of consumer protection in these markets. Even citizens who cannot afford to purchase can enjoy the environments that are created and take pride in what their cities have to offer. Moreover, getting people on to the streets during the daytime and at night is the most effective way of developing safe environments.

Sport, the arts and holidays

The old system was not wholly evil. The countries should try to salvage some benefit from their communist past. The ways in which youth arts and sport were encouraged are not incompatible with a market economy or political democracy. The decay of physical facilities and the wholesale destruction rather than the reform of the delivery systems have impaired the quality of young people's lives. A 1996 survey of high school students in a small Russian town revealed a complete absence of youth organizations (Aleshonok, 1998). None of our own research sites was quite so barren. On the other hand, very few of the young people were involved in any leisure time, or any other, organizations. The CIS countries are currently at risk of developing the worst possible versions of day-to-day Western ways of life: home-based, media-dominated leisure relieved mainly by binges in bars and restaurants. Education in sport and the arts should be maintained or reintroduced in the schools, colleges and youth centres. The systems for nurturing elite performers should be reinvigorated. Apart from providing entertaining spectacles, these can be assets that enable citizens to feel pride in their countries.

Facilities for youth travel should also be maintained or reintroduced. These need not be expensive. Indeed, they may be self-financing using low-cost accommodation and voluntary leaders, some of them young people themselves.

Endorse reform

Finally, governments and opposition parties that are so minded need to keep reaffirming their determination to press ahead with the reforms. Despite the solid body of opinion which feels that the reforms were a mistake and the even larger body of opinion which feels (with justification) that life has become more difficult, there are very few young people who wish to return wholesale to the old system. Their optimism and confidence will be best sustained by governments that express a determination to develop successful market economies, however long this might take. Before long the generation featured in our study will be satisfied by the prospect of a better future for their own children. In the meantime young (and older) people will feel that a better way of life is coming if more of the West is allowed into the countries. Governments need not spend anything. It will be sufficient if they do not try to stem the inflow of consumer goods – from cars to videotapes and satellite broadcasting.

Privatizing everything, selling off the silver cheaply if necessary, is not the answer. Dismantling the old system, whether step by step or with a big bang, does not ignite private enterprise. Governments may be unable to prevent old industries from contracting or even closing, but they can allow new ways of life to enter their countries. Even citizens who cannot afford to be active players in the new consumerism can enjoy vicarious gratification and feel that life in the countries is coming closer to their hopes. Hope and optimism are the 'bottom line' that must not be allowed to break if the transition dream is ever to become a reality in the greater part of the territories that were once communist.

Appendix I: Researching Young People in the New East

YOUTH RESEARCH UNDER AND AFTER COMMUNISM

Youth research prospered under communism, so the new East has plenty of older, experienced and expert youth researchers. The communist authorities always treated youth as an important group. They were the future, hence the official interest in what they were doing and thinking. In most communist countries there were research institutes dedicated to the study of youth. Some were based in the Academies of Science (the state-funded multisite institutions that conducted pure research). Otherwise the research was based in institutes attached to the government ministries with responsibility for youth. Sometimes the research centres were linked to the Communist Party youth organization, the Komsomol.

Priorities

The main type of youth research under communism was the (very) large-scale, quantitative survey. Huge samples were usually considered necessary due to the requirement to produce findings valid for all regions.

Some topics which featured prominently in most studies and some that were usually absent both seem rather surprising in the West. Researchers investigated youth's values repeatedly and thoroughly – the authorities were keenly interested in whether the countries were producing socialist cohorts. Cultural participation was also monitored. Once again, the authorities were interested, this time in whether young people were involved in whatever was being promoted and provided by the state and Party.

Since the end of communism local researchers have often retained these preoccupations. They (and the new governments) have been concerned about the effects of cutbacks in state spending on recreation and culture. In the 1990s and subsequently the researchers, and the governments, have also been interested in whether young people have been internalizing market values – whether they have become entrepreneurial, are prepared to be flexible and to embrace the tough demands of private enterprise. Western researchers have often been surprised at their Eastern colleagues' lack of attention to young people's various family and educational backgrounds and their precise locations in the new labour markets.

Neglected topics

The school-to-work transition was rarely tackled by youth researchers under communism. The reason is simple: it was not a problem. At any rate, it was not defined as a problem by the authorities. The system channelled school and college leavers into appropriate jobs. As far as the authorities were concerned, the system worked satisfactorily. The countries offered nothing resembling what Westerners would regard as careers guidance. The reason, once again, was that in the authorities' eyes there was simply no need. Western youth researchers' preoccupation with links between social origins and destinations, occupational choice, status attainment and social mobility, were never shared by their Eastern peers.

Young people's housing transitions was another blind spot. This may have been a problem for young people and their families (see Chapter 4) but the authorities did not adopt it as a public issue. Youth's housing transitions was also a blind spot in Western youth research until recently. It used to fall into the gap between youth and family studies. However, since the 1970s Western (British at any rate) youth researchers have been attracted by the spread of youth homelessness, the decline in the supply of affordable rented accommodation, the spread of extra-marital cohabitation, the postponement of marriage and fertility, the rise in the number of young single parents, and separation and divorce rates. In the East, under communism, these never became issues deemed to require research, and they have rarely been tackled subsequently.

Another absence in the East was research into youth sub-cultures. In the West such studies have often arisen from an interest in delinquency and related topics, including drug use in recent years. British youth sub-cultures, from the Teddy Boys in the 1950s to the rave cultures of the 1980s and 1990s, have been explored assiduously. Communism had no equivalent studies. Youth deviance was supposed to be uncommon and a result of individual pathology rather than sub-cultural. There were no ethnographic, appreciative studies of non-conformist (or conformist) youth. However, since the 1980s the East's new generations of youth researchers have been keen to learn and to practise qualitative techniques. In the process they have learnt quickly that this type of research is much more difficult to accomplish and more time consuming than may appear to be the case from the written output.

Post-1980s developments

In the West youth research has gone from strength to strength. Generally rising crime rates, the prolongation and complication of youth transitions, the spread of youth unemployment and so on have stimulated funding opportunities and scholarly interest.

Trends in the East have been rather different. The end of communism was a painful jolt. Some of the youth research institutes closed. This was most likely to happen when they had been attached to the Komsomol. When the centres survived their funding often dried up. Yet somehow, in many places, youth research continued. In Russia there were regular large-scale surveys of young people in the 1990s. Somehow research was accomplished even when research staff were unpaid for months and when budgets for other purposes shrank alarmingly. In Ukraine there had been little youth research under communism, but in the 1990s regular, country-wide surveys commenced (see Vynnychuk, 1996). In Armenia, by contrast, the former series of national surveys ended abruptly. Our own 'main survey' (see below) in Armenia was treated by the local researchers as a rather poor substitute for the lapsed, much larger-scale enquiries. In Georgia there was no major youth research under communism and this has remained so (apart from our own enquiries) since independence.

WHY STUDY POST-COMMUNIST YOUTH?

It is impossible to give a concise and honest explanation of how and why the research in this book came about. The projects involved research teams in four countries in Eastern and Central Europe (Bulgaria, Hungary, Poland and Slovakia), the three CIS countries and two European Union states (the UK and Germany). The collaborators' academic biographies and disciplines (mainly sociology, psychology, politics and economics) are quite diverse.

We can be precise about the events that made the research possible: the end of the iron curtain and the opportunities that followed to gain funding for collaborative research. All the participants had interests (albeit developed in quite different intellectual biographies in different countries), first, in young people's life stage transitions and, second, in the transitions of former communist countries. The collaborators have in fact become one of the many East–West research networks that have been created since 1989. We have been creating a new subject (post-communism) and, in the cases of the collaborators in Eastern and Central Europe and the CIS, building new types of careers whose future directions, like those of their countries, are difficult to forecast.

In practice our research was a combination of mainly Western money and mainly Eastern labour and a fusion of the collaborators' prior orientations to the topic. The reasons why we wanted answers varied, but all the research projects (there were several – see below – in terms of the funding arrangements) addressed a common set of basic questions:

- What impact are the macroeconomic and political changes in former communist countries having on young people?
- How, if at all, do these impacts vary between different socio-demographic groups and between countries?
- How are the various groups of young people in the various countries experiencing and responding to their situations?
- What are the implications for young people's day-to-day leisure activities and family relationships, and their life stage housing and family transitions?

The details of our research were underpinned by a set of agreed methodological principles:

- We believe that, in order to answer the above questions, basing studies in specimen areas is the best of all options rather than a cheaper and inferior alternative to national samples. National pictures are always aggregates of numerous local scenes, and may be very different from them all. It is far easier to trace the effects of economic changes on the job opportunities open to specific groups of young people at the local labour market level, and the same applies to housing and leisure opportunities.
- We also believe that covering adequate numbers of young people from all the main types of family and educational backgrounds is usually preferable to strict statistical representativeness of local (or any other) populations. Research resources are always scarce and, given the objectives of our enquiries (listed above), we believe that resources will always be best used to obtain as rich information as possible from the minimum numbers needed to ensure that conclusions can be drawn about all the significant groups of young people within the locality (or population).
- Our enquiries incorporate the conviction that studies of youth transitions, and how these are affected by changes in the economic and political contexts, must have an in-built longitudinal perspective. This is necessary to capture the interplay between macrohistorical changes and young people's biographies. Fortunately, gathering longitudinal information does not necessarily require research to continue throughout the period covered. If this were the case there would be no history as we know it. Individuals have sufficient powers of recall to narrate significant events in their earlier lives.
- Finally, we have acted on the assumption that all enquiries should endeavour to gather and benefit from both quantitative and softer forms of qualitative evidence, rather than opt for one or the other.

In conducting and then analysing the results of all our enquiries we adopted a strategy developed previously when investigating the impact of macroeconomic changes among young people in Britain and

Germany (see Banks *et al.*, 1992; Bynner and Roberts, 1991; Evans and Heinz, 1994).

- Identifying the main routes or pathways followed by young people from different types of home backgrounds, through different kinds of education and training, into different positions in the labour markets.
- Exploring relationships between young people's experiences on these career routes and their experiences in making other transitions, especially family and housing transitions, their peer relationships and leisure activities, and their socio-political orientations.

THE ENQUIRIES

The young people we studied were in fact aged up to 30. The CIS and Eastern and Central European researchers were comfortable with this elongated concept of youth: the Komsomol had recruited up to age 28. However, our reasons for studying up to 30-year-olds were, first, to capture higher education graduates' as well as younger school-leavers' transitions; second, in order to cover young people at various stages in their school-to-work and family transitions; and third, because we wanted information about the experiences of young people from the late 1980s when communism was in crisis and when most of our CIS respondents were still at school, usually entering their secondary schools at age 14–16, up to the late 1990s.

The main surveys

We describe these as our main surveys simply because they are in fact the main source of original evidence in this book. These surveys comprised interviews during 1997 with a total of 900 young people, 300 from each of the CIS countries, with the Ukraine sample split equally between Donetsk and Lviv. In Georgia the entire sample was from Tbilisi, the capital. In Armenia the sample was more dispersed. On the basis of previous survey experience, the Armenian investigators were able to select districts, then schools, which would provide a quasi-representative national sample. So in Armenia a third of the sample was from Yerevan, the capital, another third was from provincial towns (Abovian, Gumry and Vandazor), and the remaining third was from rural areas (Ararat and Artashat). In so far as it has been possible to check, through the proportion of the respondents' parents who had received higher education, for example, the Armenian sample does appear to be representative of the age group country-wide in 1997.

The samples were selected from elementary and secondary school registers of several years previously (1988-91) depending partly on the availability of records. When secondary school registers were used the schools were of all the main types (see Chapter 3). In the cities where survey work was conducted (Yerevan, Tbilisi, Donetsk and Lviv) half of the samples were from inner-city schools (in districts where intelligentsia families tended to live) and the other half were from the city outskirts (predominantly working-class areas). All the respondents were aged twenty-something, typically mid-twenties, at the time of the interviews in 1997. The interviews sought information about each individual's family background and current circumstances, education, labour market biography, all experiences of earning and spending money, leisure activities and socio-political values. Exactly the same fully structured interview schedule (see Appendix II), translated into each local language, was used in each location. The actual interviewing was by local teams of undergraduate and postgraduate students who traced respondents via their addresses on the school registers, which in most cases were still their addresses in 1997. When individuals had moved locally they were traced and interviewed whenever possible. It was rarely difficult to discover where and why they had gone: either parents or, in their absence, neighbours would invariably know.

Ideally all the countries' samples would have been selected in exactly identical ways. This was in fact the original intention but the plans had to be modified according to what was possible in each location, and according to each local research team's capabilities and interests. In Ukraine the samples were from the 1988 end class lists in elementary schools. So the subjects were typically aged 24-25 in 1997. In Tbilisi the 1988 elementary school end class lists had disappeared during the reforms, and the sampling was from the 1991 secondary school end classes. As in Ukraine, the respondents were typically aged 24-25 when interviewed in 1997. However, the method of sample selection in Tbilisi excluded any young people who had failed to enter, or who did not complete their secondary school courses (a very small proportion of the age group in Tbilisi by the early 1990s). As in Ukraine, the Tbilisi schools from which the sample was drawn were divided equally between the inner and outer city. Half of the Tbilisi schools used for sample selection were general (academic) secondary schools, a quarter were schools with academic specialisms (in maths or foreign languages for example), and the remainder had professional or technical specialities, which reflected the distribution of the age group between different kinds of secondary schools in Tbilisi in the early 1990s.

In Armenia the samples were from the 1991 eighth grade classes (equivalent to the end classes in elementary schools in other CIS countries), from the three types of area described earlier (Yerevan, other towns, and rural districts). Within Yerevan the sample was recruited in equal numbers from schools in the inner and outer city. The Armenian method of sample selection meant that the respondents were typically aged 20–22 in 1997, roughly three years younger than in the other two countries. The Armenia sampling differed from the approach in the other countries on account of the local researchers' ability and, certainly in their view, the desirability of achieving a nationally representative sample and results that could be compared with earlier surveys in the country.

However, in all the countries the priority in sampling was not to make the respondents representative of the entire age group in their countries or cities. Rather, the top priority was to ensure that, in each of the locations, all the main socio-demographic groups – males and females; from different types of home backgrounds; with different experiences in education; and in the labour and housing markets – would be adequately represented, and we feel that this was achieved in all the locations.

Table AI.1 contains some basic information about the samples. As can be seen, in some of the locations there had been considerable movement away from the respondents' earlier addresses. This was to be expected, given that the class lists were 6–9 years old and that by 1997 the subjects had reached the life stage where they had already, or were contemplating, moving out of their parents' homes. As explained earlier, whenever individuals had moved within the same cities or villages or to other nearby locations, they were traced and interviewed if possible. In most instances where the subjects themselves were not

Table AI.1 The samples: main surveys

	Lviv	Donetsk	Armenia	Tbilisi
Not at address	32	91	215	30
Not available, refused	38	79	36	1
Interviewed	150	150	300	300
Totals	220	320	551	331

contacted it was possible to learn from a parent or neighbour where they had gone and why. Some of the movements had been into other towns, cities or villages. In some cases the young people had been returning to their family homes, which they had left earlier in their lives for educational or housing reasons. Some had returned with their parents to the families' original villages or towns. In most ex-communist countries the 1990s saw a reversal of the earlier population flow as urban dwellers who lost their jobs moved back to the country-side where, at a minimum, they knew that they would find food and possibly work on the farms or selling the produce. In other cases the young people had moved to towns or villages where their girlfriends or boyfriends were based. Some couples had moved to places where the housing was known to be cheaper or easier to obtain.

However, a considerable volume of migration had been out of the countries. The usual motives, from all accounts, had been to escape from the difficult economic conditions and discover better life chances or, among males, to avoid army service. In Armenia young males eligible for conscription were not at liberty to leave the country unless they had already served but large numbers were obviously circum-venting this. Out of the 215 original sample members who were not at their listed addresses in Armenia, 147 had left the country. In all three countries young males appeared keen to avoid army service if at all possible. They might have approved of conscription in principle but they were less keen on setting an example. Conditions in the national armies had not improved since independence. In Armenia young men had the additional incentive for avoiding service that at least part of their enlisted time would probably be spent in a war zone – Karabakh. Avoiding conscription was not the sole reason for out-migration. A main reason everywhere was to escape from the harsh conditions of life and, in the eyes of some young people, their countries' appalling prospects. However, army service was often one of the prompts. In Ukraine the sampling and fieldwork methods ensured that there were equal numbers of male and female respondents. Elsewhere a sex control was not applied and it is instructive that in both Tbilisi and Armenia 56 per cent of the respondents were females. This would have been due to the higher levels of male out-migration to avoid army service and perhaps also because males were the more independent and adventurous sex (see Chapter 4), plus the mortalities among young servicemen during the armed conflicts.

In Tbilisi there was only one refusal and very few of the subjects the fieldworkers tried to reach were no longer at their addresses or otherwise not available, but the Tbilisi non-contact rate was minimized by the manner in which the fieldworkers approached potential subjects. The sample was in fact constructed by 'snowballing' from the class lists. Each subject interviewed was asked to identify and sometimes to phone other names on the list by way of introduction and to arrange times and places for the interviews. Very few of the individuals who were approached in this way refused to take part and first appointments were nearly always kept. This method of fieldworking avoided most of the names who had moved away; hence the relatively – apparently amazingly – low non-contact rate in Tbilisi.

When young people were at a located address but were not interviewed, this was usually because they were 'not in' on successive visits. However, there were some outright refusals. These were most common in Ukraine, especially in Donetsk. This was despite or perhaps because of the special efforts that the local researchers made to achieve a high response. Letters explaining the purposes of the survey were sent to the Donetsk sample, giving the recipients the opportunity to decline to take part. The letters of introduction mentioned a 'recompense' and some individuals telephoned to ask for details. When told that it would be a ballpoint pen or a mini-photo album no one was excited and some decided not to bother.

Many of the young people were suspicious of the survey and its purposes except in Tbilisi where the fieldwork methods did not arouse the same suspicions as 'cold calling'. Elsewhere the young people were frequently suspicious. There had been no tradition of this kind of academic research in their countries. Many suspected that persons eligible for conscription, those working in the second economies or who had undeclared incomes might be identified to the authorities.

However, the fieldworkers were always locals of a similar age and were usually able to allay these suspicions. In Georgia and Armenia the Western links usually increased respondents' willingness to take part whereas in Ukraine, and especially in Donetsk, in so far as they made any difference, these links were a disadvantage. Ukraine was the country where there was most resentment of anything that resembled Western manipulation.

Unstructured interviews

Before designing the main surveys a series of very loosely structured interviews was conducted in 1995 and 1996 with selected groups of young people in Yerevan, Tbilisi, Donetsk and Lviv. The purpose of this work was to define the issues to be addressed in the main survey that was to follow rather than, as is often the case, to explore the significance and to add 'flesh and blood' or illustrative detail to pregathered quantitative data. A total of 321 interviews were conducted. This may seem a large number for exploratory, open-ended interviews, but the fieldwork was spread across four cities, in each of which several groups of young people were targeted (see Table AI.2). Usually a fieldworker, typically a postgraduate student, interviewed 10–20 individuals in a set target group, then interpreted and wrote up the findings.

Table AI.2 The respondents: qualitative interviews

	Armenia	Georgia	Ukraine	Total
Students	45	—	40	85
Postgraduates	19	—	—	19
Artists	—	20	—	20
Workers	20	—	39	59
Self-employed	—	15	—	15
Peasants	18	—	—	18
Unemployed	20	—	—	20
Political activists	—	15	20	35
War veterans or servicemen	—	15	—	15
Refugees	—	20	—	20
Housewives	—	15	—	15
Totals	122	100	99	321

198 *Surviving Post-communism*

The groups who were studied say much about conditions in the three countries in the 1990s. There were undergraduate and postgraduate students, workers, peasants and the unemployed, but also political activists, artists, military servicemen and veterans, war refugees and housewives. All these interviews were wide-ranging and explored the respondents' experiences of family life, in education, of earning and spending money, of military affairs, religion, politics and day-to-day leisure activities.

The self-employed

This was a separately funded study, reported in detail elsewhere (see Roberts *et al.*, 1998a). Fifty self-employed young people were interviewed in each of the three CIS countries during 1996. None was merely an opportunistic trader. They all had registered businesses and were self-employed as their main occupations and had been for the greater part of the working lives. The samples were selected by quota in Lviv, Donetsk, Tbilisi and Yerevan so that all the main business sectors were represented.

Nearly all the business people had started out with very modest assets. A typical route into business had in fact been by street trading. However, by the mid-1990s some of the young people had businesses (almost always partnerships) with annual turnovers in excess of $2 million.

In the qualitative fieldwork (described above) and in the surveys of the self-employed, some joint interviewing was conducted by pairs of local and Western investigators. This method of working in cross-national pairs had been pioneered earlier in an Anglo-German comparative study (see Bynner and Roberts, 1991; Evans and Heinz, 1994). These and the other qualitative interviews were usually conducted in the respondents' own homes, businesses or other places of work. When visited in their homes by cross-national pairs of fieldworkers, the subjects and their families were invariably liberal with their hospitality. This has been the case wherever we have gone in the new East. The interviews have never been on doorsteps. We have always been invited in and served with various combinations of tea, coffee, chocolates, biscuits, cooked meals, brandy and other local beverages.

Joint interviewing can be extremely effective. People will often explain things more carefully, in much greater detail, to a naive foreigner than would be considered necessary, or maybe advisable, if addressing just another local.

We must explain, indeed stress, at this point that except in the main survey in Armenia (the most urbanized of the three CIS countries), nearly all the young people we studied were living in major cities. So our account of young people experiencing post-communism relates basically to experiences in major urban areas. In the 1980s only 4 per cent of the Armenian workforce was in agriculture, but in Ukraine it was 19 per cent and in Georgia 27 per cent (Europa Publications, 1994). Our respondents will have had better educational opportunities, and better chances of obtaining white-collar and service sector jobs than young people in rural districts who, as compensation, may have found it easier to fall back into traditional ways of life.

We must also point out that all our information is from young people who had been educated in and had remained in the countries and usually in the cities where most of our fieldwork was based. Some who had returned to family homes in the nearby countryside, with their parents or partners or to live with other relatives, were traced and interviewed, but we made no attempt to follow up young people who had left their countries (a very significant number, especially in Georgia and Armenia).

The Polish study

This is another project that has been fully reported elsewhere (Roberts and Jung, 1995). It involved interviews or self-completed questionnaires by a total of 1800 young people, equally split between three regions – Gdańsk, Katowice and Suwałki. There were also some unstructured follow-up interviews with cross-national pairs of interviewers. In the formal surveys half of the samples were in their secondary school end classes in 1993 at the time of the fieldwork, while the remainder had been in the same classes four years previously and were typically aged 22–24 when the research was conducted. The research methods used later, in the CIS countries, including the interview schedules, were developed from those used in Poland, and many identical questions were included in both enquiries.

Eastern and Central Europe studies

These were conducted in 1997, at the same time as the main CIS
survey, but in Eastern and Central Europe the samples of young people
were from two specific career groups: the young unemployed (800 in
total) and the young self-employed (400). Once again, the enquiries
have been reported fully elsewhere (Roberts, 1998; Roberts *et al.*,
1998b). The samples from both career groups were aged up to 30 and
were equally distributed across two regions, one relatively buoyant and
the other relatively depressed economically, in four Eastern and Central
European countries: Bulgaria, Hungary, Poland and Slovakia. Some of
the questions addressed to the young unemployed and the young self-
employed in these countries were identical to those used in Armenia,
Georgia and Ukraine, thus, alongside the Poland 1993 evidence,
creating a set of 'benchmarks'.

The ESRC 16–19 Initiative

The basic methods used and some questions included in the interview
and questionnaire enquiries in all the Eastern and Central Europe and
CIS countries were developed from the research conducted in the Economic and Social Research Council (ESRC) 16–19 Initiative, a longitudinal 1987–9 study of representative samples of young people from
four areas: Kirkcaldy, Liverpool, Sheffield and Swindon (see Banks *et
al.*, 1992). Thus once again it has been possible to use some of the
findings as benchmarks to assess, for example, the leisure opportunities
and activities and the political orientations of the CIS samples in 1997.

WORKING TOGETHER

The actual information gathering in all the above projects, with the
exception of the joint interviews, was by teams based in the localities.
Undergraduate and postgraduate students obtained school registers,
when necessary, selected samples, and went out and did the interviews.
The only exceptions were in Poland, where survey organizations were
used – the Government Social Survey in 1993 and the Polish Sociological Association in 1997.

The initial interpretation of the findings was always by the local researchers. The information from qualitative interviews had to be interpreted locally because it was always in the local language; and local knowledge is usually needed in order to make sense of quantitative findings.

Interview schedules and questionnaires, when these were to be used in more than one region or country, had to be designed collaboratively so as to ensure that everything was standardized in ways that remained sensitive to local particularities. The same applied with methods of sampling.

Electronic data sets were always prepared, and initially analysed, in the countries where the information was collected. In the 1993 Polish enquiry this was done in Warsaw. In the 1997 Eastern and Central Europe studies this was done in Plovdiv (Bulgaria). In the case of the 1997 main surveys in the CIS countries the data set was prepared in Donetsk. The actual questionnaires from Armenia were sent by military mail and arrived swiftly and safely. The Tbilisi data set was sent on disk and was delayed for three months in the Ukraine customs. The real problem here was probably our reluctance to use the research budget to bribe a quicker release. The complete data sets from all the countries involved in a project were always distributed to all the partners, who were then able to undertake their own analyses and reach their own conclusions.

Throughout all the research projects there were regular meetings of all the researchers from the relevant Eastern and Western countries. These meetings agreed methods of data collection and so on and, later, how the analytical work and initial report writing should be divided. Eventually the meetings had to agree the main conclusions that should be drawn from the projects.

This book is written by the Western collaborators, the lead author having co-ordinated all the projects mentioned above. The text is written primarily for a Western readership, to explain the new East. The Western authors are confident that their arguments and interpretations are sound, partly because they accord with our first-hand experience but mainly because we have been able to draw on the interpretations and advice and have had the benefit of criticisms from our Eastern collaborators.

EXPERIENCING POST-COMMUNISM FIRST-HAND

In conducting the research described above, the Western participants
have gained much first-hand experience of post-communism, but
always and only as visitors. We cannot claim personal familiarity with
what post-communism is like when it is for real, and possibly for life.

We have experienced hotels still operating in the classic Soviet style
with corridor supervisors who check rooms and their contents before
guests are allowed to depart. We have experienced hotels taking
advantage of the new market economies by charging $200 a night,
having decided, apparently, that Westerners can afford, expect and
possibly even like to pay that amount. It has not taken for long for
certain sections of the new East to adopt Third-to-First World perspec-
tives. We have also experienced hotels that have decided that their
prospects depend on keen prices and good value. By far the best deals
have been in Central Europe rather than further East where labour costs
are lower. Chapter 2 explains how this has been possible.

We are now seasoned Soviet-style air travellers. It is simply different. Passengers carry luggage aboard and store it in compartments at
the front or rear of the aircraft. Seating is usually open-plan – pick one
for yourself. The seat belts may not work. There is unlikely to be a life-
jacket under the seat or an oxygen mask that might descend. When did
you last need one?

We have also experienced rail and inter-country bus travel in the
CIS: Tbilisi to Yerevan by bus, from 6 to 8 hours, depending on the
length of border delays, at a cost of $8. The Westerners were the only
passengers to assume that there would be refreshment and toilet stops.

We have found that the taxi regimes at airports and rail stations are
quite reliable guides to the state of the local market economies. In
Tbilisi taxi drivers scuffle for a Western fare. The windscreens of many
of the taxis are fractured: a sign of wild and free capitalism. By the
mid-1990s the Central European countries had licensed taxis with
charges per kilometre on display. Western businesses had already taken
their own practices into these countries, the practices had been made
official and were being enforced. In other places the taxi trade, like
much else, is still organized by local 'mafia' who have 'bought' a
monopoly franchise. In much of the CIS valuable goods are still transported in (privately) armed convoys.

We have been caught up in political action. We have been delayed by road blockades in Bulgaria. In Ukraine, Georgia and Armenia by the mid-1990s there were mere vestiges of the earlier political mobilization. There were communist and nationalist marches with hundreds rather than thousands of participants. Groups of 10–30 males, talking politics (or anything else) in the squares of Tbilisi, Lviv and elsewhere had become more typical.

Western visitors, whether tourists or researchers, must glimpse but they can never really share the locals' problems. A confusion over arrival times left us unmet at the bus station on our very first visit to Yerevan. An attempt to instruct a taxi driver to head for the best hotel may have been unsuccessful, or he may have decided that we would be more suited to or that he would receive more commission from what turned out to be the third-best hotel. The price was fine, $23, and the facilities were acceptable except that there was no running water. The management was pleased to have paying customers, the corridor lady brewed coffee and the chef appeared to have been summoned specially to prepare breakfast the next morning. Ungraciously we transferred to the second-best hotel, $30, with continuous running water and hot water for two hours each morning and evening. The very best hotel, $80, had constant hot water. However, all these hotels had constant electricity (from their own generators). Houses in Yerevan at that time were mostly water-less and power-less for most of each day and night. The local population had endured these conditions for four years, with no end in sight. Conditions were not quite as difficult, but were not basically different, in Tbilisi, Donetsk and Lviv. Western-linked research projects have recorded all this and, together with the larger number of aid projects, have shielded their staff from local conditions, but without up to now making much impact.

Appendix II: Interview Schedule

YOUR LIFE OVER THE PAST SIX YEARS AND YOUR OPINIONS

We would like to know a little about you. Please give us some details about yourself. To answer most of the questions all you need to do is to tick one box, and sometimes you are asked to tick more than one box. A few questions ask you to write in your answer.

Please write in →

1. How old are you?

.........years

2. Are you male or female?

Male	1
Female	2

3. What is your region?

Donetsk	1
Tbilisi	2
Yerevan	3

4. What is your nationality?

Armenian	1
Georgian	2
Russian	3
Ukrainian	4
Other	5

We should like to know what you have been doing over the past 6 years.
For each year please tick one box to let us know what you were doing for most or all of that year.

	5. 1991	6. 1992	7. 1993	8. 1994	9. 1995	10. 1996	11. 1997 Jan.– June	12. NOW
In education	1	1	1	1	1	1	1	1
In a full-time job (30 hours a week or longer) with an employer	2	2	2	2	2	2	2	2
Working part-time for someone else	3	3	3	3	3	3	3	3
Self-employed	4	4	4	4	4	4	4	4
Out of work	5	5	5	5	5	5	5	5
National service	6	6	6	6	6	6	6	6
Something else (please tell us what this was in the space below)➧	7	7	7	7	7	7	7	7

A. EDUCATION

Please tell us about the main post-elementary school that you attended.

13. What type of school was it?

Vocational course	1
Vocational school	2
Secondary professional	3
Lycée	4

14. At your secondary school were you prepared for a particular occupation?

Yes	1
No	2

if YES, please tell us the occupation →

15. Was your school attached to a particular enterprise?

Yes	1	→ 16
No	2	→ 17

16. If so, did the enterprise offer you a job on completing your secondary school course?

No	1
Yes, took the job	2
Yes, did not take the job	3

17. Have you ever attended a University, Polytechnic or College of Higher Education?

Yes	1	→ 18
No	2	→ 24

If YES, please tell us the name of the institution you first attended→		

18. Was this you first choice institution?

| Yes | 1 |
| No | 2 |

19. Did you attend full-time or part-time?

| Full-time | 1 |
| Part-time | 2 |

20 Did you pay fees, or was your education free?

| Paid fees | 1 |
| Education was free | 2 |

21. Did you receive a maintenance grant?

| Yes | 1 |
| No | 2 |

22. Did you complete the course?

| Yes | 1 |
| No | 2 |

23. Have you been on another higher education course?

| Yes | 1 |
| No | 2 |

If YES, what was your specialization? →		

24. Overall, does your educational background correspond with your present / most recent job?

Wholly	1
Partly	2
Not at all	3

[There is no question 25]

207

B. YOUR JOBS

Please tell us about your experiences of paid work.

26.	How many paid jobs have you ever had?	Please write in →	
27.	How many jobs have you applied for in the last year?	Please write in →	
28.	Have you ever been made redundant?	Yes	1
		No	2
29.	Have you ever been sacked from a job for any other reason?	Yes	1
		No	2
30.	Have you ever left a job of your own accord?	Yes	1
		No	2
31.	Have you ever had a job in a state enterprise or administration?	Yes	1
		No	2
32.	Have you ever had a job in a private business?	Yes	1
		No	2
33.	Have you ever worked on your own account?	Yes	1
		No	2
34.	Have you ever done paid or unpaid work in a family business or farm?	Yes	1
		No	2

[There is no question 35]

208

Please tell us about your first main job after you left school or university.

Please tell us what this job was like during the first few months that you did it.

		Please write in →

36. How many hours did you work per week?

37. Which of the following best describes this job?

Self-employed	1
Worked for a family business	2
Worked for a state enterprise or administration	3
Worked for a co-operative	4
Worked for a private enterprise with less than 5 employees	5
Worked for a medium-sized private enterprise with 5–50 employees	6
Worked for a large private enterprise with over 50 employees	7

38. Was there a difference between your official pay and your actual pay?

Yes	1
No	2

39. In which of these groups would you classify this job?

Managerial	1
Intellectual, artistic, liberal profession	2
Clerical, office job	3
Manual work	4
Farm work	5

40. How heavy was your workload?

Very heavy	1
About right	2
Light	3

Now, please can you tell us about your present or most recent job. If you have more than one job at present, tell us about your main job.

	Please write in ➔

41. How many hours do you work per week?

42. Which of the following best describes this job?

Self-employed	1
Working for a family business	2
Working for a state enterprise or administration	3
Working for a co-operative	4
Working for a private enterprise with less than 5 employees	5
Working for a medium-sized private enterprise with 5–50 employees	6
Working for a large private enterprise with over 50 employees	7

43. Is there a difference between your official pay and your actual pay?

Yes	1
No	2

44. In which of these groups would you classify this job?

Managerial	1
Intellectual, artistic, liberal profession	2
Clerical, office job	3
Manual work	4
Farm work	5

45. How heavy is your workload?

Very heavy	1
About right	2
Light	3

46. Have you ever been unemployed for a month or more?

Yes	1 ➔ 47
No	2 ➔ 50

If YES, on the last occasion ...

47. ... did you register at the Labour Office?

Yes 1
No 2

48. ... did you receive any benefit?

Yes 1
No 2

49. ... did you earn any money during this period of unemployment?

Yes 1
No 2

C. YOUR MONEY

Please tell us how much you currently receive per month from the following sources:

	Amount per month	
	Local currency	US $
50. Earnings from main job (including any overtime or bonuses that you usually receive) <u>after</u> tax and social security deductions.		
51. Earnings from any other job		
52. Social security payments (e.g. unemployment benefit)		
53. Education grant or bursary		
54. Income from parents or other family members		
55. Any other sources, please write in ➜		
56. TOTAL		

Please tell us how much you spend in an average month on the following:

	Amount per month	
	Local currency	US $
57. Board and lodging payments to parents (if living with parents)		
58. Rent and living costs (gas, electricity, telephone, meals at home) if you live in your own place		
59. Travel to work		
60. Meals taken at work (lunch, snacks etc.)		
61. Savings and repayments of loans		
62. Things for yourself (such as cigarettes, going out, drinks, videos, records, magazines, clothes)		
63. Anything else, please write in ➜		
64. TOTAL		

[There are no questions 65–69]

213

D. YOUR PLANS FOR THE FUTURE

Thinking about the future, what do you expect to be doing in five years' time?

70. In five years time, I expect to be ...

in full-time education	1
in a full-time job (over 30 hours a week)	2
in a part-time job	3
self-employed	4
unemployed	5
something else	6

If you answered 'something else' please say what this is ➜

How likely are you to want to move out of this area to get a job in the future?

	Definitely	Very likely	Quite likely	Not very likely	Not at all likely
71. ... migrate within this country	1	2	3	4	5
72. ... go out of this country	1	2	3	4	5

73. How would you advise a friend who was wondering whether to emigrate?

Advise the friend to stay	1
Advise the friend to think carefully	2
Advise the friend to go ahead and leave	3

How would you rate the social status or prestige of the following occupations in your country?

	Very low	Low	Neither low nor high	High	Very high
74. School-teacher	1	2	3	4	5
75. Engineer	1	2	3	4	5
76. Scientist	1	2	3	4	5
77. Manager	1	2	3	4	5
78. Accountant	1	2	3	4	5
79. Businessman	1	2	3	4	5
80. Lawyer	1	2	3	4	5
81. Doctor	1	2	3	4	5
82. Army officer	1	2	3	4	5
83. Politician	1	2	3	4	5
84. Minister of religion	1	2	3	4	5

How important are the following possible life goals to you?

	Not at all important	Unimportant	Neither unimportant nor important	Important	Very important
85. Material security	1	2	3	4	5
86. Being happy	1	2	3	4	5
87. Serving my country	1	2	3	4	5
88. Having status and public recognition	1	2	3	4	5
89. Having a strong family	1	2	3	4	5
90. Becoming rich	1	2	3	4	5

[There are no questions 91–93]

E. YOUR SPARE TIME

94. Have you taken a holiday away from home in the past 12 months? Do NOT include weekends away or short visits of 2 or 3 days.

None	1
One	2
Two	3
Three or more	4

Which of the following do you have the use of if you want?

	Yes	No
95. Car	1	2
96. Personal computer	1	2
97. Video recorder	1	2
98. Room of your own	1	2
99. Satellite dish	1	2

[There is no question 100]

Please indicate how often you have done or gone to each of the following in the past year by ticking one box for each activity...

	Never	Less than once a month	1–3 times a month	1–2 times a week	3–6 times a week	Every day
101. Played sports	1	2	3	4	5	6
102. Visited pubs, cafés, restaurants	1	2	3	4	5	6
103. Gone to parties, dances, discos	1	2	3	4	5	6
104. Gone to cinema, theatres, concerts	1	2	3	4	5	6
105. Gone to watch sports (not on TV)	1	2	3	4	5	6
106. Smoked cigarettes	1	2	3	4	5	6
107. Drunk alcoholic drinks	1	2	3	4	5	6
108. Attended church services	1	2	3	4	5	6

Do you belong to.....

109. ... a trade union? Yes 1 / No 2

110. ... a political party or group? Yes 1 / No 2

111. ... a recreational club or organization? Yes 1 / No 2

112. During the past year, how often have you been to a political meeting, rally or demonstration, etc.?

Not at all	1
Once	2
Several times	3
More often	4

Have you ever been to another country to...

	Yes	No
113. ...visit relatives or friends	1	2
114. ...earn money	1	2
115. ...have a holiday, some leisure, tourism etc.	1	2

Which of the following countries have you visited?

	Yes	No
116. A West European country	1	2
117. A country of the former USSR	1	2
118. An East European country	1	2
119. North America	1	2
120. Anywhere else	1	2

217

F. YOUR ACTIVITIES AND VIEWS

People have different opinions about many things. Here is a list of some opinions. You will probably agree with some of them and disagree with others. Sometimes you may agree strongly and at other times you may disagree strongly. Now and then you may be uncertain whether you agree or disagree. Please read each opinion and put a tick in the box which is right for you.

	Strongly agree	Agree	Uncertain	Disagree	Strongly disagree
121. It is better to work for a private company than for a state firm	1	2	3	4	5
122. I would rather be employed by a large company than work on my own account	1	2	3	4	5
123. This country's enterprises should not be sold to foreign investors	1	2	3	4	5
124. I would be prepared to fight in order to maintain my country's independence	1	2	3	4	5
125. It is important to be well educated and fully qualified for one's profession	1	2	3	4	5
126. I would like to go to work in the West	1	2	3	4	5
127. Compulsory military service for men should continue	1	2	3	4	5

	Strongly agree	Agree	Uncertain	Disagree	Strongly disagree
128. Since the reforms life has become much more difficult	1	2	3	4	5
129. Important industries such as gas and electricity should remain in the public sector	1	2	3	4	5
130. Our current problems show that the reforms were a mistake	1	2	3	4	5
131. Married women with young children should stay at home and be full-time housewives	1	2	3	4	5
132. Men and women should do equal amounts of housework	1	2	3	4	5
133. It makes little difference which politicians are in power	1	2	3	4	5
134. Life here is better since the reforms	1	2	3	4	5
135. Politicians are more interested in gaining power for themselves than the good of the country	1	2	3	4	5
136. I would rather work for the public sector than for a private employer	1	2	3	4	5

219

	Strongly agree	Agree	Uncertain	Disagree	Strongly disagree
137. Poor people have only themselves to blame for their poverty	1	2	3	4	5
138. In this country being rich means hard work	1	2	3	4	5
139. I would like to have a business of my own	1	2	3	4	5

What are your views on sex before marriage for …

	Desirable	Acceptable	Usually unacceptable	Always undesirable
140. … men	1	2	3	4
141. … women	1	2	3	4

142. If there were a general election tomorrow and you were able to vote, which political party do you think you would be most likely to support?

Please write in name of party ➜

Not sure	2
Would not vote	3

143. How interested are you in politics?

Very interested	1
Quite interested	2
Not very interested	3
Not at all interested	4

144. How do you feel about the disintegration of the Soviet Union?

Very good	1
Mixed feelings	2
Too many disadvantages	3
Don't know	4

Would you like your country to develop closer ties with ...

	Yes	Not sure	No	Don't know
145. ... Russia	1	2	3	8
146. ... The West	1	2	3	8
147. ... Asia Minor	1	2	3	8

148. On balance, would you prefer...

...a free market economy	1
...the old system	2

149. What do you think should be done about nuclear generating plants which are dangerous due to age and inadequate maintenance?

They should be shut down immediately	1
They should be phased out as soon as possible	2
They should be kept going because we need power and there are other more pressing problems	3

150. Who should make key decisions for the household?

The husband	1
The wife	2
Both husband and wife together	3
The whole family	4

G. YOU AND YOUR HOME

Finally, we would like to ask you a few questions about the people with whom you share a home – that is, all those, whether family or friends, who live with you.

151. How many people are living in your home now, including yourself?

Please write in → [ ]

Which of the following people does this include?

	Yes	No
152. Father / stepfather	1	2
153. Mother / stepmother	1	2
154. Grandparent(s)	1	2
155. Brother / sister	1	2
156. Spouse / cohabitee	1	2
157. Another relative(s)	1	2
158. Own children	1	2
159. Other children	1	2
160. Someone else	1	2

Now, please could you tell us a little about your parents.

161. What was their highest education?

	Your mother	Your father
Less than elementary school	1	1
Elementary school	2	2
Vocational school	3	3

High school, lycée, gymnasium	4
College	5
University	6

162. At present is she / he…

	Your mother	Your father
Employed?	1	1
Unemployed?	2	2
Retired?	3	3
Deceased?	4	4

163. What is / was their usual occupation?

	Your mother	Your father
Managerial	1	1
Intellectual / liberal profession	2	2
Clerical / office job	3	3
Manual work	4	4
Farmer	5	5

164. Which of the following best describes your home?

Parents' or step-parents' house / flat	1
Student accommodation	2
Living in home of friends or relatives	3
My own house / flat (rented or owned)	4
Lodgings / digs	5

Other, please write in →

165. Is there anywhere in your home town where you would feel threatened during the day? And what about at night? Please tick one box for the day, and one for the night.

	A. During the day		B. At night	
	Yes	No	Yes	No
166. In the city centre	1	2	1	2
167. Where I live	1	2	1	2
168. Somewhere else, please write in below ↓	1	2	1	2
	1	2	1	2

Now that you have completed the questionnaire, is there anything else that you would like to tell us? We would be most interested to read what you have to say.
Please write down anything you want to say, and continue overleaf if you need more room.

THANK YOU VERY MUCH FOR COMPLETING THIS QUESTIONNAIRE.

224

Bibliography

Adibekian, A. (1985), *Socio-political Orientation of Armenian Graduates*, Independent Sociological Centre, Yerevan.

—— (1991), *Political Priorities in Independent Conditions*, Independent Sociological Centre, Yerevan.

—— (1992), *The New Social Stratification and Social Mobility*, Independent Sociological Centre, Yerevan.

—— (1995), *Social Integration in the Modern Period*, Independent Sociological Centre, Yerevan.

Aleshonok, S. (1998), 'Russian youth: searching for new channels of influence in society', paper presented at *International Sociological Association Congress*, Montreal.

Ashwin, S. (1996), 'Forms of collectivity in a non-monetary society', *Sociology*, 30, 21–39.

Banks, M., I. Bates, G. Breakwell, J. Bynner, N. Emler, L. Jamieson and K. Roberts (1992), *Careers and Identities*, Open University Press, Milton Keynes.

Bauman, Z. (1992), *Intimations of Postmodernity*, Routledge, London.

Bilsen, V. and J. Konings (1996), *Job Creation, Job Destruction and the Growth of Newly Established Firms in Transition Economies: Evidence from Bulgaria, Hungary and Romania*, Working Paper 59/1996, Leuven Institute for Central and East European Studies, Catholic University of Leuven.

Bogomolova, T. (1998), 'Income mobility in Russia in the mid-1990s', paper presented at *International Sociological Association Congress*, Montreal.

Bouin, O. (1996), 'Enterprise restructuring at different stages of ownership transformation: the Czech Republic and Poland', *ACE Quarterly*, 5, 9–11.

Bridger, S., R. Kay and K. Pinnick (1996), *No More Heroines? Russia, Women and the Market*, Routledge, London.

Brown, P. (1987), *Schooling Ordinary Kids*, Tavistock Press, London.

Bruno, M. (1996), 'Employment strategies and the formation of new identities in the service sector in Moscow', in H. Pilkington (ed.), *Gender, Generation and Identity in Contemporary Russia*, Routledge, London.

Bynner, J. and K. Roberts (1991), *Youth and Work*, Anglo-German Foundation, London.

Bystrova, A. (1998), 'The fate of party functionaries in post-Soviet Russia', in M. Kiviner (ed.), *The Kalamari Union: Middle Class in East and West*, Ashgate, Aldershot.

Clarke, S. (1993), 'Popular attitudes to the transition to a market economy in the Soviet Union on the eve of reform', *Sociological Review*, 41, 619–52.

—— (ed.) (1995), *Management and Industry in Russia: Formal and Informal Relations in the Period of Transition*, Ashgate, Aldershot.

Council of Europe (1996), *Cultural Policy in the Russian Federation*, Culture Committee, Strasbourg.

Dementieva, I. (1998), 'The family and professional orientations of teenagers in the changing Russian society', paper presented to *International Sociological Association Congress*, Montreal.

Eberwein, W. and J. Tholen (1997), *Market or Mafia: Russian Managers on the Difficult Road to an Open Society*, Ashgate, Aldershot.

Europa Publications (1994), *Eastern Europe and the Commonwealth of Independent States 1994*, Europa Publications, London.

Evans, K. and W.R. Heinz (eds) (1994), *Becoming Adults in England and Germany*, Anglo-German Foundation, London.

Eygendaal, W. (1992), 'The black heart: a qualitative study of the death metal culture in The Netherlands', paper presented to conference on *Internationalisation and Leisure Research*, Tilburg.

Fischer, M.M.J. and S. Grigorian (1993), 'Six to eight characters in search of Armenian civil society amidst the carnivalisation of history', in G.E. Marcus (ed.), *Perilous States*, University of Chicago Press, Chicago.

Frantisek, D.K. (1998), 'Modernisation and the lifestyles: lifestyle of the Czech adolescents', paper presented at *International Sociological Association Congress*, Montreal.

Furlong, A. and F. Cartmel (1997), *Young People and Social Change*, Open University Press, Buckingham.

Gachechiladze, R. (1995), *The New Georgia*, UCL Press, London.

Gerber, T.P. and M. Hout (1995), 'Educational stratification in Russia during the Soviet period', *American Journal of Sociology*, 101, 611–60.

—— (1998), 'More shock than therapy: market transition, employment and income in Russia, 1991–1995', *American Journal of Sociology*, 104, 1–50.

Gros, D. (1997), 'A comparative study of the causes of output decline in transition economies', *ACE Quarterly*, 9, 15–16.

Grunert, H. and B. Lutz (1996), 'A double process of destabilisation in post-socialist societies: the case of Germany', paper presented to workshop of the *European Science Foundation Scientific Network on Transitions in Youth*, La Ciotat.

Gvozdeva, G.P. (1994), 'Changes in free time utilisation by rural residents in West Siberia under the ongoing economic reform', paper presented to *International Sociological Association* conference, Bielefeld.

Holmes, L. (1993), *The End of Communist Power: Anti-corruption Campaigns and the Legtimation Crisis*, Polity Press, Cambridge.

Hutson, S. and W. Cheung (1991), 'Saturday jobs: sixth formers in the labour market and the family', in C. Marsh and S. Arber (eds), *Family and Household: Division and Change*, Macmillan, London.

International Labour Office (1995), *The Ukrainian Challenge*, Central European University Press, Budapest.

Isakova, N. (1997), 'Small business and foreign aid in Ukraine', paper presented to *Third International Conference on SME Development Policy in Transition Economies*, Wolverhampton.

Jackson, M. (1996), *Labour Markets and Income Maintenance: A Study of Transition*, Working Paper 58/1996, Leuven Institute for Central and East European Studies, University of Leuven.

Jung, B. (1994), 'For what leisure? The role of culture and recreation in post-communist Poland', *Leisure Studies*, 13, 1–15.

—— (1996), 'Current evidence on leisure participation in Poland', in G. Cushman, A.J. Veal and Z. Zuzanek (eds), *World Leisure Participation: Free Time in the Global Village*, CAB International, Wallingford.

—— (1997), 'Initial analysis of the lifestyle of young unemployed and young self-employed in Bulgaria, Hungary, Poland and Slovakia', in L. Machacek and K. Roberts (eds), *Youth Unemployment and*

Self-employment in East–Central Europe, Slovak Academy of Sciences, Bratislava.

Kharchenko, I.I. (1998), 'High school students plan their future: changes in the 1990s in Western Siberia', paper presented at *International Sociological Association Congress*, Montreal.

Kivinen, M. (1998), 'Introduction: class analysis in East and West', in M. Kivinen (ed.), *The Kalamari Union: Middle Class in East and West*, Ashgate, Aldershot, ix–xxiii.

Kolarska-Bobinska, L. (1994), 'Social interests and their representation: Poland in transition', *British Journal of Sociology*, 45, 109–26.

Konietzka, D. and H. Solga (1995), 'Two certified societies? The regulation of entry in the labour market in East and West Germany', paper presented to workshop on *Transitions in Youth: Comparisons over Time and across Countries*, Oostvoorne, The Netherlands.

Kovaleva, E. (1997), 'Institutionalisation of shadow economy and politics in Ukraine', in Z. Sevic and G. Wright (eds), *Transition in Central and Eastern Europe*, vol. 1, YASF/Student Cultural Centre, Belgrade.

Kurzynowski, A. (1997), 'Patterns of mothers' behaviour towards work after child birth', unpublished paper, Warsaw School of Economics.

Magun, V.S. (1996), 'From 1985 to 1995: revolution of youth aspirations and life strategies' [in Russian], *Sotsiologicheskii zhurnal*, 3/4, 29–48.

Marshall, G. (1996), 'Was communism good for social justice? A comparative analysis of the two Germanies', *British Journal of Sociology*, 47, 397–420.

Meek, J. (1998), 'Brown envelopes for young Russians', *Guardian*, 17 March, 11.

Meshkova, E. (1998), 'Education in restructuring Russia: history and tendencies', paper presented at *International Sociological Association Congress*, Montreal.

Mestrovic, S.G. (1994), *The Balkanisation of the West: The Confluence of Postcommunism and Postmodernism*, Routledge, London.

Michailova, S. and A. Mills (1998), 'Processual dynamics or organisational transformation in conditions of continuous disequilibrium', paper presented in *14th EGOS Colloqium*, Maastricht.

Misztal, B.A. (1993), 'Understanding political change in Eastern Europe: a sociological perspective', *Sociology*, 27, 451–70.

Oljasz, T. (1998), 'Crime busters', *Warsaw Voice*, 6 December, 16–17.

Omel'chenko, E. (1996), 'Young women in provincial gang culture: a case study of Ul'ianovsk', in H. Pilkington (ed.), *Gender, Generation and Identity in Contemporary Russia*, Routledge, London.

Piirainen, T. (1998), 'From status to class: the emergence of a class society in Russia', in M. Kivinen (ed.), *The Kalamari Union: Middle Class in East and West*, Ashgate, Aldershot, 314–41.

Pilkington, H. (1994), *Russia's Youth and its Culture*, Routledge, London.

—— (1996), 'Farewell to the tuscova: masculinities and femininities on the Moscow youth scene', in H. Pilkington (ed.), *Gender, Generation and Identity in Contemporary Russia*, Routledge, London.

Poretzkina, E. and T. Jyrkinen-Pakkasvirta (1995), 'Reconstruction of consumption patterns of St Petersburg families', paper presented to *Second Conference of the European Sociological Association*, Budapest.

Pye, R.B.K. (1998), 'From West to East: AGB Asea Brown Boveri in Central and Eastern Europe and the former Soviet Union', paper presented to Fourth Annual CREEB Conference, *Convergence or Divergence: Aspirations and Reality in Central and Eastern Europe and Russia*, Buckinghamshire Business School.

Riordan, J. (1988), 'Problems of leisure and glasnost', *Leisure Studies*, 7, 173–85.

Roberts, K. (1995), *Youth and Employment in Modern Britain*, Oxford University Press, Oxford.

—— (1996), 'Young people, schools, sport and government policies', *Sport, Education and Society*, 1, 47–57.

—— (1997), 'Same activities, different meanings: British youth cultures in the 1990s', *Leisure Studies*, 16, 1–15.

—— (1998), 'The quality jobs deficit in East–Central Europe: a prototypical case of modern youth unemployment', paper presented to International Labour Markets conference on *Skilling the Unskilled: Achievements and Under-achievements in Education and Training,* Aberdeen.

—— and B. Jung (1995), *Poland's First Post-communist Generation,* Avebury, Aldershot.

—— and T. Szumlicz (1995), 'Education and school-to-work transitions in post-communist Poland', *British Journal of Education and Work,* 8, 54–74.

——, A. Kurzunowski, T. Szumlicz and B. Jung (1997), 'Employers' workforce formation practices, young people's employment opportunities and labour market behaviour in post-communist Poland', *Communist Economies and Economic Transformation,* 9, 87–98.

——, C. Campbell and A. Furlong. (1990), 'Class and gender divisions among young adults at leisure', in C. Wallace and M. Cross (eds), *Youth in Transition,* Falmer Press, London.

——, A. Adibekian, G. Nemiria and L. Tarkhnishvili (1998a), 'Traders and mafiosi: the young self-employed in Armenia, Georgia and Ukraine', *Journal of Youth Studies,* 1, 259–78.

——, C. Fagan, K. Foti, S. Kovatcheva, B. Jung, A. Kurzynowski, T. Szumlicz, L. Machacek and J. Tholen (1998b), 'The young self-employed in East–Central Europe', in V. Edwards (ed.), *Convergence or Divergence: Aspirations and Reality in Central and Eastern Europe and Russia,* Buckinghamshire Chilterns University College, 364–94.

Ruchkin, B.A. (1998), 'The youth as a strategic resource for the development of Russia in the XXI century', paper presented at *International Sociological Association Congress,* Montreal.

Saar, E. and J. Helemae (1998), 'Intergenerational mobility and middle class formation in Estonia', in M. Kivinen (ed.), *The Kalamari Union: Middle Class in East and West,* Ashgate, Aldershot, 149–75.

Saarnit, J. (1998), 'Current trends in post-communist value shift in Estonia', paper presented at *International Sociological Association Congress,* Montreal.

Semenova, V. (1998), 'On transition to the middle class: professional strategies of young intellectuals in Russia', in M. Kivinen (ed.), *The Kalamari Union: Middle Class in East and West,* Ashgate, Aldershot, 220–9.

Sharkey, A. (1997), 'The land of the free', *Weekend Guardian,* 22 November, 14–25.

Siegelbaum, L.H. and D.J. Walkowitz (eds) (1995), *Workers of the Donbass Speak: Survival and Identity in the New Ukraine, 1989–1992*, State University of New York Press, Albany.

Sik, E. (1988), 'Reciprocal exchange of labour in Hungary', in R.E. Pahl (ed.), *On Work*, Basil Blackwell, Oxford.

Silbereisen, R.K., L.A. Vaskovics and J. Zinneker (eds) (1996), *Youth in the Reunited Germany*, Leske and Budrich, Opladen.

Slomczynski, K.M. (1998), 'Formation of class structure under conditions of radical social change: an East European experience', in M. Kivinen (ed.), *The Kalamari Union: Middle Class in East and West*, Ashgate, Aldershot.

Ule, M. (1998), 'Youth in Slovenia in the nineties: Westernisation of the transition to late-modernity', paper presented at *International Sociological Association Congress*, Montreal.

Varese, F. (1994), 'Is Sicily the future of Russia? Private protection and the rise of the Russian mafia', *Archives of European Sociology*, 35, 224–58.

Veal, A.J. (1989), 'Leisure and lifestyle: a pluralist framework for analysis', *Leisure Studies*, 8, 141–53.

Vecernik, J. (1995), 'Emerging labour market and job prospects in the Czech Republic', in S. Ringen and C. Wallace (eds), *Social Reform in East–Central Europe: New Trends in Transition*, Trevor Top, Kladska.

Vlachova, M. and M. Stanek (1992), 'Young men's value orientations and its relation to their attitudes towards the Czechoslovak military', *Sociologia*, 24, 47–8.

Vynnychuk, A. (1996), 'Youth research in Ukraine, 1991–1995: a review', *International Bulletin of Youth Research*, 13, 6–22.

Walker, C.J. (1991), *Armenia: The Survival of a Nation*, Routledge, London.

Wallace, C. (1997), *Who is for Capitalism? Who is for Socialism? Attitudes Towards Economic Change in Post-Communist Eastern Europe: A 10 Nation Comparison*, East European Series no. 44, Institute for Advanced Studies, Vienna.

—— and C. Haerpfer (1998), *The Patterns of Transformation in Post-communist Central Europe*, Institute for Advanced Studies, Vienna.

—— and S. Kovatcheva (1998), *Youth in Society: The Construction and Deconstruction of Youth in East and West Europe*, Macmillan, Basingstoke.

Watson, P. (1993), 'Eastern Europe's silent revolution: gender', *Sociology*, 27, 471–87.

Wedel, J.R. (1988), *The Private Poland*, Facts on File Publications, New York.

—— (ed.) (1992), *The Unplanned Society: Poland During and After Communism*, Columbia University Press, New York.

Wellisz, S. (1996), *Georgia: A Brief Survey of Macroeconomic Problems and Policies*, Centre for Social and Economic Research, Warsaw.

Willis, P. (1990), *Common Culture*, Open University Press, Milton Keynes.

Zubok, J. (1998), *Social Integration of Youth in an Unstable Society* [in Russian], Institute of Youth, Moscow.

Zuev, A.E. (1997), 'Socio-economic situation of the youth in a labour sphere in the modern Russia', paper presented to conference on *Youth Unemployment in East–Central Europe*, Smolenice, Slovakia.

Index

markets 89–92, 95–6, 183–4
problems 85–6, 90–92
strategies 86–9, 90–92
in transition 95–7
transitions in Lviv 97–9
Hout, M. 7, 69
Hutson, S. 145

immiserisation 112–14
incomes
declining 112–13
and leisure 143–7
mobility 125–6
sources 43–4, 117, 212–13
see also pay
independence 22–3, 164
individualization 120
industrialization 22
information technology 72, 76–7
PCs 121, 124
infrastructure 8, 9, 15, 175
initiative, individual 84
International Monetary Fund 23, 159
interviews
joint interviewing 198–9
main surveys 24, 192–7
interview schedule 204–24
unstructured 24, 197–8
Isakova, N. 152

Jackson, M. 36
jobs *see* careers; employment
Jung, B. 69, 98, 113, 143, 199
Jyrkinen-Pakkasvirta, T. 113

Kalamari Union, The 55
Karabakh Committee 14
Kharchenko, I.I. 74, 117, 144
kindergartens 66, 101
Kivinen, M. 55
Kolarska-Bobinska, L. 163
Komsomol 109, 110, 113, 127, 131
80th anniversary 155
Konietzka, D. 71
Konings, J. 40
Kovaleva, E. 171
Kovatcheva, S. 176

Kurzynowski, A. 50

labour markets 28–35
advent of 29–32
unemployment 32–5
see also employment
labour shortages 71
Labour Offices 33
language 15–16, 72
Russian 15, 77, 161
Western languages 72, 76–7
large private sector firms 38–9, 59–60
Latvia 164
lawyers 45–7
leisure and lifestyles 26, 109–48
celebration and immiseration 109–16
interview schedule 216–17
leisure activities 127–36
leisure equipment 121–7
persistence and change 147–8
policies for youth 184–5
privatism and individualization 120
resilience of basic leisure patterns 114–16
social divisions 139–47
spending 114, 116–20
what Westernization offers 137–8
life chances 25–6
elite circulation or reproduction 83–4
social origins and destinations 77–82
see also education
life expectancy 99
life goals 103–4, 165, 171, 172
lifestyles *see* leisure and lifestyles
limbo 174–8
linked schools 71, 73
Liverpool 122–31, 134, 136
living costs 118–19
living standards 8–9, 43–5
luck 84
Lutz, B. 73
Lviv 45, 70
careers 48, 51, 52, 53, 61
housing transitions 97–9